THE
SOCIAL & POLITICAL IDEAS
OF SOME GREAT THINKERS
OF THE SIXTEENTH AND
SEVENTEENTH CENTURIES

Works Edited by

F. J. C. HEARNSHAW, M.A., LL.D.

In Uniform Style and Binding

Mediæval Contributions to Modern Civilisation.

The Social & Political Ideas of Some Great Mediæval Thinkers

The Social & Political Ideas of Some Great Thinkers of the Renaissance & the Reformation

The Social & Political Ideas of Some Great Thinkers of the Sixteenth & Seventeenth Centuries

The Social & Political Ideas of Some English Thinkers of the Augustan Age

The Social & Political Ideas of Some Great French Thinkers of the Age of Reason

The Social & Political Ideas of Some Representative Thinkers of the Revolutionary Era

The Social & Political Ideas of Some Representative Thinkers of the Age of Reaction & Reconstruction

The Social & Political Ideas of Some Representative Thinkers of the Victorian Age

THE
SOCIAL & POLITICAL IDEAS
OF SOME GREAT THINKERS
OF THE SIXTEENTH AND
SEVENTEENTH CENTURIES

A SERIES OF LECTURES DELIVERED AT
KING'S COLLEGE UNIVERSITY OF LONDON
DURING THE SESSION 1925-26

EDITED BY

F. J. C. HEARNSHAW M.A. LL.D.

FELLOW OF KING'S COLLEGE AND PROFESSOR OF MEDIÆVAL
HISTORY IN THE UNIVERSITY OF LONDON

Sole distributors in Great Britain
W. HEFFER AND SONS LTD.,
Cambridge England.

NEW YORK
BARNES & NOBLE, INC.
1949

First published 1926
Reprinted 1949 by special arrangement with
GEORGE G. HARRAP & CO., LTD.
39-41 Parker Street, Kingsway, London, W.C. 2

Printed in the United States of America

NOTE

THE study of Grotius contributed to this volume
was not included in the course of lectures as delivered in King's College. Its inclusion in the
published course was, however, announced to the
audience at the inaugural lecture.

THE EDITOR

CONTENTS

7

THE SOCIAL AND POLITICAL IDEAS OF SOME GREAT THINKERS OF THE SIXTEENTH AND SEVEN-TEENTH CENTURIES

I

INTRODUCTORY

THE SOCIAL AND POLITICAL PROBLEMS OF THE SIXTEENTH AND SEVENTEENTH CENTURIES

I

THE present course of lectures is the third delivered at King's College on the subject of Social and Political Ideas.

The first course treated of the Middle Ages.[1] Its main theme was the Christian Commonwealth—the *Respublica Christiana* or *Civitas Dei*—the great mediæval Church-State which the prudence of Constantine, the genius of Augustine, and the statesmanship of a long line of Imperial Popes had established upon the ruins of Cæsarian Rome, constructing it out of the rude and crude materials furnished by the new nations into whose hands the heritage of the Western Emperors had passed. The central *political* problem of the mediæval millennium (A.D. 450–1450) was the problem of the Two Powers, that is to say, the relation of the ecclesiastical to the secular, the spiritual to the temporal, the clerical to the lay ; of the *sacerdotium* to the *regnum*, the Papacy to the Empire, or, in modern phraseology, the Church to the State. The central *social* problem of the period was the emancipation of the slave, the elevation of the serf, the edification of the freeman, and in general the establishment of conditions which would render possible the liberation and the self-realisation of the individual soul.

[1] *The Social and Political Ideas of Some Great Mediæval Thinkers* (Harrap).

THINKERS OF THE XVITH & XVIITH CENTURIES

The second course of lectures dealt with the period of the Renaissance and the Reformation.[1] Its main theme was the transition from mediæval to modern Europe, that is to say, the change which accompanied the gradual substitution of independence for authority, of contract for status, of freedom for tutelage, of movement for stability, of speculation for credulity, of progress for order. It depicted, on the one hand, the disintegration of Christendom, the decay of the Holy Roman Empire, the degradation of the papal monarchy, the disappearance of the ideal unity of the Faith. On the other hand, it displayed the formation of national states, the rise of strong dynastic kingships, the advent of the middle class to prominence and power, the revolution in the art of war due to the introduction of firearms, the emergence of the individual ; together with the moral and intellectual transformation which was effected by the Copernican discovery of the Universe, the Iberian discovery of the New World, the Humanistic discovery of Man, and the Academic discovery of Primitive Christianity as revealed in the Greek New Testament and the writings of the Early Fathers. The central *political* problem of this transitional period was the position of the new national state and its secularised government in respect of the old cosmopolitan authorities, and in relation to the Christian principles which had so long dominated Western affairs. The central *social* problem was how to restrain and limit the dangerous liberty of the emancipated individual, and how to turn to the advantage of the community the exuberance of his egoistic activity.

The present course takes up the story about the middle of the sixteenth century and carries it to about the middle of the seventeenth. It examines the ideas of eight typical and representative writers. If the biographies of these writers be surveyed, it will be found that the earliest of them, Bodin, was born in 1530, while the latest of them, Hobbes, died in extreme old age in 1679. Thus the whole period of their lives covers a century and a half. The problems with which their works deal, however, fall within a somewhat narrower field of time. They are the problems of the era of the great Wars of Religion which may be regarded as beginning soon

[1] *The Social and Political Ideas of Some Great Thinkers of the Renaissance and the Reformation* (Harrap).

10

after the Treaty of Cateau-Cambrésis (A.D. 1559) had pacified the dynastic conflict of the early part of the sixteenth century, and as terminating with the Treaty of the Pyrenees (A.D. 1659), which closed the struggles that had been generated by the Thirty Years War in Germany. This period of one hundred years was amazingly prolific in controversy, and unprecedentedly fruitful of writers of eminence. The task of selecting eight to represent the main currents of ideas has therefore been one of no small difficulty. Even now it is painful to reflect upon the great thinkers who have had to be excluded. One has only to mention such names as Hotman, Duplessis-Mornay, Barclay, Bellarmine, Mariana, Buchanan, Poynet, Althusius, Selden, Milton, Pufendorf, Filmer, to call to the minds of all familiar with the period the images of a whole galaxy of notable men of high powers and remarkable literary achievements. I think it will be found, nevertheless, that in the works of the eight selected thinkers most, if not all, of the leading principles which moved and guided the men of this era of conflict and controversy are expressed and expounded. Let us, for a short time, survey the era, note the leading movements, specify its dominant problems, mark its outstanding men.

II

The Treaty of Cateau-Cambrésis signalised a distinct turning-point in European affairs. For more than sixty years— *i.e.*, ever since Charles VIII of France, in A.D. 1494, had conducted his fateful invasion of Naples—the controlling factor in Continental politics had been the struggle between the house of Valois on the one side, and the rulers of Spain and the Empire on the other side, for dominance in Italy, for command of the Netherlands, for possession of the Rhenish Provinces, for occupation of the passes of the Alps and the Pyrenees, and generally for ascendancy in Europe. The struggle had commenced at a time when the religious horizon was clear ; when Pope Alexander VI was enjoying, in care-free profligacy, the obedience and the oblations of a Catholic world which was untroubled by any aggressive heresy and unbroken by any serious schism. In the circumstances, there was nothing remarkable or peculiarly reprehensible in a war between Most

Catholic and Most Christian kings. The Popes, in fact, had incited them to the *mêlée*, had encouraged them in it, and had joined them in the fray. All alike—kings and Popes—had been wholly engrossed in questions relating to property and power. During the long course of the conflict, however, the condition of Christendom had radically changed. The Reformation revolt had broken out in Germany, and from Germany had spread to the rest of the Continent. The unity of the mediæval Church had been rent in twain, and the very existence of Catholicism had come to be menaced. So long as the Reformation limited its subversive activities to Germany the French King welcomed it. It paralysed the arm of his enemy, the Emperor; it provided him with valuable allies in the heart of the territories of his antagonist; it saved him from too exclusive a dependence upon his other coadjutor, the Turkish Sultan. It was, indeed, to no small extent due to the fostering support of Francis I that the German Protestants were enabled successfully to defy Charles V, and ultimately to compel him to make with them the famous Peace of Augsburg (A.D. 1555) which recognised the two religions, and left the princes of the Empire free to choose between them.

By that time the Reformation had made enormous progress throughout the Continent, and the Reformers were full of hope that ere many years had passed their cause would be entirely victorious. In Germany itself, apart from the three ecclesiastical electorates, little remained to be captured from Catholicism except Austria, Bavaria, and the Palatinate. Switzerland had become the home of heresies—Zwinglianism and Calvinism—more virulent and more actively antagonistic to the old religion than was even the Lutheranism of Germany. Sweden had adopted Protestantism under Gustavus Vasa in order to inspire with religious enthusiasm her national revolt against the overlordship of Denmark. England had thrown off her allegiance to Rome in 1534, and during the reign of Edward VI (1547–1553) had drifted into an extreme anti-Papalism, which the brief but sanguinary reaction under Mary only tended to accentuate.

Scotland was still in 1559 nominally Catholic, under the queenship of the absent Mary Stuart and the regency of her mother, Mary of Guise; but Catholicism, which seemed to portend the absorption of Scotland into the French monarchy, had become anti-national and intensely unpopular, and when in that very year John Knox returned to his native land, after many years of exile and wandering, he soon kindled, far and wide, a consuming flame of patriotic Calvinism. In the Netherlands the inquisitorial rule of Philip II of Spain, combined with his determined attack upon the liberties of the seventeen provinces, had roused a passion of protest that was destined soon to break out in open revolt. In particular, during this very year, 1559, Philip aggravated and alarmed the Netherlanders when he appointed as Governor not William of Orange, as had been expected, but his own half-sister, the half-manly Margaret of Parma.

Not even the more faithful and submissive Latin countries had escaped the contagion of revolt. Italy, always indifferent to religion, seemed to be lapsing into veritable paganism. Spain, where the long crusade against the Moors had kept Christian zeal unusually quick, found it necessary, in order to retain the unity of the Faith, to immolate many hundreds of heretics in spectacular *autos-da-fé*: it was in 1559 that Philip II, newly arrived in the peninsula, initiated on a grand scale those enormous conflagrations which effectively eliminated from his kingdom both Protestantism and progress. But it was in France, above all the other Latin countries, that the struggle between the new faith and the old was fiercest and most protracted. The politic flirtations of Francis I with Lutheranism had not survived the shock of the great French defeat at Pavia (A.D. 1525). Thenceforth Francis too desperately needed papal aid in his efforts to extricate himself from the meshes of his victorious enemy, the Emperor Charles V, to venture into ways of doubtful orthodoxy. Abandoned by the Court, and suppressed by the Church, Lutheranism in France languished and died. After a brief interval, however, a much more formidable revolt against both Church and Court commenced. John Calvin was a Frenchman, and the flawless logic of his amazing system of theology made a specially strong appeal to the lucid and legal French mind. Calvin himself, from a safe distance, impudently but not wholly unhopefully, dedicated his *Institutes* to Francis I (1535). If Francis I, however, had by that date wholly purged himself of Lutheranism, which was a creed highly favourable to national monarchy, he was not likely to entangle himself with Calvinism, which (as James Stuart was later to discover and announce) was a creed that agreed with monarchy as well as God with the Devil.

Calvinism was, indeed, the creed of rebels. It reasserted the mediæval ascendancy of the spiritual over the temporal power; it regarded the State as the mere agent of the Church; it located sovereignty in the general assembly of the elect; it treated kings contemptuously as inherently inferior to saints. The measure of Francis's dislike of Calvinism was, needless to say, also the measure of the approval with which it was welcomed by feudal nobles and once-powerful communes, whose privileges and prerogatives had been diminished by the expanding and encroaching power of the Valois monarchy. Calvinism was adopted as a weapon against royalty by the decadent baronage and the anti-national municipalities. Under their formidable patronage it threatened to disrupt the newly unified kingdom, break up the central Government, destroy the royal authority, and throw France back into the chaos of the early Middle Ages. Its anti-patriotic tendency became even more clearly evident when Huguenot nobles and burgesses entered into treasonable correspondence with heretics in foreign lands, making with them defensive and offensive alliances. King Henry II (1547–59), son and successor of Francis I, felt it necessary to take decisive action. He established a suggestively named *Chambre ardente* to deal with heresy in 1549; he secured special powers for the ecclesiastical courts in 1551; he allowed the Inquisition to begin its effective operations in 1557; he gave his confidence and support to the Duke of Guise and his brother the Cardinal of Lorraine, the leaders of the ultramontane party.

Neither France nor Spain, however, could satisfactorily cope with Calvinistic rebellion if the two kingdoms continued at war with one another. Hence the negotiations which in 1559 culminated in the Peace of Cateau-Cambrésis. By the terms of the resultant treaties all outstanding territorial disputes between Valois and Hapsburg were settled or compromised, the Most Catholic and the Most Christian Kings agreed that they would join in an endeavour to secure the meeting of a General Council to restore unity of the Church; the two Courts cemented their alliance against heresy by a marriage between the widowed Philip II himself and Elizabeth, eldest daughter of Henry II.

III

The festivities which signalised the conclusion of the Peace of Cateau-Cambrésis, and the marriage of Philip II to Elizabeth of Valois, were marred by a tragedy which profoundly affected the future of European politics. King Henry II was mortally wounded in a tournament at Paris (June 1559). He was succeeded by his eldest son, Francis II, a boy of only fifteen, but already husband of Mary Queen of Scots, and through her allied to the powerful and bigoted family of Guise. The Duke of Guise and his brother the Cardinal now assumed the control of the government of France. Their sister, Mary of Guise (widow of the Stuart James V), was, as we have already noted, regent of Scotland. The forces of France and Scotland were therefore united to achieve the supreme object of the Guise ambition—the acquisition of the throne of England for Mary Queen of Scots. From the Catholic point of view her claim to the throne was incontestable. Catholics had not recognised the legitimacy of Elizabeth ; neither did they admit the validity of the testament by means of which the excommunicated Henry VIII had excluded from the succession the Stuarts descended from his eldest sister, Margaret. Mary Stuart thus became the Catholic and legitimate claimant for the English crown as against its schismatic and revolutionary appropriator, the daughter of Anne Boleyn : she assumed the arms and style of Queen of England, Scotland, and France. In order to emphasise the religious character of Mary's claim ; in order to secure the active support of the large Catholic faction in England ; and in order to win the powerful assistance of the papal Curia, the Guises initiated a policy of severe persecution of heresy in both France and Scotland. In neither country was it accepted without demur. In Scotland there was an instant conflagration. The Calvinistic " Lords of the Congregation," incited by John Knox and his brethren, and secretly encouraged by Elizabeth, rose in revolt, drove out the French garrison, repudiated the papal authority altogether, and established a Presbyterian Church system (1560). In France events did not move so rapidly or so easily. Catholicism had not there become associated with a foreign yoke and an alien tyranny. Rather, on the contrary, was it the national cause maintaining itself against those who would revive an antiquated feudalism, and would introduce disruptive novelties from Germany and Geneva. Nevertheless, the policy of the Guises roused a formidable opposition organised and led by the Prince of Condé and the Admiral Coligny—an opposition which, for purely political reasons, received at first the support of the crafty queen-mother Catherine de' Medici.

It would be beyond our province to follow in detail the dramatic events of the three years 1559–62 in French history. Suffice it to say that growing friction between Catholics and Huguenots culminated in armed conflict—the so-called Massacre of Vassy—on March 1, 1562. Following that unhappy episode France was torn by religious civil wars which lasted, with intervals, until, thirty-six years later, the Edict of Nantes (1598) gave to the distracted and devastated country, not a peace based on principle, but a truce imposed by exhaustion. By that time the leaders of both Huguenots and Catholics had perished by assassination; both Valois and Guise had been eliminated from the political scene; the massacre of St Bartholomew had disgraced and degraded France in the eyes of the world; the land had been overrun by English, Dutch, Germans, Swiss, Italians, and Spaniards, called in by one or another of the warring factions; more than a million Frenchmen had lost their lives, and a large proportion of the wealth of the kingdom, including many of its most precious art treasures, had been destroyed.

The Edict of Nantes satisfied neither of the contending parties. To the chagrin of the Catholics it allowed the Huguenots freedom of worship in a large number of towns and castles, besides admitting them to office. To the disgust of the Huguenots it left Catholicism as the religion of the State, and it excluded the reformed faith from Paris and many other important localities. It was, indeed, a compromise, based on mere expediency and political necessity. It was the work not of men of lofty principles inspired by the great idea of religious toleration, but of statesmen indifferent to religion and anxious only to find any sort of settlement which would save their unhappy country from being entirely ruined by the sanguinary fanatics who for three dozen years had wasted it in their frantic and interminable conflicts. It established in France for eighty-seven years not toleration, but a separation of the spheres of the rival intolerances; not freedom of worship, but a specification of the localities in which each of the two tyrannies should be enforced. It was an improvement on the ubiquitous and indiscriminate battle, murder, and sudden death which had prevailed in France for more than a generation. It gave the nation tranquillity at the cost of dividing it into two antagonistic and segregated sections. It meant that if a citizen changed his religion he had no longer to send for the undertaker, but merely for the furniture-remover; he had to prepare not for a precipitate journey from this world to the next, but only for a comparatively easy transit from Paris to La Rochelle, or *vice versa*.

The statesmen whose compromising expedients it embodies were the so-called *Politiques*. Inaugurated about 1561 by the noble and large-minded Chancellor L'Hôpital, they had gradually gained in number and in influence as the civil war had run its disastrous course, until finally under Henry IV they had obtained sufficient power to impose peace upon the combatants and issue the famous edict of compromise. But it was clear that, although it gave tranquillity and effected a truce, it settled no question of principle, and left the vital problem of the limits of religious liberty to be dealt with from the very rudiments. It merely indicated one method by means of which it could be temporarily shelved—a method practicable only when politicians were indifferent to orthodoxy, and the orthodox were too much exhausted to continue to fight.

IV

While the French were embroiled in their suicidal Wars of Religion, their neighbours, the men of the Netherlands, were engaged in a life-or-death struggle for emancipation from the horrors of the Inquisition and from the tyranny of Spain. The very year which saw in France the Massacre of Vassy (1562) witnessed also the dispatch from the Low Countries of a petition to Madrid, begging Philip II to put a stop to religious persecution, to withdraw Spanish troops, to recall

Cardinal Granvella, the chief agent of Catholic autocracy, and to summon the States-General. The reply to the petition, delivered in what was for Philip the unusually short time of three years (Edict of Segovia, October 1565), was a general refusal of all concessions, and in particular all concessions on the matter of religion. Then the trouble began. A League of Confederates, *Les Gueux*, was formed—anti-Spanish and, as was almost inevitable, anti-Catholic. Popular riots broke out in Antwerp and other large towns, tumultuary risings marked by violence, bloodshed, and destructive iconoclasm. To deal with the new situation Philip dispatched the Duke of Alva from Spain with large reinforcements of Spanish troops and Catholic inquisitors. He was resolved to suppress rebellion, stamp out heresy, and completely re-establish the authority of Spain and the Church over the recalcitrant provincials. For five years (1567–72) he worked his will. It was a time of unprecedented horror. Alva's own reports to Philip convey the appalling information that 18,600 people were destroyed in the general inquisitorial massacres which raged during this sanguinary lustrum. Alva's merciless severity, however, had precisely the opposite effect to what he and his even more severe master had intended. Instead of crushing the Netherlanders it stirred them up to a ferocity of hatred and a passion of resistance which could be satisfied by nothing short of the complete expulsion of the Spaniards from their land. In 1572 open rebellion began in the North, and soon Holland, Zealand, Guelderland, Overyssel, Utrecht, and Friesland were at open war with Spain and in active search for allies in Huguenot France and Protestant England. They elected as their Stadtholder William of Orange, who had discarded his original Catholicism for Calvinism, and had declared himself an enemy of the foreign oppressor.

Once again we must pass over the details of the terrific struggle which raged throughout the Netherlands, with intervals of attempted conciliation, during the twenty years 1572–92. All the bands of both morality and compassion seemed to be loosed. Burnings, lootings, assassinations, massacres, every imaginable kind of fury and abomination, wasted and devoured what once had been the richest, most populous, and most highly developed region of Northern

18

Europe. The one point which we have carefully to note is this, viz., that in the Low Countries, as in France, neither Catholic nor Calvinist could achieve a complete victory. In both regions a division and a separation had to be made. In the Netherlands, however, it was a more permanent, more satisfactory, and more hopeful division than that instituted by the Edict of Nantes. It was, that is to say, not a mere perpetuation of a stalemate, with the combatants all intermingled and intolerant; it was a territorial and, to some extent, a linguistic and even racial division, clear-cut and definable, rational and durable. The ten Belgian provinces were retained by Catholicism and Spain; the seven Dutch provinces secured independence as a federal and Calvinistic republic. The Spaniards were slow, however, to recognise and acknowledge the *fait accompli*: not till 1609 did they nominally bring hostilities to an end; not till 1648, amid the general pacification of Westphalia, did they formally abandon their claim to sovereignty over the Dutch.

V

The Peace of Westphalia, contemporaneously with which the independence of the United Provinces was recognised, was primarily the means by which the third and most terrible of all the great Wars of Religion was terminated, viz., the Thirty Years War in Germany. Germany was not a unitary state like France, nor a federation of provinces like the United Netherlands; it was the ragged remnant of the mediæval Holy Roman Empire, a congeries of principalities, dukedoms, counties, baronies, free cities, and what not—some three hundred and fifty items in all—held loosely together by the bonds of a nominal allegiance to the elected Emperor, and by a shadowy recognition of the authority of an Imperial Diet. We have seen how Lutheranism disintegrated this already nebulous mass, and we have noted how the Treaty of Augsburg (1555) aggravated this disintegration by recognising the curious principle *Cujus regio ejus religio*, that is to say, the principle that each prince should be free to choose between Catholicism and Lutheranism, and, having chosen, should be free to compel all his subjects to conform to his creed. The Treaty of Augsburg gave Germany an uneasy peace for sixty-three years. During the first half of that period Protestantism continued to make headway. Much ecclesiastical property was secularised; many bishoprics and abbacies with their endowments were conveyed into Lutheran hands; above all, Calvinism spread from Switzerland into Germany, early capturing the Palatinate and causing much commotion by its militant antagonism to Catholicism and Lutheranism alike. The bitter controversy between Calvinism and Lutheranism which marked the closing decade of the sixteenth century in Germany gave the Counter-Reformation its opportunity to commence its recoveries for Catholicism. Inspired by the Jesuits, encouraged by the Papacy, led by Maximilian of Bavaria and his clerical brother Ernest (who ultimately became Archbishop and Elector of Cologne), it made rapid progress in expelling Protestants from Catholic fiefs, in recovering properties wrongfully secularised, in stopping the transference to Protestants of ecclesiastical reservations. The Calvinists, who were not protected by the Augsburg settlement, were particularly hard hit. Finding that from the Lutherans they could expect neither sympathy nor support, they organised in 1608 a Calvinistic Union under the presidency of the Elector Palatine—its members were mainly princes and cities of the region of the Upper Rhine. To this challenge of the Calvinists the immediate reply of their chief opponents was the mobilisation of a Catholic League (1609) under Maximilian of Bavaria, with the Pope and the King of Spain as supporters. The clouds of war began ominously to darken the horizon of the Empire. For ten years the rival alliances faced one another with growing animosity. In 1618 the conflict was precipitated by a dispute respecting the Bohemian succession.

In spite of the fact that Protestantism—Lutheran or Calvinistic—had captured the major portion of Germany, the Imperial Government (such as it was) had been kept in Catholic hands, because out of the seven electorates three (Cologne, Mayence, Trèves) were Archbishoprics, while a fourth (Bohemia) was a Hapsburg preserve. Thus the three Protestant electors (the Duke of Saxony, the Margrave of Brandenburg, and the Count Palatine) were impotent. In those circumstances, however, it is obvious that the key of the situation was the Bohemian electorate. If that could be secured for a Protestant, the Empire itself, with all its machinery of central government, might be captured and used against the Papacy. With one of the two great Powers of the Middle Ages—the one exalted by Dante and extolled by civilians; the one which inherited the autocratic and divine traditions of the Roman Cæsars—in the hands of the Reformers, there would be endless possibilities of revival of Imperial authority, total suppression of Catholicism, unification of Germany, conquest of Italy, and revenge upon the Curia for a millennium of insult and injury. Now the Bohemian crown, which carried with it the electoral dignity, was an elective one. For many years the form of election by the Diet had been nominal only, the head of the Hapsburg house being uniformly chosen. But the Emperor Matthias in 1617 perceived that on the next occasion of a vacancy there would probably be a formidable revival of the ancient claim to freedom of choice, and a dangerous attempt to secure a Calvinistic successor to the crown. For Bohemia, strongly inclined to heresy and schism since the days of John Huss and Jerome of Prague, had developed a large Genevese, nationalist, and anti-Hapsburg faction among its native nobility. In order to guard against the possibility of this disastrous contingency, he used his authority as king and Emperor to proclaim the Bohemian crown hereditary in the Hapsburg house and to indicate his nephew, Ferdinand of Styria, a Catholic zealot, as his heir. This act precipitated the long-pending religious war in Germany. The Protestant faction, headed by Count Henry of Thurn, refused to recognise the Imperial proclamation. Emissaries of the Emperor who came to Prague to negotiate were incontinently " defenestrated," that is to say, hurled from a window seventy feet high into a convenient dung-heap. Thus was argument cut short and violence invoked.

The conflict which began as a mere local struggle in Bohemia, rapidly spread until it not only involved the whole of Germany, but also drew into its vortex, on one side or the other, Denmark, Sweden, England, France, and Spain. It was an awful contest, prolonged throughout an entire generation (1618–48), and it was marked by atrocities so horrible that even the barbarities of Alva in the Netherlands, and the ferocities of St Bartholomew's Day in France, seemed mild in comparison. Germany was wasted from end to end; its prosperous cities reduced to ruins; its commerce and industries rooted up; its churches and monasteries laid low. Of thirty-five thousand villages in Bohemia only six thousand survived. A total population in Germany of some sixteen millions in 1618 was represented, it is estimated, by not many more than six millions when at length the Peace of Westphalia was concluded. Scarcely, even in the present day, has Germany recovered from the devastations of that appalling catastrophe— a catastrophe brought upon her not by act of God or accident of nature, but purely and simply by the wickedness and folly, the fanaticism and fury, of her own demented sectaries.

The Peace of Westphalia (October 1648) settled nothing which could not have been readily and easily arranged, after brief discussion, thirty years before, by men of moderation and good will. It admitted the Calvinists to equal privileges with the Lutherans; it made an equitable division of the ecclesiastical lands; it effected certain territorial adjustments; it compensated Sweden and France for their kind interventions with some valuable German dominions; it recognised the independence of Switzerland and the Netherlands, thus excluding them from the confines of the Empire. Its net result was to leave the Empire shattered, divided, weakened beyond all hope of restitution—the mere shadow of a great name. Perhaps the best thing it did was to proclaim aloud to all mankind the impossibility of settling the religious differences which separated the sects of the period by either political persecution or military repression. It compelled all practical statesmen, and even many devout churchmen, to realise that *autos-da-fé* and dragonnades, however effective they might have been in the Middle Ages, were worse than impotent against the new and virulent heresies of the modern era. It forced them to face the problem of toleration, and to devise some sort of means by which men of different creeds could live together within the bounds of one and the same state. Hence the Peace of Westphalia marked the end of the Wars of Religion and the beginning of the end of active ecclesiastical persecution.

VI

England fortunately escaped the Wars of Religion. She had warnings of what they would be like in the Pilgrimage of Grace (1536), the Western Rebellion of 1549, and the Revolt of the Northern Lords in 1569. At the beginning of Elizabeth's reign, indeed, the stage seemed to be set for a conflict on a large scale, and it appeared probable that the British Isles would constitute the battlefield on which the supreme issue between the Reformation and the Counter-Reformation would be fought out. Ireland was eager to rise on behalf of Papacy and independence. Scotland was sharply divided between Catholic supporters of Queen Mary and Calvinistic adherents of the Lords of the Congregation. England, however, was the key of the position. It is estimated that of her population of some five millions about one-half still clung to the old faith, while the other half leaned to the new. Hence in a struggle there would have been a fair equality of forces. The leaders of each side, moreover, were in a state of intense exasperation—the Catholics because of the spoliation and depredation of Edward VI's reign, the Protestants because of the burnings and outlawries of the Marian persecution. Each side—apart from the ambiguous Elizabeth, whose reign was not expected to be a long one—had its candidate for the throne : the Catholics, Mary of Scotland ; the Protestants, the Lady Catherine Grey, sister of the martyred Jane. In these circumstances any spark might have started a conflagration which would have wasted the British Isles from end to end.

Elizabeth and her chief adviser, William Cecil, were entirely aware of the acute peril of the situation. They made it their first business to see that no pretext for controversy or conflict should arise. They were greatly assisted in their task of keeping the peace by the fact that the bulk of the English people—whether nominally Catholic or nominally Protestant —were not fanatically interested in religion at all. On the one hand, the Catholic Church had lost its hold over the nation, and had become unpopular, long before Henry VIII severed his connection with Rome. On the other hand, the Protestant

23

Reformation had been carried through by a handful of politicians amid the comparative indifference of the population at large. The bulk of the English people, in fact, were believers in the State rather than in any Church; they were concerned with the maintenance of social order more than with the enforcement of religious orthodoxy; they dreaded the return of anarchy more acutely than any lapse into heresy; they were prepared in the interests of tranquillity to accept any reasonable settlement which the Government in its wisdom might institute. They looked upon religion not as a private matter for the consideration and determination of the individual mind, conscience, and will, but as a public affair to be settled for them by the appropriate authority. They took, that is to say, the view of religion which had prevailed in the Athens of Pericles, in the Rome of Julius Cæsar, and in the Constantinople of Justinian. It was essentially a pagan view of religion, but it was the one which (with many other pagan elements) had been imported into Christian society by Constantine the Great, his associates, and their successors. It was the Byzantine view of religion—misnamed the Erastian—which Henry VIII embodied in his Act of Supremacy. It was the view which was defended by Richard Hooker, and the view which is still maintained by those who contend that every Englishman is *ipso facto* a member of the Church of England. It is a view which obliterates the distinction between sheep and goats; a view which ultimately and inevitably involves the identification of God and Mammon.

Unless we realise that this political conception of religion was the one which dominated Tudor England we shall misjudge such persons as the Vicar of Bray, or William Cecil, or even Elizabeth herself. Cecil, for example, conformed to most possible forms of worship—Anglican, Zwinglian, Lutheran, Calvinistic, Catholic—during the course of his respectable career; but he did so without any suspicion that he was laying himself open to an accusation of inconsistency. At all times and in all circumstances he obeyed the law. What more could be asked of a good man? When he himself had a hand in the making of the law, that is to say in 1559, he showed clearly that he conceived a moderate and tolerant Protestantism to be the form of religion demanded in England by the political exigencies of the moment. In the interests of national independence he felt it necessary to break the connection with Spain and with Rome which Mary Tudor had instituted. In the interests of national security he had to make and keep peace with France and Scotland. In the interests of national unity he had to frame a religious settlement which would be accepted not only by the accommodating Vicar of Bray and the indifferent majority, but also by as many as possible of those zealous minorities—both Catholic and Puritan—who, rejecting the prevalent Byzantine view of the Faith, were coming to regard religion as a personal matter, a matter of conviction, conscience, conversion, consecration, and, if necessary, martyrdom.

The main lines of the Elizabethan settlement of religion were laid down in the Act of Supremacy (1559), the Act of Uniformity (1559), and the Thirty-nine Articles (1562–71). The general principle was compromise in the interest of peace. The one decisive and provocative, but wholly unavoidable, step taken was the severance of the English Church from the Church of Rome by the renewal of the royal supremacy. But even this critical act was made as inoffensive as possible by the abandonment of Henry VIII's obnoxious title " Supreme Head of the Church " in favour of the less aggressive " Supreme Governor of this Realm as well in all Spiritual or Ecclesiastical things or causes as Temporal "; by many explanations and apologies to the papal Curia; and by a confidential assurance that, so soon as political circumstances should permit, Elizabeth would return to the bosom of the Church in which she had found security during her sister Mary's reign. For the nation at large the significant measure was the Act of Uniformity. Its title provides the clue to its nature. Abandoning the attempt made by both Henry VIII and Mary to enforce an essential *unity* of faith, it contented itself with insisting on an external *uniformity* of worship. What Englishmen were required to do, as part of their duty as citizens, was to attend their parish church with regularity— under penalty of nothing more serious than a small pecuniary fine if they absented themselves. That was all. No inquisition whatsoever was to be made into the worshippers' personal beliefs or private opinions. The form of worship, too, was so ordered that it should offend as few of the pious as possible ; the ritual remained as nearly Catholic as Protestants could tolerate, the doctrine became as nearly Calvinistic as Catholics could conceivably digest. Even when the Thirty-nine Articles were framed and promulgated, they were not used, like the Six Articles of Henry VIII, as a scourge for the community ; they were employed merely as a test for those who voluntarily offered themselves for ecclesiastical ordination, or university degrees, or service under the Government.

Thus Cecil and Elizabeth secured peace in their time. Under pressure of urgent political necessity they abandoned an inquiry into men's beliefs which would inevitably have precipitated a conflict with both Papists and Puritans, and contented themselves with a demand for mere external conformity. By doing so they established a larger measure of religious toleration than was at that time known elsewhere in Christendom. The immense mass of Englishmen, whether inclined to the old ways or to the new, welcomed the relaxation from the oppressive Protestantism of Edward VI's later days on the one hand, and the sanguinary Catholicism of Mary's troublous reign on the other. They willingly went to church and there composed themselves to sleep, thus gaining refreshment and vigour for the secular enterprises on which their hearts were set. Only gradually did the zealous minorities wake up to the fact that the Elizabethan Church was a mere political organisation, having the outward form of a religious communion but being devoid of spiritual life. Not till 1570, and then only under the stimulus of a tremendous papal bull, did a remnant of faithful Catholics decline any longer to bow down in the House of Rimmon ; not till the defeat of the Spanish Armada had removed the fear of a Catholic reconquest of England did the growing company of Puritans withdraw from the Erastian Church and begin to set up conventicles of their own. By that time the perils which had beset the early path of Elizabeth had passed away. Firmly established upon her throne, and strong in the devotion of the overwhelming majority of her subjects, she was able to punish with a severity hardly exceeded by her father or her sister those who refused to recognise her authority as asserted in the Act of Supremacy, or to obey the reasonable requirements of the Act of Uniformity.

Thus the persecutions which marked the closing years of the sixteenth century in England showed that the principles of 1559 had not altogether solved the problem of the relation of religion to politics. They provided relief for the Laodiceans, that is to say, for that large majority of people whose interest in religion was secondary; but they did not furnish a way of peace for those whose consciences demanded either the consolations of Catholicism or the liberties of Congregationalism. Hence the seventeenth century had once again to face the question of toleration. This question of toleration was in fact the dominant problem of an age which was primarily the age of transition from the mediæval world ruled by the Church to the modern world ruled by the State. Not until the State was fully established in its sovereignty could it afford to allow liberty to its dispossessed rival.

VII

Perhaps enough has now been said concerning the Wars of Religion and the embittered theological controversies which raged round them during the century 1559–1659. For though they were the outstanding feature of the period, they were by no means its only characteristic. The century was one of amazing activity, both physical and mental, a time of rapid developments in many directions—a period of bewildering changes. These developments and changes all gave rise to social and political problems of considerable perplexity and magnitude. Six in particular seem worthy of special mention and of brief discussion. They were as follows: first, the increase of the power and the pretensions of kings; secondly, the decay of the feudal aristocracy, the rise of the capitalist middle class, and the increase of a pauper proletariat; thirdly, a revolution in the art of war; fourthly, an extension of geographical discovery, accompanied by the founding of colonies on the part of the exploring peoples, and resulting in the expansion of Europe into the New Worlds; fifthly, the spread of the Renaissance, with its essential secularism and its fundamental individualism, into fresh countries and into hitherto prohibited spheres of thought; and, finally, the development of natural science.

(1) *The increase in the power and pretensions of kings.* Mediæval monarchs had, as a rule, been impotent and inconsiderable folk, doomed to a harassed and ineffectual life, liable to a premature and violent death. In general their territories had been small, their revenues smaller, their dignity least of all. They had been merely *primi inter pares*, chosen by fellows who proclaimed themselves as good as they, limited by courts and councils which exercised independent authority, bound by constitutional oaths and feudal obligations, shepherded by confessors, watched jealously by bishops, visited by legates, and if necessary excommunicated by Popes. As the Renaissance dawned, however, their fates and fortunes began to improve. They were assisted in the sphere of practical politics by the decay of their rivals, the feudal nobles and the ultramontane clergy; they were exalted in the sphere of political theory by both the Law and the Gospel. On the one hand, the growth of industry, the development of commerce, the rise of a middle class, the increase of towns and cities, gave the kings natural allies in their struggles against lawless feudatories and extortionate churchmen. On the other hand, the revised study of Roman Law revealed a polity in which the sovereignty of the people displayed itself through the autocracy of the monarch—a polity in which nobles were nothing, and ecclesiastics mere ministers of the prince's will; while the reading of the New Testament and the rediscovery of primitive Christianity revealed the duty of obedience to kings and magistrates, as to officers appointed by God Himself. So early as the fourteenth century the doctrine of the Divine Right of Kings had begun to be promulgated; it was familiar alike to John Wycliffe (who clearly proclaimed it) and to Richard II (who acted upon it prematurely, with fatal results). As the fifteenth century ran its turbulent course, circumstances increasingly called for a strong executive. Within the newly formed national states civil wars and criminal anarchy cried out for a royal dictatorship capable of restoring and maintaining order. In the international sphere too the decay of the old cosmopolitan authority of the *Respublica Christiana* left the European peoples face to face with one another in a State of Nature which knew no law. Only a wisdom and a power concentrated in a king could hope to display the alertness and the

ability necessary for survival in so deadly a struggle for existence. The outbreak of the Reformation and the consequent Wars of Religion threw a still further burden of responsibility upon the royal autocracy; even in Catholic countries the control of ecclesiastical affairs passed largely into the king's hands. Hence one of the new and great problems of the period was the question of the source, the nature, and the limits of monarchical authority.

(2) *The decay of the feudal aristocracy, the rise of a capitalist middle class, and the increase of a pauper proletariat.* Feudalism had been fundamentally a military system : its focal features had been the walled castle and the armoured knight. It had sprung up spontaneously, naturally, and inevitably in Western Europe during the period of the great invasions—particularly the ninth-century invasions of Danes, Magyars, Saracens, and Slavs—when the Empire was gone, the kingdoms not yet come, the peoples helpless in the presence of merciless depredators. It had done a great and indispensable work during the ninth and tenth centuries in saving Christendom from submergence beneath the floods of paganism and infidelity. By the time, however, that the millennial year (A.D. 1000) dawned, feudalism had fulfilled its function. But, like most human institutions, it was not ready to disappear when it had completed its usefulness. Feudal nobles clung to their powers, cherished their privileges, declined to make way for the new order of merchants and artisans, civilians and bankers, for whose advent they had prepared the way. One of the leading features of the social history of the later mediæval period (A.D. 1000–1500) is the gradual rise of the middle class—with its gilds, corporations, boroughs, and cities—and its steady supersession of the rustic knighthood and baronage. The strength of the middle class lay in the power of the purse ; its agents were such representative assemblies as the English House of Commons; its allies and coadjutors the rising national kings. By the sixteenth century the middle class had definitely arrived. The feudal nobility, ruined by the Crusades and by suicidal civil wars, was everywhere in decline. Merchant princes were busy buying up derelict fiefs, revolutionising modes of agriculture, enclosing common lands, converting unprofitable arable to lucrative pasture, transforming

the traditional village economy of mediæval Christendom. They were establishing a new *bourgeois* nobility, inept indeed for war, but incomparably more efficient than the old in all that appertained to the creation of wealth. Unfortunately, the rural revolution effected by the new men, although it was essential to progress, and although it tended ultimately to a general and widespread increase of prosperity, nevertheless for the moment had a disastrous effect upon the peasantry. Unable to adapt themselves to the novel conditions, they drifted in large numbers into pauperism and vagrancy and so gave rise to a problem of poverty (amid rapidly growing wealth) which was one of the gravest and most insistent of the sixteenth century.

(3) *The revolution in the art of war.* The rise of the middle class and its success in its struggle with the feudal nobility was materially assisted by the change in the art of war which transpired between the fourteenth and sixteenth centuries. The invention of firearms, and particularly the development of artillery, rendered obsolete the fortified castle and the armoured chivalry. If as yet swords were not beaten into ploughshares or spears into pruning-hooks, at any rate once-formidable fortresses were reduced to the ranks of interesting historical monuments, and suits of mail, which had erstwhile rendered their wearers immune from plebeian attack, were rendered useless except as exhibits for antiquarian museums. The common soldier of the third estate—the yeoman of the rural manor, the craftsman of the city gild—who had been gradually acquiring military value by means of the bow and the pike, suddenly attained the place of predominance. The promise of Courtrai, Bannockburn, and Crécy was more than realised in Ravenna, Novara, and Marignano. Just as the printing press destroyed the monopoly of learning which the first estate of the clergy had enjoyed during the mediæval millennium, so did gunpowder sweep away the military ascendancy which the knightly order had possessed without dispute almost from the days of the battle of Adrianople (A.D. 378). There could have been no modern Europe without the Renaissance; there could have been no Renaissance without the middle class; there could have been no middle class without the printing press and gunpowder. It is, therefore, an

interesting tradition that Europe owes both the art of printing and the new instrument of warfare to the Chinese. If the tradition be founded on fact, to China must be assigned no small share of the responsibility for our present civilisation.

(4) *Extension of geographical discovery, etc.* Another invention of first-rate importance also attributed to the Chinese is that of the mariner's compass. Whatsoever may have been its origin, there can be no doubt that it—together with quadrant and chronometer—effected a revolution in the art of navigation, and made possible the great voyages of discovery in the fifteenth and sixteenth centuries. Between the death of Henry the Navigator in 1460 and the Treaty of Cateau-Cambrésis in 1559, no less than two-thirds of the land area of the globe had been revealed for the first time to the eyes of the adventurous West. Little more than revealed, however; for though Portugal had opened up trade with India by way of the Cape, and though Spain had laid hold of Mexico and Peru, the vast task of appropriating and developing the enormous regions of the New World had hardly begun. The Dutch, the French, the English, had, as yet, scarcely commenced their intrusive voyages. The succeeding century (1559–1659), with which we are specially concerned, saw prodigious activity in the development of commerce, the establishment of factories, the making of plantations, and the settlement of colonies. The East Indies were exploited by Portuguese, Dutch, French, and English; while Spaniards, Dutch, French, and English wrestled with Nature, with natives, and with one another in the West Indies and North America. Now these important developments overseas gave rise to several groups of novel problems of the gravest character. First, they gave rise to moral problems: what principles should guide and control European peoples, nominally Christians, in their dealings with native races, and in their dealings with one another *in partibus infidelium*. Secondly, they gave rise to legal problems: what rules should be recognised as to the acquisition and ownership of newly discovered territories; how far should the high seas be regarded as the legitimate property of individual states; and so on—an interminable series of difficult juristic questions. Thirdly, they gave rise to political problems—problems of sovereignty; problems of jurisdiction; problems of

international relations—a bewildering complex of novel conundrums.

(5) *The spread of the Renaissance*, and (6) *the development of Natural Science.* These striking features of the age need, for our present purpose, be no more than mentioned. They gave rise to problems, it is true, of a formidable character. But these were moral and intellectual problems primarily, and only indirectly social and political. They must not be wholly forgotten or ignored, however ; for the growth of rationalism, the advancement of learning, and the dissemination of the scientific habit of mind profoundly affected the spirit and attitude in which all problems of every sort were confronted and solved. The influence of the Renaissance tended to increase the secularity of the age, to lessen its interest in the battling theologies, to render it impatient of religious intolerance, and anxious to find some way of escape from irrational persecution. The influence of the new science, and particularly of the new astronomy of Copernicus and Galileo, tended to foster a general scepticism respecting the teaching of Churches which had committed themselves so irrevocably to a cosmogony proved to be false.

VIII

We are now in a position to summarise briefly the leading social and political problems of the sixteenth and seventeenth centuries, and to indicate the lines along which solutions to them were sought.

(1) First and foremost there was the problem of *religious toleration*. For a thousand years the principle of the freedom of faith had been foreign to the mind of Christendom. In the days of the early Church, amid the great persecutions of pagan Rome, the plea of the first disciples had been for liberty, and they had claimed that their religion was a matter purely personal, a relation established between the individual soul and its Creator. Even Constantine, the great perverter of the Faith, had so far recognised the validity of this contention as to leave his subjects free to choose between Christianity and the manifold paganisms of Old Rome.

Freedom of choice, however, was not long continued. It

32

was alien from the Roman mind, which regarded religion as a political concern to be controlled by a department of State. Hence within eighty years of Constantine's edict of toleration paganism had been proscribed and Orthodox Christianity established as the sole legal religion of the Empire (A.D. 392). A last echo of the larger and more liberal principle was heard when Theodoric the Ostrogoth (died A.D. 526) uttered the words which Bodin was so fond of repeating during the French Wars of Religion : " It is not possible to command in the matter of faith, because no one can be compelled to believe against his will." From that time to the end of the Middle Ages the pagan conception of the single politico-religious community, the *Respublica Christiana*, prevailed ; the citizen and the church-member were one and the same ; heresy was a form of treason ; excommunication implied complete ostracism, and infidelity involved death.

That there was a fine and glorious aspect of this mediæval attempt to commandeer the World for Christ is not to be denied. The attempt did not, however, succeed : from the nature of the case it could not succeed. The effort to capture and con-secrate the World resulted as a matter of fact in the secularisation and perdition of the Church. The Reformation marked the revolt of religion from its bondage to mammon ; its emancipation from politics ; its return to its long-sundered alliance with ethics ; its reaffirmation of the primary importance of the personal relation of the individual with his God. The religious leaders of the sixteenth century, filled with mediæval preconceptions, were slow to recognise the principle of the freedom of faith which their own revolt against the authority of Rome necessarily implied. Only the awful experiences of the Wars of Religion, and the failure of force to restore unity to Christendom, brought them at last to see the need for some form of toleration. The first people of importance to advocate the restoration of political unity by means of the recognition of religious diversity were, as we have noted, the French *Politiques* led by the Chancellor L'Hôpital and the lawyer Bodin. " Let us do away," said L'Hôpital, " with these diabolical terms, Lutherans, Huguenots, and Papists— the names of parties, factions, and seditions ; let us cling to the title of Christians."

c

As for Bodin, he wrote a long work entitled *Heptaplomeres*, in which, after discussing seven widely different forms of religious belief, he came to the conclusion that the State should tolerate them all, and that the devotees of all should live together in peace and charity with one another. No principle actuated the *Politiques* except the principle of expediency and the interests of the State. This was the sole idea embodied in the Edict of Nantes (1598), and it did not suffice to save the Edict from revocation when Louis XIV considered the Huguenots weak enough to be crushed (1685). Stronger and better grounds for toleration were sought and found by thinkers and statesmen of the seventeenth century.

For example, John Milton contended that the interests of truth demanded freedom of expression. " Let her and falsehood grapple—who ever knew truth put to the worse in a free and open encounter ? " Oliver Cromwell and the Independents generally urged the view that freedom of worship was one of the natural rights of the individual, anterior and superior to the enactments of all Governments ; John Locke, following Roger Williams of Connecticut, was content to stress the negative argument that the functions of the State were limited, and that they did not include any interference with religion, provided always that the religion did not menace the security of the State itself ; Benedict Spinoza took the more positive line that the very interests of the State demanded the freedom of the individual in matter of faith. Thus gradually the coincidence of political necessity with philosophical conviction led to the abandonment of the worst forms of persecution and to the wide establishment of some form or other of religious toleration.

(2) Closely connected with the primary problem of religious toleration was the general question of the *relation between Church and State*. Four divergent lines of opinion can be distinguished. First, there were those who maintained the mediæval Catholic tradition of the single and indivisible Christian society—the Church in its spiritual aspect, the State in its secular aspect—in which the ecclesiastical authorities, by reason of the superior importance of their functions, should exercise supreme control. This view was essentially the same as that adopted by John Calvin and his disciples in Geneva and

elsewhere, except that the Christian society which they contemplated was local and sectional, not cosmopolitan and universal.   Secondly, there were those—mainly national kings such as Henry VIII of England, Philip II of Spain, or Louis XIV of France—who, while vehemently insisting on the maintenance of the single society, free alike from traitors and from heretics, yet equally strongly emphasised the royal supremacy, and demanded the full submission of the clergy to the monarchical authority.   The judicious Hooker, the timorous Hobbes, and the politic Barclay all lent support to this view of the relation of Church to State.   A third view was that with which the great Jesuit publicists—such as Mariana, Bellarmine, Suarez—were specially associated.   They abandoned the mediæval and essentially pagan conception of the single and indivisible *Respublica Christiana*, and reverted to the view of the New Testament, the Early Fathers, and St Augustine, viz., that there are two separate and distinct societies—a *Civitas Dei* and a *Civitas Terrena* ; that the *Civitas Dei* or Catholic Church is divine in origin and organisation, and inherently the higher of the two ; and that the *Civitas Terrena* or national state is human in origin, a mere creature of contract, deriving such scanty authority as it possesses simply from the sanction of sinful men.

The fourth view, closely akin to that of the Jesuits, was the Puritan view, expressed, for example, by John Milton.   It too emphasised the separateness of Church and State.   It too treated kingship and civil government as mere human conventions dependent upon contract and consent.   But it did not accept the Jesuit conception of the exaltation of the Church. It considered the ecclesiastical polity, equally with civil polity, to be simply a matter of human convenience and social agreement.   The ultimate authority which has to decide how far obedience shall be rendered to either Church or State is the individual conscience, guided and directed by the inspiration which comes from personal communion with God.   Of these four views the two which ultimately divided the bulk of the world between them were the Erastian view of Henry VIII and the Puritan view of John Milton.

(3) A third problem—one which was inevitably raised by the discussion concerning the relation between Church

and State—was the problem of the *nature and source of royal authority*. For the new national State was in a peculiar manner centred in, and represented by, the king. The aphorism *L'état c'est moi* not inaptly sums up the situation. National consciousness was as yet weak and immature, incapable of realising abstractions. Electorates were narrow, provincial, unrepresentative ; Parliaments and States-General decadent and discredited ; Cabinets not yet arisen. The king tended to be everything. Hence champions of the State almost necessarily exalted the king, while opponents of the State concentrated their attack upon the royal authority, and in the sphere of action cultivated the practice of tyrannicide. (*a*) On the one side, *advocates of State-sovereignty* as a rule relied on the doctrine of the Divine Right of Kings. This doctrine had been first developed in the fourteenth century as a support for the Germanised Emperor Lewis IV in his controversy with the Gallicised Pope John XXII. But it had been taken up by national kings such as Henry VIII of England and Henry III of France, and had been used by them as a defence not only against Papalist, but also against Calvinistic rebels, common lawyers, recalcitrant Parliaments, and social revolutionaries. James I of England and Henry IV of France, both of whom had to argue for their thrones against opponents who denied the validity of their titles, restricted the doctrine to the narrow limit of *hereditary* right, making royal authority a bequest transmitted by primogeniture from the Old Testament patriarchs. In doing so they made the doctrine ridiculous, and laid themselves open to the attack of anyone who cared to investigate their genealogies and demonstrate the obvious fact that they were not Jews.

In the seventeenth century the sceptical Hobbes, unable to accept the doctrine of Divine Right in any shape or form, and yet anxious to assert the supreme authority of the secular ruler over all persons and in all causes, developed an alternative theory according to which the sovereignty of the State is derived from purely human sources by a process in which the main elements are perception of utility, consensus of opinion, social covenant, and perpetual popular surrender. This naturalistic teaching of Hobbes, although most obnoxious to the pious, as well as to the Jacobite clergy, was welcomed by the later defenders of State sovereignty from Spinoza down to Hume and Austin. (*b*) On the other side, *opponents of Erastian monarchs*—in particular Calvinists like the author of the *Vindiciæ contra Tyrannos*, or Jesuits like Francisco Suarez—propounded the sharply antagonistic contract theory of the origin of the authority of kings. Repudiating with contempt the doctrine of Divine Right, they asserted the popular source of all executive power. Rejecting, also, Hobbes' idea of any perpetual surrender of sovereignty on the part of the people, they contended that kingship is a matter of bilateral convention, subject to conditions and liable to determination in case of breach of the agreement by either party : if subjects break their oaths to obey, kings are freed from their obligation to administer justice ; if kings violate their duty to administer justice, then subjects are freed from their obligations to obey. But what is justice ? Who should judge as to whether or not kings are administering it ? This was one of the problems of the period. The religious zealots, both Catholic and Calvinist, identified injustice with the maintenance of heresy, and they defended the right of resistance to unjust, that is, heretical, kings, even to the limit of tyrannicide. Thus the Catholic Mariana and the Calvinist Beza both proclaimed in general terms the right of assassination ; thus, too, when ghastly murders had taken place at the hands of devout fanatics, the horrid deeds were justified by men so eminent for piety as John Knox and Pope Sixtus V. Hence the monarchs of the period of the Wars of Religion went about in constant peril of their lives. William of Orange had survived five attacks upon his life before he fell in 1584 to the pistol of Balthazar Gerard ; Elizabeth of England told a French ambassador that she had captured no fewer than fifteen emissaries of Philip II who had confessed that their mission was her murder; Henry IV of France had escaped nineteen times from assassins before he was caught by Ravaillac in 1610. It was against sanguinary zealots of this type that sober *Politiques* like Bodin urged the sanctity of sovereignty, the duty of obedience, the need of toleration, and the urgency of peace. The issue, however, between supporters of Divine Right and believers in the contract theory was too acute and emotional to be settled by argument. It had to come to the arbitrament of the sword. The British Isles saw the grim adjudication. The verdict was writ large on the page of history when on January 30, 1649, King Charles I stepped from the window of the banqueting chamber of Whitehall to be divested alike of royalty and life.

(4) The establishment of national states, the growth of strong monarchies, the formulation of the doctrine of sovereignty, the repudiation of the cosmopolitan authority of both Pope and Emperor, the extension of European dominion over newly discovered lands—all these things forced upon the attention of statesmen and publicists the problem of *international relations*. Mediæval Christendom had been for many purposes a single society acknowledging a common authority and obeying a common law. It had, of course, always been in contact with an alien and non-Christian world, but not until the time of the Crusades had it urgently felt the need of a code of international morality independent of theological sanction. The opening up of the New World in the sixteenth century, coupled with the schism of Christendom in the Reformation, and the outbreak of the ferocious Wars of Religion, strongly emphasised the need. Where could be found a body of law of universal validity, which was binding on men as such, apart from race, locality, or creed ? By what restraints could limits be imposed upon the lawless ferocity of men like Cortez and Pizarro, who, with firearms in their hands, found themselves in presence of the helpless multitudes of Mexico and Peru ? Whence could be drawn rules capable of mitigating the appalling barbarities which marked the Wars of Religion in France, the Low Countries, and Germany ? This was the problem faced by such humane thinkers as Suarez and Grotius. Suffice it here and now to say that they discovered the solution in the stoic *Lex Naturalis* and the Roman *Jus Gentium*. On the basis of these two they, and other toilers in the same field, built up the magnificent fabric of modern Public International Morality and Custom—misnamed International Law.

(5) The difficult question raised by the contact of sovereign states with one another in the new European anarchy, and by the contact of the civilised peoples of the Old World with the primitive nations of the New, led the more philosophic minds

of Christendom to ponder the whole problem of *Law*—its nature, its sanction, its variety, its classification. They found their way prepared for them by the speculations of the Roman jurists, by the scholastic discussions of St Thomas Aquinas and his followers, and by the investigations of the early modern civilians. Among the sixteenth- and seventeenth-century thinkers who devoted special attention to this problem of Law were Hooker, Suarez, Grotius, and Selden. They came to a general agreement that it was possible to distinguish four different kinds of law, viz., Divine Law, Natural Law, the Law of Nations, and Civil Law. They disagreed, however, seriously, first, as to Natural Law, whether to regard it as unrevealed Divine Law, or merely as a moral code of purely human origin based on man's social instinct ; secondly, as to the Law of Nations, whether to regard it as public International Law proper or merely as the highest common factor of the private laws of the leading civilised peoples. None of them succeeded in reaching any clear conception of the fundamentally important distinction between law in the juridical sense of command and law in the scientific sense of generalisation—the one imperative, the other merely indicative ; the one capable of violation, the other open only to disproof. The ferocity with which the theologians attacked Grotius because he took a secularist view of the *Jus Naturæ*, and the acerbity with which the civilians assailed him because he treated the *Jus Gentium* as true International Law, showed that there were deeper issues involved in the controversy than appeared on the surface.

(6) The problem of the nature and validity of law had close relation to the *social and economic problems* which became acute as mediæval agrarian society was transmuted into modern capitalist society. We have noted that the period was one of deep disorganisation and distress, marked by the decay of old classes and the rise of new ones, by the rapid accumulation of wealth associated with a lamentable spread of pauperism. Bodin, a pioneer in so many directions, made a careful study of economic conditions, and he was followed by an increasing number of amateur investigators. But the most remarkable group of thinkers who made the ' condition of the people ' problem the subject of their speculation was that which imitated Sir Thomas More in constructing Utopias descriptive of

a better state of things than that which actually existed. Never had Utopian dreamers been so numerous as they were during the century under review. Most noteworthy among the ideal commonwealths which they depicted were the *Mundus Alter et Idem* of Hall (1607), the *New Atlantis* of Bacon (1627), the *Civitas Solis* of Campanella (1637), and the *Oceana* of Harrington (1656). But there were a dozen others. Of the whole series, however, the most remarkable was that of Harrington. In a unique manner it anticipated the modern economic interpretation of history. In the present course, therefore, it is taken as the most important of the group to which it belongs.

IX

Such were, it seems to me, the leading social and political problems of the sixteenth and seventeenth centuries, and particularly of the central portion of the period which lies between the dates 1559 and 1659. It merely remains to add a closing word or two respecting the eight thinkers who have been selected as representative of the era. *Jean Bodin* (1530–96), the French lawyer, was prominent as an advocate of toleration, a defender of royal authority, and a pioneer in the formulation of the doctrine of sovereignty. *Richard Hooker* (1553–1600), admirable as a writer and inimitable as a controversialist, took the lead in defending the Elizabethan settlement of religion against both Papalists and Puritans ; incidentally he did much to develop the conception of the contractual basis of society. *Francisco Suarez* (1548–1617), the Spanish Jesuit, was eminent as an exponent of the conception of law, and as a defender of the natural right of the uncivilised peoples of the newly discovered lands to just treatment at the hands of explorers and exploiters. *James I* (1566–1625) was the interested champion of the fully elaborated doctrine of the Divine Right of Kings, and important as the spokesman of the most extreme theory of irresponsible royal autocracy. *Hugo Grotius* (1583–1645), the Dutch lawyer and statesman, was eminent as the founder of the first effective code of International Law. *Thomas Hobbes* (1588–1679), the greatest political philosopher of the age, and one of the greatest of all time, was notable for his psychological approach to politics, for his naturalism and materialism, for his formulation of the doctrine of utility, for his capture of the contract theory and his use of it as a weapon against rebellion, but above all for his development and purification of Bodin's conception of sovereignty. *James Harrington* (1611–77) we have already noted as a man keenly interested in the social problems of the period. He was also a radical, a republican, a democrat, with strong and clear views respecting the natural equality of men, the sovereignty of the people, and the necessity of wide popular education—a seventeenth-century Rousseau. Finally, *Benedict Spinoza* (1632–77), noble and illustrious representative of a persecuted race, made for himself a name for ever honourable by his curbing of the *Leviathan* of Hobbes, and by his impassioned yet convincing plea for toleration and freedom.

THE EDITOR

BIBLIOGRAPHY

BUTLER, G. : *Studies in Statecraft.* 1920.
EINSTEIN, L. : *Tudor Ideals.* 1921.
FRANCK, A. : *Réformateurs et publicistes de l'Europe.* 1864.
JOHNSON, A. H. : *Europe, 1494–1598.* 1897.
OGG, F. A. : *Europe in the Seventeenth Century.* 1924.
POLLARD, A. F. : *Factors in Modern History.* 1907.
STUBBS, W. : *European History, 1519–1648.* 1904.
WAKEMAN, H. O. : *Europe, 1598–1715.* 1897.

II

JEAN BODIN

A GREAT deal has been said and written about Bodin; and there yet remains a good deal to be said. The study of his writings leaves on one's mind an impression perhaps best described as one of vastness. There is vast book-learning, vast confusion, and an enormous, all-embracing effort. The man's reading and his writing were alike prodigious in amount. He knew nothing of relaxation or of recreation. He knew Hebrew and Greek and was in some degree acquainted with German and Italian. He knew the Talmud and Plutarch and the orations of Demosthenes. He knew the Roman historians and drank deeply of Cicero. He had some knowledge of the mediæval scholastics, though he knew the jurists better. He knew something of the law and constitution of all European states, and made a special study of certain of them. He knew the chronicles of France and studied with profit the writings of the historian Du Haillan and the registers of the Parlement of Paris. He knew the Old Testament line by line, though his acquaintance with the New Testament seems to have been slighter. He studied, as best he could, the strange jumble of the sciences of his day : astronomy and astrology, geography, physics, medicine and magic. He even made, himself, experimental investigations. The chief of the influences in his intellectual life seem to have been the Old Testament and New Platonic philosophy as interpreted by the Italian Platonists.

From about the time when he left Toulouse for Paris, in 1560 or 1561, Bodin seems to have been engaged in an effort, ceaseless and prodigious, to synthesise all human knowledge. When he wrote the *Methodus* he had in mind the plan of a synthetic philosophy of the universe. The rest of his life was occupied with the execution of that plan. In the *Methodus* he established a base of operations and a plan of attack. There

42

he laid it down that knowledge of God, without which there is no real knowledge, is best attained through the study first of man and then of non-human ' nature.' Then, for a time, he turned his attention to the study of economic conditions in France, convinced already that these were fundamentally important. In 1568 he published the *Réponse*, a book of which it has been said that it founded political economy. Certainly no earlier writer had seen so clearly the nature or the importance of economic processes or had dealt with them so definitely as a whole.

These were but preliminary studies for the great work which appeared in 1576, *The Six Books of the Republic*. With that book Bodin finished his studies of man and of human society : he went on to complete his programme. The *Démonomanie* is an essay on one very serious and practical consequence of man's constant relation to a world of active spirits. Bodin was profoundly convinced that man lives under constant influence, good or evil, of beings of another world. The *Heptaplomeres* is a demonstration of the failure alike of Christianity, Mohammedanism, and Judaism to give a satisfactory account of the universe. His own account was supplied by Bodin in his *Universæ Naturæ Theatrum*, published in the last year of his life. I can only hope he found it satisfactory.

But Bodin was far from being only a speculative philosopher. In his *Republic*, at least, he desired above all to be practical. He wrote, avowedly, in view of the evils of the time. Since the ship of state, he says, is struggling in a storm so violent that captain and mariners are worn out with toil, needs must the passengers themselves lend a hand and let those who have not strength to pull a rope at least give advice and warning.[1] He set himself, accordingly, to deal with every question of the moment that seemed to him important. He wrote the *Republic* not only to expound the nature of political society, but also to lay down general rules of policy and to advocate a number of specific reforms in France. It is useless, he declared, merely to imagine such a state as we should like to see. What is needed is understanding of things as they are, not dreams of what they might be.

Bodin's political philosophy as a whole is too complex and

[1] See the *République*, Preface.

comprehensive to be dealt with here and now.   But there is just one thing to which his importance in the history of political thought is commonly attributed and that is his theory of political sovereignty.   The best thing that can be done under the circumstances is, I think, to concentrate on that.   If I can succeed, within the limits appointed, in giving a clear exposition of that, with all its confusions and ambiguities, I shall have done what I rather think is impossible.

If you read certain modern writers you might suppose that Bodin's theory of sovereignty is a tolerably simple thing ; you will not think so if you read Bodin.   That, after all, seems the right thing to do.   I cannot resist the temptation to remark here that the study of the history of political thought seems to be still in adolescence.   We seem to me to be just emerging from a stage of preliminary generalisations, frequently based on rather hazy impressions.   Guesses may be useful as hypotheses to work on : they may even be valid.   But sooner or later all students of the history of political thought will have to do what some do now, and study their texts with as much minuteness and interpret them with as exact a precision as is bestowed upon even the most insignificant constitutional documents.   Harsh experience compels me, indeed, to admit that to read Bodin's *Republic* is a far from easy thing to do.   He was, apparently, incapable of grouping his facts or arranging his argument in any tolerable order.   The plan of the book is so confused that one sometimes wonders, in reading it, what he thought it was all about.   In the first three books the arrangement, in which he seems to be guided by Aristotle, is tolerably orderly ; all the rest is chaos.   All the later books are miscellanies ; even the chapters tend to be miscellaneous. He goes back and forth and back in the same chapter ; he turns from ideal considerations to actual France without seeming aware of the change of subject ; he discusses the means of guarding against revolution in one chapter and the question whether the property of felons should go to the treasury in the very next ; he repeats himself continually and from book to book ; he overwhelms his reader with illustrations that do not illustrate, with irrelevant references and with remarks on Roman and other history ; he interlards the discussion with lengthy disquisitions on astrology and the magic that is hidden in numbers. His verbosity, his enormous prolixity, above all his immense seriousness unrelieved by the least gleam of humour, reduce one to something like despair. Nor has he any saving grace of style. His style has merits. There is no affectation; his pedantries and his verbosity are natural; he is always trying to say what he means. His style has power and weight; generally too much weight, but never too little. But it lacks grace and balance; it is positively harsh and arid. It lacks completely that quality of charm which is as important to a writer as to a woman. Powerful and original thinker as Bodin certainly was, he was, in the highest degree, a bore. For all that, painful as it may be to read him, if we are to explain his thought it has got to be done. And not only must the French text originally published in 1576 be studied, but all its important passages must be compared with the Latin text first published ten years later.

It was, perhaps, the very worst of Bodin's failures that he did not definitely connect his theory of sovereign power with his theory of the effects of what he calls climate. But this failure at least relieves one of the necessity of considering the latter here. His theory of climate does, indeed, connect very closely with his discussion of the question as to the best form of sovereignty ; but I do not propose now to enter into that. On the other hand, his theory of sovereignty is inseparably connected with his conception of social structure and more loosely with his view of the ends for which the state exists.

Bodin saw France disorganised by faction and increasingly disordered. On all sides irreconcilable views were being expressed as to the nature of the French monarchy, the nature of political authority, and the duty of subjects. Bodin set himself to deal with every aspect of the problem; and all the questions debated in France at the time received reasoned answers in his *Republic*. He dealt, generally, with questions of policy and method in relation to circumstance, he warned of actual and immediate dangers, he suggested positive remedies and reforms. But he was aware that no argument from mere circumstance and immediate needs could satisfy in the long run or even at all. Most important of all was it that agreement should be reached on fundamental questions, for only so could order be permanently established. Formulæ had to be found of general application by which all vexed questions of duty could be decided.   What, above all, was wanted was an understanding of the nature of political authority.   Bodin tried to show that the nature and extent of such authority was involved in the history, the structure, and the end of political society.   He strove to find some principle of order and unity that should reconcile liberty and subjection, define political obligation, and satisfy conscience and reason.   In his doctrine of sovereignty he imagined he had found what was needed.

The source and origin of every political association, Bodin declared, is to be found in the family, and always the family remains the essential unit in the structure of ordered society. He repeats this assertion again and again.   The *ménage*, consisting of man, wife, and children, together with such property as is necessary for its maintenance, forms a " natural community."[1]   It is natural because it arises of necessity from the nature of man and woman.   It must have come into existence with man.   It does not necessarily, or even rightly, include slaves, but it does involve property.   Private property, or, at least, property attached to households, was to Bodin as primitive and natural as the family itself.   He was assured that without property the family could not maintain existence.   The state is an association of families and could in his view be nothing else.   It followed that the state rests absolutely upon the recognition of private property.   A communistic state was to Bodin a contradiction in terms.   " Take away the words *mine* and *thine* and you wreck the foundations of any state whatever."[2]   These conceptions are absolutely fundamental in Bodin's system of thought.

Not only does the family involve private property, it involves also rightful authority and government.   It is not woman's relative physical weakness that makes of her the natural subject of a man ; it is her moral and intellectual inferiority.   It is a primary law of nature, Bodin declares, that reason should rule appetite : in relation to woman, man represents reason, however poorly.   To emancipate her would be disastrous, since this would be to disregard unalterable facts.   So Bodin claims power for the husband to divorce his wife if he is not satisfied with her.   He also claims for the father of a family the

---

[1] *République*, ii, 7.   [2] vi, 4.

right to put his children to death, at least in certain cases. He was convinced that much of the moral and political disorder of the time was due to the reduction of paternal authority. " It is needful," he roundly declared, " in the well-ordered state, to restore to fathers that power of life and death which God and nature give them."[1] No state, he declares, in which the family is not rightly constituted can possibly be well ordered.

It might be said that, to Bodin, the family constitutes the primitive form of the state. But under his definitions the *ménage* is not a state. The state is an association of families recognising what he calls *puissance souveraine*. In the order of time the formation of civil societies preceded that of the state. Families grouped themselves about advantageous sites, were drawn into trading relations and into co-operation for defence, developed a common worship. The process ended, or it sometimes ended, in the recognition of sovereign power. But how was it, or rather why was it, that these more or less loose associations of families came to recognise sovereign power ? To this crucial question Bodin returns only a confused answer.

Puissance souveraine, whatever exactly it is, is, by definition, the mark of the fully formed state. But, obviously, it can only be an instrument : the state could not conceivably be formed for the sake of sovereign power. What were the ends for which the state came into existence and for the sake of which, presumably, sovereign power was recognised ?

Bodin, following Aristotle, seems to conceive of the state as distinguished from the *ménage* by the recognition of higher and larger ends. The end of the state, however, he declares emphatically is not mere happiness. It cannot be conceived as less than the realisation of all manner of good for mind and body. In a sense the body must come first. A state that lacks means of subsistence will have little care for moral or for intellectual values. All the same, it is the realisation of virtue, which includes both moral and intellectual values, that is the justifying end. " The primary and chief end of every state," he says, " must be virtue."[2]

Bodin, however, does not say that the state comes into existence through an increasingly clear recognition of its true end. He did not clearly see any such recognition as a process

[1] i, 4.   [2] iv, 4.

in time past.   Never anywhere does he give a clear account of
how or why the loose, early associations of families were trans-
formed into states.   He says that the recognition of sovereign
power may be completely voluntary and he says that it may be
compelled by force.[1]   In either case a state is created.   He
certainly imagined that the state very commonly originated in
some kind of conquest: monarchy, he seems to think, always
did.   But all his language on the subject is confused and in-
conclusive.   If the state be founded by conquest, who and
what is the conqueror ?   Is he already the head of a state,
possessing sovereign power ?   In that case what happens is
not the creation of a new state, but the extension of an old one ;
and we are no nearer the origin of the state than before.
Bodin could not have thought that the state was created by
mere force, because it is impossible to think so.   The human
exercise of force can be nothing but an expression of will ; and
to say that anything is created by force is not so much an
erroneous as a meaningless assertion.   But Bodin was caught
in the net of his own definition.   All he meant was that since
wherever there is sovereign power there is a state, and since the
recognition of sovereign power may be compelled by force,
states may be and have been created by force.

It is clear that when a state is, in this sense, established by
conquest, the process involves no recognition of what Bodin
describes as the true end of the state.   The state, therefore,
may exist without any reference to its end.   This, in fact, is
precisely what Bodin did think.   His famous definition of the
state, so far as it defines anything, is a definition of the *république bien ordonnée* rather than of the *république* pure and simple.
He defines it as an association of families, under *droit gouvernement* by *puissance souveraine*.   But in the course of his exposition it becomes perfectly clear that he regards *puissance
souveraine* as sufficient alone to constitute a state without anything that can be called *droit gouvernement*.   Much of the confusion of his language is due to the fact that he often does not
know whether he is writing about the state in itself or about
the state well ordered.   But always the distinction is in his
mind somewhere.

What it seems to amount to is this.   Bodin asserts that no

[1] iv, 1, ed. 1591 (Latin), p. 580.

less comprehensive end than that which he describes can justify the existence of the state to reason. The well-ordered state will be conscious of its end : how far conscious may be matter of degree only. But in any case the state cannot be rationally conceived as existing merely for the sake of peace and order and material prosperity. Man needs very much more. The fully developed state is one that endeavours to satisfy all the needs of man. Even though acceptance of *puissance souveraine* will make a state of sorts, it will not make a well-ordered state. But Bodin thought that the ends of the well-ordered state implied and necessitated that acceptance.

So we come, at last, to the question : What, exactly, is this *puissance souveraine* ? Here Bodin's formal definition helps us hardly at all. He expounds it at great length. And if we faithfully read his exposition, with the sole desire to understand what he means, we come painfully and inevitably to the conclusion that Bodin himself did not know exactly what he meant by *puissance souveraine*. If, in one passage or another, he seems to be making the matter clear, we have only to read on to find confusion.

Up to a certain point all goes easily. It looks as though we were going to arrive either at a Hobbesian conclusion or at a statement of a legal fiction conceived as necessary. It seems clear that, to Bodin, sovereignty consists essentially in an unlimited authority to make law. We are told, over and over again, that the essential feature of sovereignty is the right to impose law on all and sundry without consent of anybody. Yet, even from the first, there is a suggestion of confusion. Bodin does not seem to see that a strictly unlimited right to make law must include all other conceivable powers. He explains that the sovereign possesses right to make peace or war, to appoint magistrates, to decide all causes, to grant pardons, and so on. It would seem that he has not clearly separated the idea of sovereignty from the idea of a group of legal prerogatives. All the same he asserts quite distinctly that law is nothing else than the command of a sovereign. Mere customary law derives authority only from the sovereign's sanction. It holds good only so long as the sovereign pleases to treat it as law.

We are told, further, that sovereignty is not the same thing

D

as mere power to make law. A dictatorship, absolute while it lasted but limited in time, would not be a sovereignty. It could only be the creation of a sovereign. Sovereignty can suffer no limitation in time, in function, or in law. For, rightly considered, sovereignty belongs rather to the state itself than to the actual sovereign. It is, Bodin says, "la puissance absolue et perpétuelle d'une République," [1] absolutely vested or actualised in a sovereign. It may, he says quite explicitly, be conferred by voluntary act ; but it cannot be conferred conditionally. If ruling power were conferred conditionally, sovereignty would remain with those who conferred it.

There are things, Bodin points out, that, just because he can always do anything, the sovereign can never do. He cannot bind his successors, because in the nature of the case his successors cannot be bound. What is even more important to understand is that he cannot bind himself. He cannot conceivably limit his own powers. Essentially, it would seem, sovereignty consists in a continuous right to do anything. Obviously such a right is incapable of limitation. A sovereign ought, no doubt, to hold himself bound by any promises he makes, so far, at least, as consideration for the general welfare will allow him to keep them. But that is a matter between himself and God, to whom all promises are made. Legally he can never be bound, even though he wish to be : he must always remain *legibus solutus* whether he like it or not. It seemed strange to Bodin that anyone could conceive of a sovereign as bound by his own law ; for that means simply by his own will, " a thing," he says, " by nature altogether impossible." [2]

Sovereignty was conceived by Bodin quite independently of its form. In a monarchy it is vested in a single person, in an aristocracy it belongs to some relatively small group, in a democracy it lies with a numerical majority. Quite explicitly Bodin defines democracy as the sovereignty of a numerical majority. It seemed to him, however, that the sovereignty of any group must always be theoretical rather than real. He makes this point not in the course of his exposition of sovereignty, but in connexion with his discussion of the question how sovereignty is best actualised practically. He explains

[1] i, 8.   [2] vi, 4.

JEAN BODIN

that the craving for equality expressed in democracy is a rebellion against nature. The radical and inescapable fact is the
natural inequality of man. He explains, also, that there is less
real liberty in a democracy than in any other form of state.
For the liberty that is worth having does not consist in or
depend upon a fictitious share in political power, but depends
upon order and stability in the state. " True popular liberty,"
he says, " consists in nothing else than ability to enjoy one's
goods in peace, fearing not at all for one's life and honour
or that of one's wife and family." [1] But in a democracy
nothing can be expected but chronic disorder. Why is this ?
Radically, it seemed to him, because only in a single will can
sovereignty actually exist. In a democracy, as in an aristocracy, the majority is sovereign at any one moment. But this
majority is a constantly shifting thing that may, and does,
change from day to day. A majority of wills has neither
definite form nor constant substance. A group is always
divided ; it has, strictly speaking, no will at all. Its decisions
tend to be compromises which express the will of no one.
Compromise distorts and confuses its action, and faction disorders it. The sovereignty attributed to an aristocracy or to
a whole people is necessarily fictitious. A monarch alone can
give real unity to society and establish definitely the distinction
between sovereign and subject.

That essential feature of the state which is sovereignty
cannot, then, quite strictly speaking, really exist except
in monarchy. For all that, Bodin admits that wherever
sovereignty is recognised as existing, whether in a single
person or in a body of persons, there sovereignty in a sense,
and therefore the state, exists. But in whatever form
sovereignty may exist, it is always, he insists, absolutely indivisible. An unlimited authority to make law is not ideally
divisible. To talk, therefore, of mixed sovereignty or of
partial sovereignty is to talk mere nonsense. The ' mixed '
state, in this sense, cannot exist : it cannot be conceived as
existing. Under a constitution in which division of sovereignty
is attempted " it will always," he says, " prove necessary to
come to blows to decide whether sovereignty lies with a prince
or with a part or with the whole of the people." [2]

[1] vi, 4.   [2] ii, 1.

It seemed to Bodin that the very existence of law implied the existence of a sovereign in his sense.   For law, he thought, must be conceived as command, and command is an act of will, and the expression of will must be single or there is no command, and once a sovereign will is recognised its action cannot logically be limited by law.   Evidently, however, this absolute law-making power cannot be merely a legal fact.   If you say it is so, you might as well say that it is mere legal fiction ; since, whatever law may say, no ruler can actually do anything he pleases.   The question, to Bodin, was never one of mere legal fact : it was always, essentially, a question of the obligation to obedience.   He was asserting the existence in all ' republics ' of an unlimited legal authority to which all owe obedience as a duty.   But to the question whence is this authority derived Bodin gave no distinct or coherent answer.   Plainly this sovereignty of his rests always on recognition : he never suggests that he conceived of sovereignty as capable of existing unrecognised.   But he thought of this recognition incoherently. He thought of it now as creating the state, now as simply something highly desirable, now as connected with the true end of the state or even as necessary in view of that end.   But he gives no clear account either of its origin or of its purpose.   He speaks of sovereignty being established or appropriated by force ; but evidently a sovereignty that is either inherent or necessary is not created by force in any sense, though an actual sovereign may be.   He speaks of it, also, as being conferred. But whoever confers it must in some sense have possessed it.

Confusedly, Bodin seems to have thought that legal sovereignty must be the formal expression of a sovereignty inherent in the nature of human association and determined by its ends.   If the end of political association be the realisation of all possible good—if, therefore, Government should have power to control all relations, the recognition of a sovereignty unlimited in law might seem to be a necessity.   Since the end of the state is an unlimited good, the state must itself possess sovereignty in this absolute sense or contradict itself by admitting that its end is unattainable.

To say that Bodin thought of the recognition of sovereignty as the only radical remedy for the disorders of his own France is true, but is far from the whole truth.   To him it seemed that

52

the conception of a legally complete sovereignty at once explained and justified political society. It ensured order and unity, it defined the duty of the citizen, it answered all questions. Bodin argued that it had long existed and did still exist in fact and in law. He was still more concerned to show that it must exist. It must exist because it is implied in the very notion of man-made law, and because it alone is sufficient to the needs of man in society.

There was, to Bodin, really no need to inquire how political society, in which it seemed to him that sovereignty was logically implied, had come into existence. In connexion with his political conceptions it is necessary to realise the man's profound religiousness. Unless this be realised it is impossible to understand his *Republic*. I do not know precisely what were his religious beliefs at the time he wrote the book ; but I do not think that, at that time, he was either a Catholic or what is commonly called a Protestant. Later in his life he was quite clearly not a Christian at all in any tolerable sense. But always he saw the state as a manifestation of God's will. In all inevitable sequences and associations, in all enduring conditions and institutions, even in successful enterprises, he saw, always, a revelation of that will. The long continuance of political society proved to him that it is the will of God that man should so realise the good. This it was that led him sometimes to use language that might have been used by Barclay. " Whoso contemns his sovereign prince, contemns God whose image he is." But such language was equally used by Calvin. Bodin believed in a Divine Right in Kings only because to all religious men, at least of the sixteenth century, all right is divine and all obligation is to God. But sovereignty and sovereigns were, to Bodin, created by no special act of God. Sovereignty was to him of man's creation, in the only sense in which man creates anything. It arose from the nature of man and from human need and aspiration. Barclay's prince is sovereign by virtue of a special divine commission. You can eliminate from Bodin's *Republic* all his few references to princes as the lieutenants of God, and the whole structure will stand unaltered. If you eliminate God's direct action from the system of Barclay, nothing whatever will remain.

So far, in spite of certain confusions and unanswered

questions, Bodin's conception of sovereign power would seem to be fairly clear and coherent. But we have only to read on to find confusion confounded. It appears that Bodin did not really mean quite what I have so far represented him as thinking. It appears, after all, that he did not conceive of sovereignty as necessarily involving a strictly unlimited power, even in law. He recognises, indeed, a form of sovereignty which does involve such power : it is that of the *dominatus* or *monarchie seigneuriale*, in which the monarch is proprietor of all goods and rules his subjects as slaves. But this Bodin regards as a primitive and imperfect form which, in Christendom at least, has disappeared. It can never constitute a well-ordered state. The monarchy of every *république bien ordonnée* is a *monarchie royale*. And Bodin makes it quite clear that in a well-ordered state sovereignty is, in more than one sense, limited.

It is limited, in a sense, first of all by that law of nature which, Bodin says, shines on all like the sun, unmistakably ; by those eternal principles of right and wrong obedience to which constitutes *droit gouvernement*. All the princes of the earth, he declares, are subject to those laws, and none can break them without committing treason against God. It is, indeed, quite clear that he views the obligation of the sovereign to obey Natural Law as in no sense a legal obligation. There can be no lawful means of compelling the sovereign to obey Divine Law. It might seem, therefore, that if any question arises it is a question for the sovereign's conscience only. But this is not, and could not be, the case : the consciences of other people also may be concerned. Bodin himself states and discusses the difficulty clearly and frankly.[1] What, he asks, is the duty of a subordinate magistrate who receives from the prince an order to do something manifestly unjust and wicked ? He distinguishes between an order which merely contravenes the prince's own law and an order inconsistent with the Law Natural. In the former case the prince is acting inconsistently with his own standing orders. That is not the magistrate's business, and, his conscience unconcerned, he is bound to obey. But what if the prince should order a massacre of manifest innocents ? Bodin's answer is emphatic. The magistrate must be quite sure of his ground, but, in such a case, he is

[1] iii, 4.

bound to disregard the order. The unfortunate official is not, indeed, entitled, like the magistrate of the *Vindiciæ*, to set about organising armed revolt. He is bound to disobey and take the consequences. But what consequences, logically, can there be ? How is the recalcitrant to be punished ? An order for his punishment would be manifestly unjust, and all would be bound to ignore it. Ideally, on the principle laid down by Bodin, an order of the sovereign seen by all to be iniquitous could not be carried into effect, nor would punishment for disobedience be practically possible, if all did their duty. There is no ground whatever for supposing that Bodin would have sought to escape from this conclusion. No more than mediæval believers in Natural Law could Bodin believe in a sovereignty strictly unlimited.

It appears, in the second place, that sovereignty may, and apparently should, be limited by what Bodin calls *leges imperii* or fundamental laws. He speaks of them as laws with which the sovereign power is itself absolutely associated.

In the kingdom of France he recognises only two such laws, and they are those which were recognised as 'fundamental' by all French jurists of his time : the Salic Law and the law prohibiting alienation of domain. His discussion of these things is a discussion of mere French constitutional law. But it becomes clear that sovereignty need not, and in Bodin's view should not, be unconditioned by law, though he has declared elsewhere that it cannot be conferred on conditions. How did these *leges imperii* come into being ? They cannot have originated in an act of the sovereign, for no such act would bind future sovereigns. A law of succession may perhaps be conceived as necessarily binding on the prince who owes his crown to it. But the difficulty about domain remains. "Le Domaine," says Bodin, "appartient à la République":[1] it does not belong to the sovereign. But what, then, is the republic apart from its sovereignty ? We had been given to understand that there was no such thing. It would seem that sovereignty, viewed in abstraction, in a world void of circumstance, is not the same thing as actual sovereignty.

I will go no farther into this matter here. There is evidently

[1] vi, 2.

serious confusion, nor do I think it is possible satisfactorily to clear it up. But far more important and bewildering is Bodin's declaration that the sovereign can, normally, take no part of any man's property without obtaining, in some sense, his consent. Sovereignty, it appears, does not necessarily include a right to levy what we call direct taxation without consent of the tax-payer. In a seigneurial monarchy, indeed, the monarch will possess this right ; but it does not exist in well-ordered states.

After all that has gone before this assertion is rather astounding. It is yet more astounding to find that it is made by Bodin almost incidentally, and that no great stress is laid on it. This fact seems significant ; but it is not easy to be sure what it signifies. Much of Bodin's language on the subject is ambiguous in phrasing or in reference. When he denounces the arbitrary seizure of private property by the prince as mere robbery, he is thinking not of taxation, but of occasional and irregular confiscations. He is merely denouncing a breach of the Law Natural. Yet at times he seems to confuse such arbitrary confiscation of the property of individuals with actual taxation. In any case he asserts explicitly, in one place, that it is not within the power of the sovereign prince to levy taxation at his will and pleasure : and he quotes with approval the famous remark of Philippe de Commines to the same effect.[1] Elsewhere he implies clearly that, in France, direct taxation cannot be levied except under a grant from the Estates of the realm. " If need be to raise money," he says, " that can only be done by the Estates." [2] And again, in another passage, he lays down that, if urgent need suddenly arises, the prince will be justified in levying a tax without waiting for a grant. Assuming that sovereignty lies with the prince, the implication that the right to tax property at will does not attach to sovereignty is completely inevitable.

It is certainly astonishing that Bodin should have made these assertions almost casually, almost without argument, without any attempt to reconcile them with or exhibit their relation to his conception of sovereignty. He makes them almost as though they were self-evidently true and needed no explanation.

[1] i, 8.   [2] iii, 7.

Now in discussing the financial position and resources of the French monarchy Bodin dealt last of all with direct taxation ; and he spoke of it as though it were to be considered as a last resource, exceptional always and only justified by dire need. Is it possible that he thought of such taxation under normal conditions as indistinguishable from brigandage and a manifest breach of the Law of Nature ? If he did, he is still not released from his logical difficulty, but his confusion is to some extent accounted for. But such an interpretation ignores the fact that Bodin knew better. In the very chapter just referred to [1] he pointed out that it would be absurd to advocate the reduction of the taxes on property even to what they had amounted to under Louis XII. He knew that the king could not possibly, in any case, " live of his own." He knew that regular direct taxation was absolutely needed to maintain government.

Is it possible, then, that when he said that no prince on earth can tax his subjects without consent he only meant that, by common consent, it has been established that in practice the prince shall not do so ? His words and his references to Estates will hardly bear that interpretation. It has, on the other hand, been maintained that, in giving the Estates power to grant or refuse taxation, Bodin not merely took away with one hand the sovereignty he had given to the prince with the other, but handed it over to the Estates. Sovereignty, in this view of his meaning, belongs really and perpetually to the community itself. It is indivisible and unconditioned save by the Law of Nature. The legal sovereign is merely a delegate and does not really possess sovereignty, even though no one may command or punish him.

I am quite sure that this way of putting the matter does not express what was in Bodin's mind. Since, according to Bodin, sovereignty may be conferred by a people, it may indeed be argued that, on his own showing, sovereignty must in some sense have originally belonged to ' the people '—that is, apparently, to a numerical majority. In a democracy it remains with that majority. But, at least, Bodin makes it clear that when conferred it is conferred entirely and absolutely. Sovereignty may be conceived as, in his own phrase, " the

[1] vi, 2.

power of a state "; but clearly Bodin thought of it always as power actualised in a legal sovereign. Essentially it is a power of making law, and what Bodin above all insists upon is that such power cannot be conceived as divided or as legally conditioned. There is not a phrase in the *Republic* that suggests that he ever thought of the king in France as not possessing full sovereignty in his own sense. He was emphatic in declaring that in France neither Estates nor Parlements have any share in sovereignty : that in France the king is sole sovereign.

We are forced, I think, to conclude that, to Bodin, the sovereign has no right to levy taxation at his pleasure, because a power of arbitrary taxation seemed to him inconsistent with the purposes for which sovereignty exists or with the nature of the state itself. We must be careful not to misrepresent Bodin by representing his thought as clearer than it was ; and that his thought on this matter was confused is not doubtful. But the root of it seems to be his conception of the relation of the family and of property to the state. The family was to him the indispensable unit of political society, and private property he associated absolutely with the family. An unlimited right to tax private property is, logically, a right to destroy it. To say that the sovereign is not bound to respect property is to say that he is not bound to respect the state itself, since the destruction of one would be the destruction of the other. The necessity, for the prince, of obtaining consent to the levy of direct taxes on property is not, in Bodin's system, derived from any sort of sovereignty of the people, but simply from the fact that to allow the sovereign a right to destroy the state is inconsistent with the ends for which sovereignty exists. Bodin, of course, knew that French lawyers had long been claiming an unlimited power of taxation for the King of France. To him, I suggest, they seemed to have done so just because they had never understood the basis and the implications of sovereignty. Sovereignty must be conceived as absolute and as legally unconditioned in relation to the ends for which the state exists : to conceive of it without reference to those ends is to make of it mere nonsense. Bodin's admission that in case of sheer urgency the prince might rightfully levy taxes without waiting for consent was logically quite consistent with the principle. Such a right involved no power to destroy. The assertion that the legal sovereign cannot tax without consent is, of course, inconsistent with the Hobbesian conception of sovereignty. But that fact is irrelevant. Between Hobbes and Bodin is no mere difference of degree, but a great gulf fixed.

Bodin saw sovereignty as something necessarily limited by that Natural Law the measure of which is the common consciousness of right and wrong. He saw no difficulty here : he refers always to this Natural Law as something that is clearly known to all men. A conception of sovereignty as actually creating right would have seemed to him an atheistic blasphemy. Not only so : to Bodin the structure of the state implies, at least in all well-ordered states, a recognition of further limitations to sovereign power. Three things, to Bodin, were essential in political society : sovereignty, the family, and private property. And the last were first. The sovereign can no more tax at pleasure than he can bind himself. To do the one would destroy sovereignty ; to do the other might destroy the state.

It may be pointed out here that in a bare conception of legal sovereignty as unlimited there was nothing new. The French civilians of the reign of Francis I had actually claimed for the French king a right less limited than was claimed by Bodin. It is true that they had not troubled to generalise their conception : they were thinking of France and its law, and not of the state as such. But neither the conception of law as command, nor the perception that there can only be one sovereign in a state, nor the idea that sovereignty consists essentially in a right to make law, were in any sense new. I am inclined to suggest that William of Occam and Wycliffe were nearer to a conception of unlimited secular authority than ever was Bodin. It may, indeed, be said that Bodin was the first to declare that the distinguishing mark of the state was its recognition of legal sovereignty. But this assertion does little more than illustrate Bodin's love of formal definition. It may be said that what Bodin did was to detach the notion of sovereignty from circumstance and see it as legal theory logically necessary in all associations for other than specifically limited purposes. In doing this, in detaching the idea of sovereignty from all association with Emperor, Pope, or king, and attempting to define its nature apart from all circumstance, he was doing, perhaps, what had never quite been done before.

But, in relation at least to the thought of his own day, the originality of Bodin's theory of sovereignty consisted, I think, mainly in the fact that he did not connect it specifically and directly with the will of God. To Bodin sovereignty was created by need, which was just what the thinkers of the 'Divine Right' school believed to be impossible. Bodin's *Republic* is, among other things, an attempt to show that political authority is derived from human nature and from human need. Viewed as a complex whole, his theory of sovereignty may certainly be fairly said to be original. But of the various elements that went to its construction the only one that can be called new is the conception of political society as absolutely and necessarily associated with the existence of the family and of private property, and the derivative conception of a consequent limitation of all political authority. In view of a good deal that has been written about Bodin this conclusion may seem a little surprising; but I do not see how it can be escaped.

I will conclude with a few words of warning. To isolate Bodin's theory of sovereignty is to present it in a form in which it did not exist in his own mind. But it is not because I am painfully conscious of this fact that I have refrained from all criticism except such as is designed to elucidate. I have not, I hope, indulged in a word of praise or censure. No light can be thrown upon Bodin by our censure or by our approval; nothing is thereby revealed but our own opinions. My beliefs, if I have any, and your beliefs, if you have any, are strictly irrelevant. When Bodin is spoken of as having made a contribution to political thought, there seems, sometimes, to be an implication that this contribution was made to some body of truth concerning political society which has been slowly accumulating. The existence of that body of truth requires a demonstration, at present somewhat evidently lacking. Bodin's claim to special honour consists, I think, in the fact that he, almost alone among sixteenth-century thinkers, made an honest attempt to construct a comprehensive theory of political society. All that we are rationally entitled to demand of such a system of thought is that it should be coherent and intelligible and that it should not ignore or distort indisputable facts. In such a connexion there seems to me nothing more presumptuous than praise, except condemnation.

I have endeavoured to represent Bodin's thought about sovereignty as substantially coherent. He himself has made it difficult to do this; and I think it must be admitted that it is ultimately impossible. I think that much of Bodin's confusion and all his important inconsistencies connect with a radical flaw in the foundations of his great construction. That flaw, I think, consists in his failure definitely to connect his theory of sovereignty with his conception of the end of the state and in his failure to adjust both to his own theory of climate. As a consequence he left many essential questions unanswered and some unasked. Some of them I have indicated already. He saw sovereignty as limited by a law of conscience and by the nature of the structure of society. Is recognition of all this involved in the act or the process that creates sovereignty? In what sense is sovereignty the power of a state as distinguished from that of a legal sovereign? Whence, after all, is the obligation to obey the sovereign derived? For all his pains Bodin has answered the question so obscurely and so indirectly that we are not sure he has answered it at all. Vaguely we apprehend that sovereignty is somehow inherent in human association and that obligation to obey is derived from recognised ends. Bodin's theory of the state is a grand edifice in the very latest Gothic, built up on disjointed foundations. In consequence it tended from the first to disintegrate, crumble into ruin, and disappear. But, after all, to say this is to say little. Omitting the word ' grand,' may not the same be said of all similar structures?

J. W. ALLEN

THINKERS OF THE XVITH & XVIITH CENTURIES

BIBLIOGRAPHY

A. PRIMARY SOURCES

BODIN, JEAN : *Les six livres de la république.* 1576.
De republica libri sex. 1586.
The Six Books of a Commonwealth, translated into English by Richard Knolles. 1606.

B. SECONDARY SOURCES

BARTHÉLEMY, E. DE : *Études sur Jean Bodin.* 1876.
BAUDRILLART, J. : *Jean Bodin et son temps.* 1853.
CHAUVIRÉ, R. : *Jean Bodin, auteur de la " République."* 1914.
DUNNING, W. A. : *History of Political Theories,* vol. ii. 1910.
FOURNOL, E. : *Bodin, prédécesseur de Montesquieu.* 1896.
FRANCK, A. : *Réformateurs et publicistes de l'Europe.* 1864.
HANCKE, E. : *Bodin : Studien über den Begriff der Souveränität.* 1894.
JANET, P. : *Histoire de la science politique dans ses rapports avec la morale,* vol. ii. 1887.
PLANCHENHAULT, N. : *Études sur Jean Bodin.* 1858.

III

RICHARD HOOKER

IN a moment of patriotic optimism a Hebrew prophet of the
seventh century B.C. indulged the bold vision of a time when
"Israel should be the third with Egypt and with Assyria,
a blessing in the midst of the earth." A fancy hardly less
ambitious than the dream of the Judæan patriot, and apparently hardly less difficult of realisation, was that of the English
statesmen of three and a half centuries ago who aspired to
make Canterbury a third with Geneva and with Rome. The
Elizabethan Church Settlement, following upon the extremist
examples of Edward VI and of Mary in turn, marked the
determination of the Queen and her advisers resolutely to tread
the *via media*, and to steer their course between the Scylla of
Popery and the Charybdis of Calvinism. Thus the Church of
England received the impress of its peculiar character, at once
as the embodiment of a standard of doctrine and worship which
should be acceptable to the majority of the nation, and as the
expression of a type of Christianity combining some of the
elements of both Protestantism and Catholicism. From the
outset the venture was of doubtful promise. In an age of
strong religious feeling, when the European stage was being
set for a decisive struggle between the forces of the Counter-
Reformation and of the Protestant Movement, a policy of
cautious mediation was singularly difficult. The Elizabethan
Settlement provoked much abusive comment from the zealots
of both parties. "Rome I know, and Geneva I know, but
who are ye?" was the theme of not a little bewildered interro-
gation and angry repudiation. It was the good fortune of the
Church of England that from the midst of the controversy and
of the controversialists there arose an apologist, in the person
of Richard Hooker, whose defence of its position was based
upon lines so broad and deep that his work was not only effective as a refutation of his opponents' contentions, but has won

a recognised place as a classic of English theological literature. In *The Laws of Ecclesiastical Polity* Hooker cast his net wide. Repelled by the narrowness of the Puritan position which sought to secularise all that was not expressly commanded and prescribed in Holy Scripture, Hooker reviewed the whole sphere of human activity, insisting that the law of reason which governed the thoughts of men, and the laws of conduct which bound them into political societies, were equally divine in origin and binding in character with the especial laws of religion revealed in the Bible, which directed them as members also of a spiritual society. Behind this exposition of the laws of human societies lay the investigation of the function and province of law in the whole created universe. It is this breadth of vision and of thought which is the characteristic feature of Hooker's writings; this, too, which justifies his claim to be regarded as a notable political thinker. Inevitably, however, he was concerned first to defend the doctrine and discipline of the Church of England, and so he was only able to adumbrate his scheme of political philosophy. Since also it was the narrowness of the Puritan attitude which moved him to undertake the wider investigation, attention must first be turned to the controversy which occasioned his writing.

Of the Protestant Reformation of the sixteenth century it would be hazardous to attempt to say anything new, and tedious to repeat views which are already old. Yet something must be said by anyone who would aspire to expound Hooker. The call for reformation was neither new in the ears of the sixteenth century nor in any sense a peculiarity of that era. What was strikingly new was the actual rebellion of a large part of Europe against the papal obedience and the permanent separation of some of its most important nations. This rebellion had been presaged, as Dr Figgis was wont to insist, by the failure of the Conciliar Movement. The milder methods of a 1689 being unavailing, recourse must be had to the surgery of a 1789. In the sixteenth century the demand for reformation had been strengthened by the influence of the Renaissance. Of that influence all that can be affirmed here is the fact that the reforming movement received a new impetus and a fresh orientation when the enthusiasm which in Italy had led to the avid perusal of the literature of classical Greece and Rome was

64

turned into a zeal in other countries for the study of the New
Testament in its original language. Not only could students
compare the incipient Church Order of the Pauline Epistles
with the elaborate organisation of the papal hierarchy, but
the weapon had been forged which broke down for ever that
mediæval exegesis which had seen in Old Testament texts
a prediction of the papal supremacy. Along such lines the
Oxford Reformers desired to work to effect a reformation
within the bosom of the Church. Other motives inspired
other leaders and issued in different methods. In Germany
Luther led a revolt against the mercenary and worldly spirit
which had captured much of official Catholicism, and affirmed
that the foundation and mainspring of true religion is the in-
ward experience of justification by faith. His was an essentially religious protest which centred in the actual conversion
of the individual. But the strength of such a position was also
its weakness. Luther was not endowed with the gifts of the
founder of a theological system nor of the creator of a new
Church Order. He did not even build up a " kingdom of
fairies," as Hobbes pleasantly calls the ecclesiastical hierarchy.
Consequently Lutheranism, lacking a system of reasoned
theology and a definite Church Order, was impotent before the
Catholic revival, supported by the scholastic theology and the
organisation of the Church, now strengthened by the new
religious order of the Society of Jesus. But the movement
which Luther had founded Calvin saved. In him and in the
system which bears his name Protestantism found a defence
against the Counter-Reformation. For Calvin had a *penchant*
for systematic theology and a genius for Church organisation.
To the Christian who followed his standard he gave a self-
contained and consistent system of theology and a practical
interest in the constitution of a new Church polity.

The differences thus outlined between Lutheranism and
Calvinism mark the essential features of a change which was
passing over the Protestant Movement. From the position of
" a movement for the reform of doctrine and worship it passed
into the form of a rival Church over against the old Catholic
system." Calvin not only worked out a system of dogmatic
theology, but claimed that his new Church Order was commanded in Holy Scripture and was therefore the only lawful

65

form of Church government. The implications of this claim were of great importance. If the only true models of ecclesiastical polity were the Presbyterian government of the Church and the Consistory as established at Geneva, it was evident that the greater part of the traditional organisation of the Catholic Church was not only mistaken, but to be condemned. " He that is not for us is against us " became a test of potent strictness and severity in discriminating between idolaters and followers of the truth. Everything in which Rome differed from Geneva savoured of Antichrist, things indifferent became occasions of stumbling, and ceremonies which were not clearly prescribed in Holy Scripture were denounced as superstitious. The ideal of Calvin was to establish a Church as far removed as possible from the Catholic system.

Meanwhile the reforming movement in England had pursued a markedly insular and independent course. From the outset its development was profoundly affected by the policy of the Tudor sovereigns. In his youth Henry VIII had been trained in theological studies, when the sudden death of his brother Arthur called him from the field of devout speculation to that of kingly action. " From following the ewes great with young ones he was taken to rule Jacob his people and Israel his inheritance." During his reign the Reformation, though a breach with Rome was effected, did not involve doctrinal changes. True to the orthodoxy which had gained him the title of Defender of the Faith, Henry, when occasion arose for him to define it also, frowned upon all departures from Catholic theology. After his death the inevitable advance toward a more definite Protestant standard was essayed by Edward VI only to provoke a reaction under Mary. During the Marian persecution several of the leading Protestant divines found an asylum and a school of discipline in Geneva, whence they returned full of determination to introduce Calvinistic theology and polity into England when Elizabeth succeeded to the throne.

With the accession of Elizabeth the really critical phase of the English Reformation began. The Queen and her advisers were resolved " to keep the mean between the two extremes " of Rome and Geneva. The Reformed Church was to retain episcopacy, to have a public liturgy in the vulgar tongue, and in particular the use of the traditional Eucharistic vestments—the alb and chasuble or cope—was enjoined. It was evident that this settlement was intended to be a halfway house between the two extreme positions, and it was hoped that this halfway house would be sufficiently commodious to include the great majority of the people. The difficulties of such a position were obvious. At the accession of Elizabeth the political situation was full of danger. " England," as has been well observed, " seemed but a bone cast between two dogs," the only question being whether France or Spain would seize the tempting morsel. In such circumstances the fiery reformers who returned from Geneva desired a more effective bulwark against Roman Catholicism than they believed to be offered by the Reformed Church of England.

The controversy at first centred round the wearing of vestments. Not only were the cope and chasuble very generally disused, but the surplice became an object of contention, together with such nocent ceremonies as the sign of the Cross in baptism, the use of the ring in marriage, and the kneeling to receive the Communion. This phase of the dispute culminated in the issue of the *Book of Advertisements* in 1566. Far more serious were the issues upon which the opposition party, who received the name of Puritans, next challenged the position of the Church. The nonconforming movement entered upon a new and clearly marked phase, which was distinguished by the rise of new leaders and the moving of emphasis from points of outward ceremony to fundamental matters. The most important of the leaders of the Puritan party was the learned and able Thomas Cartwright, who held the office of Lady Margaret Professor of Divinity at Cambridge. He was soon recognised as an avowed Presbyterian, and the controversy now turned upon the question as to whether the National Church could be considered a truly reformed Church at all, since it retained such symbols of Antichrist as archbishops, and bishops with their minor officials, the archdeacons and the hierarchy of ecclesiastical courts. The reformers demanded the reconstruction of the Church entirely after the pattern of Geneva. They became so bold in their demands that in the third Parliament of Elizabeth in 1571 their champions in the House of Commons endeavoured to debate the question there. The Queen, however, checked this discussion, and by her orders the Court of High Commission took action to secure a stricter conformity on the part of the clergy. This opposition led to the framing of the First Admonition to the Parliament, which, although not formally presented to the House—as is demonstrated by a recent biographer of Cartwright—is of great importance because it sets forth the new demands of the malcontents. Dr Scott Pearson, in his life of Cartwright, fully recognises the gravity of this new departure. "Puritanism," he observes, "had travelled far since the vestiarian quarrels of the 'sixties and was now recognised as a complex movement, the chief feature of which was an avowed endeavour to presbyterianise the Church of England."[1] The Puritans now concentrated their forces upon "great matters concerning a true ministery and regiment of the Church according to the Word"; which being interpreted meant the adoption of the entire platform of Geneva.

There could be no greater tribute paid to any man than this slavish imitation of all that Calvin had said and done. The Puritans were awed by the power and wisdom of the authority which he wielded. "Of what account the Master of the Sentences was in the Church of Rome, the same and more amongst the preachers of the Reformed Churches Calvin had purchased ; so that the perfectest divines were judged they which were skilfullest in Calvin's writings. His books almost the very canon to judge both doctrine and discipline by ; French churches, both under others abroad and at home in their own country, all cast according to that mould which Calvin had made. The Church of Scotland in erecting the fabric of their reformation took the selfsame pattern. Till at length the discipline . . . began now to challenge universal obedience."[2]

There remained, however, some independent and vigorous thinkers who had not bowed the knee to this fashionable Baal ; and among them was the Master of the Temple, Richard Hooker, to whom there was given alike the ability and the opportunity to write in defence of the established order of things, "that posterity might know that he had not loosely

[1] *Thomas Cartwright and Elizabethan Puritanism*, p. 107.
[2] Hooker, Preface to the *Ecclesiastical Polity*, ii, 8.

through silence, permitted things to pass away as in a dream."
Hooker had been born in 1554 at Heavitree, near Exeter, and
had passed from a school in that town to Corpus Christi College,
Oxford, at the early age of fourteen, thanks to the generosity
of an uncle, John Hooker, and the interest of Bishop Jewel of
Salisbury. Both at home and in college the religious influences
brought to bear upon him were predominantly Calvinistic in
character. In academic studies Hooker justified the confidence of his friends and became in turn scholar and fellow of
his college; shortly afterward he lectured for the Regius Professor of Hebrew during the latter's illness. Meanwhile he
had received as pupils Edwin Sandys, whose father was then
Bishop of London and afterward became Archbishop of York,
and George Cranmer, great-nephew of Archbishop Cranmer.
His connexion with Sandys was of service to him later. The
date of Hooker's ordination is not known, but in 1581 he was
appointed to preach the open-air sermon at St Paul's Cross.
During recent years some of the preachers selected for this
office had given umbrage by their avowal of Puritan sympathies ; but Hooker distinguished himself by enunciating
certain opinions which were deemed by some " to cross a late
opinion of Mr Calvin's," thus giving a sign that he was
already acquiring a valuable independence of thought and
judgment. Unfortunately this soundness of judgment did
not prevail in other fields, for the visit to London resulted in
Hooker's making an unhappy marriage with Joan Churchman,
the daughter of one John Churchman, at whose house he had
lodged. Since marriage meant his removal from Oxford, he
was instituted in 1584 to the living of Drayton Beauchamp
near Aylesbury. There he was visited by his former pupils,
Sandys and Cranmer, and it was not improbably the result of
the report which Sandys presented to his father that Hooker
was offered shortly afterward the Mastership of the Temple.
His appointment was a compromise, since many of Puritan
sympathies desired to promote Walter Travers, the Reader of
the Temple, and others favoured one of the Queen's chaplains,
a certain Dr Bond. Somewhat reluctantly Hooker accepted
the office, for he may well have foreseen that it would plunge
him into the centre of the Puritan controversy.

This controversy indeed was domesticated within the

Temple Church itself in the person of Travers, the Reader, who had only received Presbyterian ordination, and who sought at once to persuade the new Master not to enter into his office until notice had been given of him to the congregation " so that their allowance might seal his calling." Hooker refused to countenance this suggestion, but it was evident that there could be little hope of harmony, since beneath the difference of opinions as to Church government there lay deeper differences in theology. The result was that " the pulpit spoke pure Canterbury in the morning and Geneva in the afternoon," for Travers felt it his duty to correct the unsoundness of Hooker's theology. Such a state of affairs could not continue long, and after a year's controversy the Archbishop served Travers with a notice forbidding him to preach any more. Inevitably this led to further acrimonious writing, and Hooker's position was by no means freed from difficulty by the silencing of his assistant.

The real importance of the events lay in the fact that they suggested to Hooker the task and design of his *Ecclesiastical Polity*. Not doubting either the goodness or the learning of his opponent, he was driven to examine carefully and minutely the foundations of his own position in order to commend to others what seemed so reasonable and convincing to himself. The scope of his design broadened under the influence of his studies, until it came to embrace the ambition to display the universal field of law. This breadth of conception was characteristic of his work, for he had been repelled by the narrowness of the Puritan position. First he disliked the excessive authority ascribed to Calvin's work and words. Although willing to admire Calvin as " incomparably the wisest man that ever the French Church did enjoy," and to admit the legality of the *régime* which he had set up at Geneva, Hooker refused to accept the elaborate pretensions built upon it. " That which Calvin did for the establishment of his discipline seemeth more commendable than that which he taught for the countenancing of it established." Secondly, Hooker refused to admit the Puritan tendency to exalt Holy Scripture as the sole rule of life and to depress all traditions of corporate life which could not claim direct sanction in its pages. Also he denied that there must necessarily be found in the Bible one particular form of ecclesiastical polity, from which no deviation was allowable.

This restriction of outlook on the part of the Puritans was a result of their reaction from the authority of Rome, which led them to despise all human conventions and to profess to lead a purer life guided solely by the precepts of the Bible. Dr Scott Pearson acknowledges that Cartwright was convinced "that God who made provision for the tabernacle and the temple even to the pins, snuffers, and besoms, was sure to lay down in His Word the essentials and ornaments of His Church, and that in Scripture He does enjoin Presbyterianism as the only government of the Church." [1] Further, Cartwright did not differentiate between the degrees of authority to be ascribed to the various books of the Bible. He held "that all Scripture is equally binding and that therefore the death-penalties announced in the Old Testament for blasphemy, murder, adultery, and heresy are valid still and ought to be put into force." [2] It was against this attempt to found an ecclesiastical polity, and in large part a civil polity also, upon the sole foundation of the Scriptures that Hooker was moved to make emphatic protest.

In his endeavour to elucidate the several kinds of law by which the universe is governed Hooker followed with deliberate fidelity the system expounded by the mediæval scholastics. He started from their fundamental conviction that the world was a cosmos, not a chaos, and that the idea of law is traceable to the very Being of God Himself. Although it is not possible fully to comprehend the mystery of the Divine Nature, Hooker felt himself on sure ground in affirming that "the Being of God is a kind of law to His working" and that "God is therefore a law both to Himself and to all other things besides." There is thus an Eternal Law, which is the eternal purpose by which God does all things. Hooker called it "that order which God before all ages hath set down with Himself, for Himself to do all things by." In its relation to the working of God Himself this law is termed the "First Law Eternal"; but there is also a sense in which we may speak of a second Eternal Law, namely, the law which governs the entire creation in its several parts, a law which is eternal because it is set down by the Creator "to be kept by all His creatures according to the several conditions wherewith He hath endued them." [3] It is

[1] *Thomas Cartwright and Elizabethan Puritanism*, p. 90. [2] *Ibid.*
[3] Hooker, *Ecclesiastical Polity*, I, iii, 1.

evident that the entire universe is under the reign of law as there defined ; for, on the one hand, " all things which are as they ought to be "—that is to say, all creatures which conform to the law of their own particular state—" are conformed unto this Second Law Eternal," while, on the other hand, even those things which are evil and contrary to this law are nevertheless permitted and allowed by God and so come within the scope of " the First Law Eternal."

From this general definition Hooker advanced to a careful examination of the created world. It is clear that the " Second Law Eternal " embraces several different classes of creature, some belonging to inanimate and some to animate creation, which have therefore each a different law. Hooker pointed first to Natural Law, the law which governs the non-rational creatures, the " natural agents which keep the law of their kind unwittingly." The obedience of these is entirely involuntary and unconscious, but yet it is " the stay of the whole world." Such creatures are therefore " nothing else but God's instrument." This world governed by Natural Law, however, is but the scene upon which is staged the activity of self-conscious rational creatures, whose co-operation with the Law of God is self-determined. Of this class of beings Hooker distinguished two species, angels and men. He defined the nature of the law which angels must observe, of which it is not necessary to speak here, save to notice that the angels, like men, are capable of transgression.

More important was the problem of human society and government. The questions of the origin of the State and of the authority of the laws by which Governments enforce their will upon their subjects have provoked a great variety and con-trariety of answers. To some thinkers, who have dreamed of a time when men were little lower than the angels, organised society has been an instrument of depression and degradation ; others have abhorred the State of Nature and have seen in the escape to society the only elevating power which has raised man above the animals. Hooker, while convinced that in the State of Nature men were not left a prey to lawlessness and ignorance, was nevertheless equally sure that the State marked an immeasurable advance upon the natural condition. In con-sidering the nature of Man he enunciated as an axiom the principle that Man was superior to the animals by the possession of " natural reason." This natural reason was the birthright of all men, and by its means they were able to know good from evil, right from wrong. There was therefore no such possibility as a wholly lawless evil state for men, for they had at all times knowledge of " Law Rational "—that is, " the law which human nature knoweth itself in reason universally bound unto." The scope of this Law of Reason was declared by Hooker to embrace " all those things which men by the light of their natural understanding evidently know (or at leastwise may know) to be beseeming or unbeseeming, virtuous or vicious, good or evil for them to do." All men were bound by this law "absolutely even as they are men," so that none could claim that its observance was a matter of free choice. If men had this natural understanding of the Law Rational, all that remained was that they should conform their actions to its precepts. Granted this correspondence between the understanding and the will, the State of Nature would indeed approach an idyllic happiness. Hooker himself was driven to admit in one place that there was " no impossibility in nature considered by itself, but that men might have lived without any public regiment." [1] None the less the fact remained that there had been a transition from the State of Nature to organised society, of which some explanation must be furnished.

In creating a bridge to span this gulf Hooker followed the teaching of the scholastic theologians, who had found in the story of the Fall an explanation adequate to account for all the lack of harmony between the ideal and the actual, and who also had the fortune to live in an age when the historicity of the alleged event was unquestioned. He therefore fell back upon the supposition of " the corruption of our nature," which accounted not only for the inability of man to observe the Law of Reason, but also for the imperfections in the natural creation, the " defect in the matter of things natural," which, although evident to reason, was only explicable by revelation with its doctrine that this was the result of " divine malediction laid for the sin of man upon those creatures which God had made for the use of man." Having thus admitted the corruption of human nature, Hooker was able to turn aside

[1] I, x, 4.

vigorously to belabour those who raised the cry of " Back to Nature." Nothing could be more foolish than to suppose that the solution of difficulties lay in the return to the State of Nature. The Old Testament afforded convincing evidence of the depravity to which the natural man could descend upon occasion, so that although Elizabethan England might be far from perfect it was a happy age compared " with those times wherein there were no civil societies, with those times wherein there was as yet no manner of public regiment established, and with those times wherein there were not above eight persons righteous living upon the face of the earth."[1] So far was Hooker from sympathising with the idea that the natural state was to be preferred to the present that he declared that " the Law of Nature doth now require of necessity some kind of regiment, so that to bring things unto the first course they were in and utterly to take away all kind of public government in the world, were apparently to overturn the whole world."

There remained the question of the mode by which mankind passed from the State of Nature to that of government, and in considering this Hooker seems to have been somewhat perplexed by the contrast of theory and practice. Theoretically he had no doubt that the creation of a government was the voluntary and deliberate act of the community, which originally possessed full power over itself. " Unto me it seemeth almost out of doubt and controversy that every independent multitude, before any certain form of regiment established, hath under God's supreme authority full dominion over itself " ; and again, " God creating mankind did endue it naturally with full power to guide itself in what kind of societies soever it should choose to live ; a man which is born lord of himself may be made another's servant ; and that power which naturally whole societies have, may be derived unto many, few, or one under whom all the rest shall then live in subjection."[2] There could be no difference of opinion in Hooker's judgment that " the end whereunto all government was instituted was *bonum publicum*, the universal or common good," nor that the appointment of governors was by the free consent of the people, " without which consent there were no reason that one

[1] I, x, 3.   [2] VIII, ii, 5.

man should take upon him to be lord or judge over another."
Characteristically too, he suggested two reasons for this voluntary creation of government: the one a natural result of man's
reason, namely, the desire "to seek communion and fellowship with others," and the other the consequence of man's
depravity—" to take away all mutual grievances, injuries and
wrongs there was no way but only by growing unto composition
and agreement amongst themselves by ordaining some kind of
government public and by yielding themselves subject thereunto." From these statements it would appear that Hooker
believed in a social contract of the sort which Locke later expounded, a voluntary institution of government by the entire
multitude for its own corporate advantage and profit. On the
other hand, he realised that history afforded many examples of
government by right of conquest, and therefore, while maintaining his thesis that the basis of society was consent and regarding this as the normal method of establishing a state, he
allowed exceptions, since in certain cases God permitted rulers
to govern by another authority. In the case of the Hebrews
the divine regulation of their civil government was part of the
providential ordering of their history. Their circumstance
was exceptional. But in other cases the right of conquest
might be recognised as a permissive departure from the normal
rule of consent. " Some multitudes," Hooker observed, " are
brought into subjection by force, as those who being subdued
are fain to submit their necks unto what yoke it pleaseth their
conquerors to lay upon them; which conquerors by just and
lawful wars do hold their power over such multitudes as a thing
descending unto them, divine providence itself so disposing.
For it is God who giveth victory in the day of war; and unto
whom dominion in this sort is derived, the same they enjoy
according unto that law of nations, which law authoriseth
conquerors to reign as absolute lords over them whom they
vanquish." [1] Despite this recognition of the lawfulness of
dominion by conquest, Hooker did not waver in his conviction
that it was only an exceptional form, and he was solaced by the
reflection that " by means of after-agreement " such dominion
could be converted " even by little and little into that most
sweet form of kingly government," a constitutional monarchy.

[1] VIII, ii, 5.

The institution of the State, however, is but the prelude to the making of laws; accordingly, Hooker continued his examination of the different kinds of law which legislators enact. At the outset he insisted that law is essential to social life. " Politic societies could not be without government, nor government without a distinct kind of law from that which hath already been declared." This " Law of a Commonweal " he called " the very soul of a politic body, the parts whereof are by law animated, held together and set on work in such actions as the common good requireth."[1] In accordance with this thesis Hooker affirmed that law was not an infringement, but a protection, of individual liberty. A state governed by a tyrant according to his whim and caprice lacked the very elements of liberty, namely, a clearly defined system of laws. If laws were the guardian of liberty, they must receive whatever force they possessed from the consent of the whole society. " By the Natural Law (whereunto God hath made all subject) the lawful power of making laws to command whole politic societies of men belongeth so properly unto the same entire societies that for any prince or potentate of what kind soever upon earth to exercise the same of himself, and not either by express commission immediately and personally received from God, or else by authority derived at the first from their consent upon whose persons they impose laws, it is no better than mere tyranny."[2] The only basis of law is public consent; " laws they are not therefore which public approbation hath not made so." But this consent may be of several kinds, tacit no less than active. Hooker distinguished personal consent—signified by voice, sign, or act—from representative consent—given by authorised representatives in Parliaments and councils ; and more far-reaching and powerful than both of these was the silent influence of custom, the accumulated experience of generations which is crystallised in the traditions of a corporate society. " To be commanded we do consent when that society whereof we are part hath at any time before consented without revoking the same after by the like universal agreement." So " the act of a public society of men done five hundred years sithence standeth as theirs who presently are of the same societies because corporations are immortal."[3] The doctrine that laws

---

[1] I, x, 1.   [2] I, x, 8.   [3] *Ibid.*

derive their authority only from public assent, therefore, neither destroys the continuity of social life nor yet ascribes an unalterable finality to the laws of the past.

Much of the error of Hooker's opponents sprang from a mistaken idea of the immutability or otherwise of laws. The Puritan tended to suppose that the finality of the law depended upon the authority of the lawgiver rather than upon the matter contained in the law. Thus the only immutable system of law was that of the Bible, whose author was God. Hooker perceived the falsity of this notion and proceeded to correct it. He cut at the root of the error by pointing out the distinction between Natural Laws and Positive Laws, a difference which underlies all legislation whether civil or ecclesiastical. " Laws natural do always bind ; laws positive not so, but only after they have been expressly and wittingly imposed." [1] Nor were positive laws confined to the enactments of human legislators, as the Puritans held ; they were part of the Divine Law revealed in Scripture. Therefore they were " either permanent or else changeable according as the matter itself is concerning which they were first made; whether God or man be the maker of them, alteration do they so far forth admit as the matter doth exact." Consequently legislation which enforces observance of the moral law by the enactment of penalties is permanent, because the moral law is part of the Natural Law ; and conversely the ceremonial law of Israel, although of divine authorship and also incorporated in the laws of the Jews, was only temporary, because the matter was not permanent. Positive laws might vary according to the circumstances and condition of different nations. In democracies Hooker thought it wise to have laws which made " common smaller offices to go by lot, for fear of strife and division likely to arise," and the greater offices, " whereof but few are capable, to pass by popular election." [2] From these principles it followed that human laws might either re-enact precepts to which men were already bound by the Law of Nature, or might make that a duty which was not so before. The former kind of law Hooker termed "mixedly" human, the latter "merely" human. A "mixedly" human law added penalties to compel the observance of duties to which men were already bound by reason ; a "merely"

[1] I, xv, 1.   [2] I, x, 9.

human law dealt with matters of expediency, such as the regulation of the descent of land by primogeniture.

In addition to laws concerning civil affairs, Man also had need of laws of religion, since he was a citizen of a heavenly as well as of a terrestrial commonwealth. These laws Hooker called supernatural laws, since they dealt with matters such as Man could not know by the use of his natural reason. Consequently laws which concerned supernatural duties were all positive, since they were not binding upon Man by Nature, but only by being imposed through revelation. In many cases they were repetitions of the Law of Nature, for " when supernatural duties are necessarily exacted, natural are not rejected as needless. The Law of God therefore is, though principally delivered for instruction in the one, yet fraught with precepts of the other also." [1] The Scriptures were in part a republication of the Law of Nature. Therefore the Puritans were foolish to urge " that the only law which God had appointed unto men . . . is in the Sacred Scriptures," since Scripture itself embraces many precepts of the Law of Nature.

Finally there remained the Law of Nations, an International Law governing the relations of different peoples. Man's capacity and desire for fellowship was not satisfied wholly by the nation, but extended to the wish for " a kind of society and fellowship with all mankind." Hence there grew up a Law of Nations, which had its counterpart in religious matters in the decrees of General Councils, which are " laws of spiritual commerce between Christian nations." In the sphere of international relations it was especially evident that statesmen had to reckon with the depraved nature of man, as well as with his natural instincts toward goodness. Laws therefore were in part directive and in part penal. They directed men's impulses toward the attainment of virtue, but also, " presuming man in regard of his depraved mind little better than a wild beast," they restrained him from anti-social acts by threat of punishment.

It is unnecessary to emphasise the detailed correspondence between Hooker's exposition of the universal province of law and that of the Thomist philosophy. In reaction against the Puritan narrowness he had deliberately turned back to the

[1] I, xii, i.

traditional scholastic doctrine, and his contemplation of the majestic dignity of law moved him to utter a splendid panegyric upon it. " Of Law there can be no less acknowledged than that her seat is in the bosom of God, her voice the harmony of the world ; all things in heaven and earth do her homage, the very least as feeling her care, and the greatest as not exempted from her power, both angels and men, and creatures of what condition soever, though each in different sort and manner, yet all with uniform consent, admiring her as the mother of their peace and joy."

The student of political philosophy may perhaps indulge the regret that Hooker was not born again in the century which saw the attack upon the Stuart monarchy, for his defence of monarchy would have been no less valuable than his apology for prelacy. Although he detected with dislike a revolutionary tendency in some of the Puritan writings, yet in his time the attack upon episcopacy had not involved the fortunes of the monarchy, so that his remarks on the subject of government by kings cannot be construed as an oration upon the theme " No bishop, no king." Nevertheless, in view of the later controversy, Hooker's opinions on this subject are of great interest. He thought it "no improbable opinion" that "when numbers of households joined themselves in civil society together, kings were the first kind of governors among them," so that kingship was an extension of the supreme power which fathers had over their private families. But this did not imply that monarchy was of divine prescription. On the contrary, Hooker maintained, " That the Christian world should be ordered by kingly regiment, the Law of God doth not anywhere command" ;[1] and as a fact of experience monarchy often taught men that " to live by one man's will became the cause of all men's misery,"[2] so that it had been superseded by another form of government. Notwithstanding this possibility of tyranny, monarchy had been so widespread and prevalent in human societies that the conservative nature of Hooker's mind led him to a strong predilection for it as the best practicable form of government, if under due regulation, to prevent the abuse of power. In words prophetic of an age not far distant he wrote : " If it should be at this day a controversy whether kingly regiment were lawful

[1] VIII, ii, 7.   [2] I, x, 5.

or no, peradventure in defence thereof the long continuance which it hath had sithence the first beginning might be alleged"; and if its opponents should point to its abuses, surely the best defence would be " to show the nature of sovereignty, to sever it from accidental properties, make it clear that ancient and present regality are one and the same in substance, how great odds soever otherwise may seem to be between them." [1] Hooker was a convinced advocate of constitutional monarchy. Although he had no belief in monarchy as an institution of divine prescription, nor did he view with favour the kingship based upon conquest and involving the exercise of absolute power over the conquered, he welcomed the development of absolute monarchy into constitutional. But the existence of a limited monarchy raises difficult questions. What are the precise limits which may be imposed upon kings ?   Is it lawful to extend these checks ?   And, in the last resort, if the kings should overstep their bounds, may the people depose their rulers ?   Such questions are necessarily involved in a constitutional monarchy, and Hooker could not avoid attempting to answer them.

In his view the normal manner of instituting kingship was by the Social Contract, which expressed the desire of an ungoverned multitude to enter into organised social life.   In such cases he suggested that the extent of the limits imposed upon the kings could be ascertained by examining this original compact.   "Touching kings which were first instituted by agreement and composition made with them over whom they reign, how far their power may lawfully extend, the articles of compact between them must show "—a thesis of incontestable soundness in theory, but open to the unfortunate practical objection that history has no record of the text of a single compact whereby the solution may be known.   For like the Fall of Man of which it was a consequence, the Social Contract would seem to be a necessary hypothesis in the school of philosophy, though an unprovable fact to the school of history. Hooker realised the difficulty of the loss of the Social Compact, which, like the Mosaic Tables of Stone, had perished in the hands of its authors.   Therefore he allowed a dominant determining power to written law and present custom.   The limits

[1] VII, ii, i.

of kingly power are to be known by consulting " not the articles of compact only at the first beginning, which for the most part are either clean worn out of knowledge, or else known unto very few, but whatsoever hath been after in free and voluntary manner condescended unto, whether by express consent, whereof positive laws are witness, or else by silent allowance famously notified through custom reaching beyond the memory of man." [1] The present, therefore, is to be the interpreter of the past, yet nothing can be done in the present to make of none effect the original agreement by which " original influence of power from the body into the king is the cause of the king's dependency in power upon the body." An absolute monarchy may become constitutional, but a limited monarch may not make himself a tyrant. But suppose he should seek to do so ? " May then a body politic," asked Hooker, " at all times withdraw in whole or in part that influence of dominion which passeth from it, if inconvenience doth grow thereby ? " The problem was difficult, and the answer given was hesitant and uncertain. " It must be presumed that supreme governors will not in such cases oppose themselves and be stiff in detaining that, the use whereof is with public detriment ; but surely without their consent I see not how the body should be able by any just means to help itself saving when dominion doth escheat. Such things therefore must be thought upon beforehand, that power may be limited 'ere it be granted." [2] This answer can scarcely be called a solution. Hooker, not unlike the harassed Pilate, had raised a question of acute complexity, and had sought rather to evade than to answer it. His words could afford no guidance in case of practical urgency. Within a century his countrymen were faced for the second time with this problem. Like himself, they hoped that dominion would escheat, but the birth of a son to James II frustrated their hope, and they had to act rather than to speculate. Perhaps in expelling James II and admitting William of Orange to be king with " power limited 'ere it be granted," they were acting in the spirit of Hooker's counsel, if not according to the letter.

The problem of placing practical checks upon the king did not present itself to Hooker as a matter of urgency, so that he

[1] VIII, ii, 11. [2] VIII, ii, 10.

did not make definite suggestions. His chief point was that the consent of the whole people was necessary to make laws, and if the laws were good, then the State would be happy, for he insisted that the king was subject, not superior, to the law. " The good or evil estate " of a commonwealth " dependeth so much upon the power of making laws, that in all well-settled states, yea, though they be monarchies, yet diligent care is evermore had that the commonwealth do not clean resign up herself and make over this power wholly into the hands of any-one." [1] In particular Hooker admired the English Constitu-tion, in which, he asserted, the laws " are not by any of us so taken or interpreted as if they did receive their force from power which the prince doth communicate to the Parliament, or to any other court under him, but from power which the whole body of this realm being naturally possessed with, hath by free and deliberate assent derived unto him that ruleth over them." [2] The two principles upon which he insisted were the necessity of the consent of the whole people to legislation, and the subordination of the king to the laws of the nation. In such a State Hooker judged the people to live in great pros-perity. "Where the king doth guide the State and the law the king, that commonwealth is like an harp or melodious in-strument the strings whereof are tuned and handled all by one, following as laws the rules and canons of musical science." [3] Upon such a pattern was the English monarchy modelled, " wherein though no manner of person or cause be unsubject to the king's power, yet so is the power of the king over all and in all limited, that unto all his proceedings the law itself is a rule. The axioms of our regal government are these : *lex facit regem* ; the king's grant of any favour made contrary to the law is void ; *rex nihil potest nisi quod jure potest.*" [4]

The monarchy was not the sole glory of the English nation. Hooker rejoiced with equal enthusiasm in the prospect of the close alliance of Church and State and of the government of the National Church by bishops. In his scheme of society there could be no divorce between religion and politics. Not only were all true virtues " to honour true religion as their parent," but " all well-ordered commonwealths [were] to love her as

---

[1] VIII, vi, 2.   [2] VIII, vi, 11.
[3] VIII, ii, 12.   [4] VIII, ii, 13.

their chiefest stay." [1]   The same men who were citizens of the State were also members of a celestial kingdom.   The Church therefore was both a natural society—the expression of men's desire for fellowship in religious matters—and a supernatural society—being governed by a " law supernatural which God Himself hath revealed concerning that kind of worship which His people shall do unto Him." [2]   In the early centuries of Christianity, when it was a persecuted religion in the Roman Empire, the Church had necessarily to organise itself apart from the State, but once the Emperors had adopted Christianity as the official religion of the Empire the opposition between the Church and the civil power ceased.   Thus Hooker reached his characteristic conclusion that in a nation professing Christianity Church and State were but two aspects of the same body. He maintained that " seeing there is not any man of the Church of England but the same is also a member of the Commonwealth, nor any man a member of the Commonwealth which is not also of the Church of England . . . so albeit properties and actions of one kind do cause the name of a Commonwealth, qualities and functions of another sort the name of a Church to be given unto a multitude, yet one and the selfsame multitude may in such sort be both, and is so with us that no person appertaining to the one can be denied to be also of the other." [3] There could hardly be found a stronger affirmation of the identity of Church and State in respect of members, the difference consisting only in divergence of function.   This doctrine naturally led Hooker to approve the Royal Supremacy and the Parliamentary Establishment of the Church.   For although it was proper that the Convocations should debate and consider what measures were necessary for the welfare of the Church, even as men expert in Civil Law should frame measures for the State, yet their recommendations could not have the force of law until they had received the consent of the people.   " Howbeit, when all which the wisdom of all sorts can do, is done for devising of laws in the Church, it is the general consent of all that giveth them the form and vigour of laws." [4]   This consent could not be otherwise given than in Parliament, which was not a court " so merely temporal, as if it might meddle

<hr/>

[1] V, i, 1.   [2] I, xv, 2.
[3] VIII, i, 2.   [4] VIII, vi, 11.

with nothing but only leather and wool." Ecclesiastical laws, therefore, must be approved by Parliament and accepted by the king, for if all the people had a right to give their consent by representation it would be absurd that the sovereign alone should be denied the liberty of assent or dissent. "Against all equity were it that a man should suffer detriment at the hands of men, for not observing that which he never did either by himself or others, mediately or immediately, agree unto ; much more that a king should constrain all others unto the strict observation of any such human ordinance as passeth without his own approbation." [1]   This doctrine of the Establishment of the Church and of the Royal Supremacy has proved the most controversial of Hooker's contentions.   It was dissented from strongly by the Puritans forthwith, and it is a stumbling-block to many of Hooker's own communion in the present century.   " This man might have been set at liberty, if he had not appealed unto Cæsar."   Yet it was to the union of prelacy and monarchy that Hooker looked for the happiness of England.   Of episcopacy, as of kingship, he held no doctrinaire theories.   He did not affirm that it was of express Dominical appointment, nor that it could be proved from Scripture to be the only form of Church government.   But his respect for tradition caused him to regard it as of the *bene esse* of the Church, and he was anxious that bishops should hold civil offices also.   " If it please God," he urged, " to bless some principal attendants on His own sanctuary and to endue them with extraordinary parts of excellency " then it was proper that they should concern themselves with affairs of State, since the Commonwealth " must needs suffer loss, when it hath not the gain which eminent civil ability in ecclesiastical persons is now and then found apt to afford." [2]   It was a matter of great concern to Hooker that there should be so much dishonour offered to prelacy, of which he wrote that it is " the temperature of excess in all estates, the glue and soder of the public weal, the ligament which tieth and connecteth the limbs of this body politic each to other " [3]—a more than adequate defence of that gift of treading the *via media*, miscalled compromise, which has been thought by some to be the peculiar grace of the Anglican Episcopate.

[1] VIII, vi, 8.   [2] VII, xv, 6.   [3] VII, xviii, 12.

RICHARD HOOKER

Upon a general reading of the *Ecclesiastical Polity* perhaps the most striking characteristic which impresses itself upon the student is the author's gift of historical thinking. Few have had a finer sense of the value of historical tradition than Hooker. To him the unity and continuity of history was neither a phrase nor a fallacy, but a practical truth as well as an inspiration. The sense of the importance of custom and tradition was strong in all his defence of the Church of England. The very keynote of his writings is the wisdom of the scribe who " brought out of his treasure-store things old and new." Hooker insisted that the Reformation had not broken the continuity of the Church of England. " We hope that to reform ourselves . . . is not to sever ourselves from the Church we were of before. In the Church we were, and we are so still." The same principle governs his defence of the retention of ceremonies. The arguments which he used in this connexion are equally cogent in the political sphere, and he applied them in defence of orderly and stable government. The sense of continuity with the past is stimulated in the minds of the people by symbolic ceremonies and pageantry. " We must not think but that there is some ground of reason even in nature, whereby it cometh to pass that no nation under heaven either doth or ever did suffer public actions which are of weight, whether they be civil and temporal or else spiritual and sacred, to pass without some visible solemnity ; the very strangeness whereof and difference from that which is common, doth cause popular eyes to observe and to mark the same." [1] Public actions should be solemnised by public ceremonies ; still more should public officers be marked out for esteem by the bestowal of honours and dignities. The problem of the use and abuse of badges and titles has been a matter of controversy often, and there was a tendency in some Puritan circles to despise all adornments save those of godliness and virtue. It was urged that, at best, honours were but outward tokens and things indifferent. Hooker replied that they had a significance and influence which demanded their retention. " Weigh these things in themselves, titles, gestures, presents, other the like external signs wherein honour doth consist and they are matters of no great moment. Howbeit,

[1] IV, i, 3.

take them away, let them cease to be required, and they are not things of small importance which that surcease were likely to draw after them. Let the Lord Mayor of London, or any other unto whose office honour belongeth, be deprived but of that title which of itself is a matter of nothing ; and suppose we that it would be a small maim unto the credit, force and countenance of his office ? " [1] Governors of all kinds were but human beings, fallible and errant, and particularly open to the slander and misrepresentation of those who were ignorant of the difficulties of statesmanship, and therefore every means should be contrived to maintain the dignity and repute of their position. " The good government either of the Church or the Commonwealth dependeth scarcely on any one external thing so much as on the public marks and tokens, whereby the estimation that governors are in is made manifest to the eyes of men." [2] Although Hooker was firmly convinced of the necessity of public consent to the making of laws, he was no champion of an unbridled democracy. In no place does the essential caution of his judgment find expression more clearly than in his reluctance to alter laws and traditions handed down from the past, so long as they serve any good purpose. " The wisdom which is learned by tract of time, findeth the laws that have been in former ages established, needful in later to be abrogated. . . . But true withal is it, that alteration though it be from worse to better hath in it inconveniencies and these weighty. . . . Further, if it be a law which the custom and continual practice of many ages or years hath confirmed in the minds of men, to alter it must needs be troublesome and scandalous. . . . What have we to induce men unto the willing obedience and observation of laws but the weight of so many men's judgments as have with deliberate advice assented thereunto, the weight of that long experience which the world hath thereof with consent and good liking ? So that to change any such law must needs with the common sort impair and weaken the force of those grounds whereby all laws are made effectual." [3] Some laws must be abrogated when they have become harmful to the welfare of the State. But a passion for change is altogether to be discouraged. " As for arbitrary alterations . . . if the benefit of that which is newly devised

---

[1] VII, xvii, 4.   [2] VII, xix, 1.   [3] IV, xiv, 1.

be but small, sith the custom of easiness to alter and change is so evil, no doubt but to bear a tolerable sore is better than to venture on so dangerous a remedy." [1] Even in the case of necessary alteration it is more advisable to leave evil laws " to be abolished by disusage through tract of time " than to risk disorder by the disturbance of change. Hooker placed great emphasis upon stability of government as the surest means of preserving public tranquillity, and his love of tradition and continuity disposed him to an almost excessive distrust of innovation and change.

Before the completion of the great task which he had set himself, there had been a change in the circumstances of Hooker's life and in the controversy which had evoked his writing. The Temple was a restless and unquiet place, even after the departure of Travers, and there can be little doubt that the Master felt the hindrance of contention and hostility to the execution of his design. After six years he was presented by Whitgift to the living of Boscombe, near to Salisbury, in accordance with his petition to the Archbishop to be allowed to retire to some country rectory where " I may study and pray for God's blessing upon my endeavours, and keep myself in peace and privacy, and behold God's blessing spring out of my mother earth, and eat my own bread without oppositions." At Boscombe Hooker finished the first four books of the *Ecclesiastical Polity* and published them in 1594. In the following year the Queen presented him to the rectory of Bishopsbourne, near Canterbury ; and there he finished the fifth book and published it in 1597. The few remaining years of his life were devoted to the completion of the task, and he succeeded in finishing the last three books, though the effort not improbably cost him his life, for he died on November 2, 1600. After his death the final draft of the last three books could not be found among his papers, but only some rough copies. These were examined by the author's friend, Dr Spencer of Corpus Christi College, Oxford, and with his reconstruction of this part of the work we have to rest content.

Meanwhile, the influence of the published books had

[1] IV, xiv, 2.

changed the character of the Puritan controversy. A generous recognition of Hooker's work is contained in the most recent biography of Cartwright, to which reference has been made before. " This classic defence of the Church of England," writes Dr Scott Pearson of the *Ecclesiastical Polity*, " is a product by reaction of Cartwrightian Puritanism. In the calm air of the detached philosopher the tenets of T. C. are analysed, their implications set forth, and the universal principles of Church government expounded. Hooker discusses the broad question of divine revelation and exposes the narrow view of Scripture held by the Puritans. . . . Hooker's work is a great and lasting achievement. He certainly discloses the deficiencies of the Puritan conception of revelation and introduces a strong humanist element into theological thought. . . . The Puritans recognised the weight of their latest opponent. Their only reply, *A Christian Letter* (1599), is an insipid production that reveals the consciousness of defeat." [1]

If it be true that Hooker " hastened his own death by hastening to give life to his books," it is certain that his work is a worthy memorial of him. A few points of his philosophy have been touched upon in these pages, too few to do justice to the richness of his thought, yet perhaps enough to suggest the justice of his claim to be regarded as a political thinker as well as a great divine. None can read his *Ecclesiastical Polity* without realising the versatility of his genius. Yet the most powerful impression produced upon one reader is that of the reverence for the historic past which characterised Hooker. He lived in an age of great change, and amid a company of reformers zealous for more radical changes than had yet been attempted in England. In face of the exaggerated enthusiasm for the innovations of Calvin and the desire of his disciples to make an end of old traditions, Hooker turned back deliberately to seek the old paths and to walk in them. His return to the scholastic philosophy was not a mere controversial *ruse de guerre* ; rather it was the expression of his deep conviction of the value of historical tradition and of the continuity of corporate life. The wisdom of Hooker is the principle of true

[1] *Thomas Cartwright and Elizabethan Puritanism*, pp. 371-372.

conservatism, and he realised the abiding significance of this principle as an essential constituent of human nature. " For no man having drunk of old wine, straightway desireth new ; for he saith, ' The old is better.' "

NORMAN SYKES

BIBLIOGRAPHY

HOOKER : *Works*, arranged by Keble, revised by Church and Paget. 3 vols. Oxford, 1888. [These include Walton's *Life of Hooker*, the *Ecclesiastical Polity*, the *Supplication* of Travers and Hooker's *Answer*, and Hooker's *Sermons*.]

F. PAGET : *Introduction to Book V of Hooker's "Ecclesiastical Polity."* Oxford, 1899.

R. W. CHURCH : *Introduction and Text of Book I of Hooker's "Ecclesiastical Polity."* Oxford, 1876.

A. F. SCOTT PEARSON : *Thomas Cartwright and Elizabethan Puritanism.* Cambridge, 1925.

IV

FRANCISCO SUAREZ

I

UNTIL at any rate quite recently it has been held as beyond the possibility of challenge that physical nature was the peculiar domain of practically constant and immutable law. It is indeed possible that if we could see human history from a sufficient distance we might conclude that it too was the expression of an uniform order. But, living within history as we do, we are aware of a twofold attitude toward law which seems to embrace and to exhaust all the possibilities and resources of our human energy. For us men life is first an impatience of or revolt against law, and afterward the recognition of its indispensableness and the gradual recovery of it as a guide. In the case of the individual these two attitudes, or rather moments of energy, are represented by youth and middle age. And as the members of each human generation, as we ordinarily reckon that period, survive for the most part throughout its successor, these movements are always contemporary and are able therefore normally to supplement and correct each other.

But in contrast with the generations composed of individuals born round about the same point in time history has its more protracted moments of youth and middle age which are purely successive. The six centuries, for instance, which followed upon the disruption of the Roman Empire formed a period during which it might have seemed as though the Western peoples would never grow tired of sowing their wild oats. That period of anarchy gave way at last, however, to the Middle Age, which deserves its title not only because it formed the chronological bridge between primitive Western barbarism and our modern world, but also because it was really middle-aged. It was middle-aged especially in that it envisaged all human society as a vast hierarchy of law and spent

90

all its energy in the effort to translate that vision more closely into fact. But the mediæval conception of society was not confined to the human world, nor was its order derived from any merely human law or legal system. Above and beyond the highest human society extended the angelic orders to which was committed the administration of that Eternal Law by which the Divine Providence governed the universe. And it was from this Eternal Law of the Divine Providence that all positive human law down to that which regulated the pettiest feudal jurisdiction was derived.

It is unnecessary here to attempt any enumeration of the converging causes which led to the wild riot of youthful self-assertion which followed, and which we know as the Renaissance. Nor is it necessary to survey the area of demolition which that whirlwind of human energy left in its train. It is enough to say that it passed and left to its successor the work of necessary restoration and reconstruction. The latter half of the sixteenth century and the earlier half of the seventeenth were engaged upon this task. In them the heady youth of the Renaissance sobered down to the temper and the methods appropriate to the prosaic work of making the best of things which always falls to the lot of middle age. Now the task imposed upon middle age always seems to involve reaction, and often seems to be much more of a reaction than it really is. It often tries to get back behind the changes wrought by what it regards as the thoughtless inconsequence of youth, but never quite succeeds in doing so. On the other hand, it sometimes recognises frankly certain changes in the situation as assured, and resolutely sets itself to make the best of them. Both these attitudes are represented in the period with which we are now concerned, but it is with the first only that I have to deal.

II

The Renaissance had laughed the old scholasticism out of court. There was perhaps excuse for even the wildest buffoonery of its derision, for the later scholasticism had by the thinness of its substance and the increasing subtlety of its distinctions become frankly ridiculous. But behind this scholasticism of the decadence there lay a body of the sanest and exactest thinking which has ever been enlisted in the service of religion. It was to this scholasticism of the thirteenth century that the new defenders of the faith resorted for weapons which they might adapt to the needs of their new warfare. Indeed, it may be said that it was the requirements of the sixteenth- and seventeenth-century theologians that first gave to St Thomas the undisputed position as supreme doctor and theologian which he still holds in the Roman schools. Even in the sixteenth century and even in the Spanish universities which were the chief seats of Dominican learning the tradition still very widely obtained which made the *Sentences* of Peter Lombard, not the *Summa* of St Thomas, the text-book on which professorial lectures were based. There are few beliefs more widely held than that the Jesuits have always been the bitterest opponents of the Thomist theology. In so far as such a belief implies, as it is usually taken to imply, that the greater Jesuit theologians have either disparaged or even been indifferent to the merits of St Thomas, there is none less grounded in fact. Indeed, it may be said, without at all overlooking the contributory zeal of sixteenth-century Spanish Dominicans like Melchior Cano, Soto, Victoria, and Covarruvias, that the exaltation of St Thomas to his position of unchallenged theological supremacy was in amplest measure due to the fervent, if discriminating, discipleship of a distinguished group of Spanish Jesuits inspired directly by the express injunctions of their Founder. Of this group Francisco Suarez has unquestionably achieved the most lasting celebrity and influence.

The life of the member of a religious order, apart from those engaged in missionary enterprise, is not likely to abound in thrilling incident. It is as a rule devoted to a single pursuit with a tenacity of concentration which leaves no room for anything beyond, save the exercises of that spiritual discipline by which it is sustained and inspired. Such at any rate was the life of Suarez. It extended to a period of almost seventy years, and more than forty of those years were engaged, *ohne Hast ohne Rast*, in the erection of a theological edifice which, while necessarily resembling its predecessors both in general design and in use of materials, yet bears all the marks of a

singular originality and force. Born at Grenada on the fifth
of January in the year 1548 of an old Castilian family settled
now for two generations in the ancient capital of the Moors,
Suarez was admitted to the Jesuit novitiate at the Salamanca
house of the Society in the June of 1564. The next six years
were spent in the ordinary course of philosophical and theological studies required for the baccalaureate, and in October
1571 he began his career as a teacher, first of philosophy, then
of theology, which was to continue practically without inter-
ruption until his death on September 25, 1617. For nine
years he taught in the Castilian colleges of the Society at
Segovia, Avila, and Valladolid, then for five years at the Roman
college, after which he returned once more to Spain, where he
taught for eight years at Alcala and then for four more at
Salamanca. In 1597 Philip II with great difficulty induced
him to accept the chief chair of theology in the University of
Coimbra in Portugal, and there he remained until his death.
It was at Coimbra in the first two university years of the
seventeenth century—from October 1601 till July 1603—
that he delivered his lectures on those portions of the Second
Part of the *Summa* which deal with law and. justice, lectures
which formed the substance of his *Tractatus de Legibus ac Deo
Legislatore* published only in 1612. In the following year
appeared his *Defence of the Catholic and Apostolic Church against
the Errors of the Anglican Sect,* a work undertaken by him at the
request of Pope Paul V as an answer from the point of view of
Catholic theology to James I's *Apology* for the oath of fealty
exacted by him from his Catholic subjects. In these, the last
two of Suarez' works published during his lifetime, is contained the whole of his contribution to political theory.

III

Like most of the Spanish theologians Suarez preserves
throughout his writings an air of supreme scientific detach-
ment. He displays none of the heat, the passionate parti-
sanship, the almost instinctive chicane, of the controversialist.
If the process of his argument seems to us often tortuous and
not infrequently to lead to conclusions which are in violent

contrast with the general principles from which he set out, that may be after all less his fault than ours. We can deal directly with facts as history gives them to us and frame whatever theory fits them independently of the prescriptions of past theory. The authority of the past is for us not only revisable, but something which calls for revision in the degree that fuller historical knowledge enables us to correct our view of the facts. And therefore we find it difficult to be fair to those thinkers of the past whose interpretation of changing fact had to be made to conform somehow to the requirements of a sacrosanct theory. That was roughly the position of the Jesuit thinkers of the later sixteenth century in so far as they aimed at being political theorists, as indeed it was of all the orthodox Christian publicists of the time whether Catholic or Reformed. The facts with which they had to deal were novel facts, and they were by no means unconscious of their novelty. But they held themselves bound by a theory which corresponded naturally only to a very different set of facts. In the attempt to be true both to the altered fact and to the authoritative theory they seem to us either confused or evasive where to themselves they seemed only to be making the necessary distinctions. Hence the appearance of tortuousness in an intellect so peculiarly simple and straightforward as that of Suarez.

But further the conflict between fact and traditional theory need not have seemed to the sixteenth-century thinker so violent as it does in the retrospect to us. For us the mediæval theory is given in its integrity in the thought-system elaborated by St Thomas. But as matter of fact that system had been modified in many of its details by the work of later thinkers, and such modification, though it seemed to those thinkers themselves to be a product of their own free speculation, was in reality an unconscious reflection of the changing political order in which they lived. Now it was this modified theory, firm in its central substance, but plastic in its wide variety of detail, that the Christian and especially the Catholic thinkers of the sixteenth century inherited. Here again, therefore, the reconciliation of fact and tradition would have seemed to them no intellectual *tour de force*, but the steady continuation of a task bequeathed to them by a long line of predecessors.

FRANCISCO SUAREZ

IV

Now let us try to consider this task from their point of view. And first of all let us look at the theological conception of law, the central substance of all the political thinking which derived from the Middle Age. For us law is primarily the mass of regulative custom in which actual human societies have found a principle of enduring order and by which that order is continually being perfected. It may therefore—nay, it must—have a large historical variety even though its various forms may evince a certain generality of principle. But for the Middle Age and all the later thinking it inspired, law was an eternal reality, the one unchanging principle of all order, the principle from which every form of order proceeded. All earthly law was an emanation from the Eternal Law by which the Divine Providence governed the universe. Though that Law, existing eternally in the Divine Mind and guiding the Divine Will, could never be known to man in its completeness, yet inasmuch as man was created in the Divine image in virtue of his rational nature its principles were a constitutive part of his reason and existed there as the Law of Nature. The Law of Nature was therefore a universal Divine revelation prior to every immediate and particular Divine revelation. Special Divine revelations might add to, but could not abrogate or annul, the commands and prohibitions of the Natural Law. As for positive human law, whether civil or ecclesiastical, it must conform to the principles of the Natural Law or to legitimate inferences from them. Every positive law which was a clear violation of the Law of Nature thereby ceased to be law, and not only did not bind in the court of conscience, but created an actual obligation of resistance to itself. All law, therefore, was in the strictest sense one, and was of the same Divine substance and origin. The Law of Nature was the divinely given norm by which all other law was to be tested and approved.

Corresponding to the hierarchy of law was a hierarchy of society as constituted by law. Theoretically there was only one society, only one at least which came within the theologian's purview, the Christian Republic. Theoretically again

this society was a single unit of government under the joint
rule, in different but strictly parallel spheres of authority, of
Pope and Emperor.   Theory was, of course, grossly at war
with fact.   Nearly half Europe could and did make an effective claim to independence of the Emperor.   The rulers of
France, England, Denmark, of the petty kingdoms of the
Iberian peninsula, of the Slav states of the Eastern March, all
claimed supreme temporal authority within their respective
domains.   But here again theory was powerful enough to re-
dress fact.   For all these rulers had at some time or other to
acknowledge an immediate vassalage to the Papacy.   Their
right to rule had somehow to be brought within the theoretical
system of the one Christian Republic.

But by the end of the sixteenth century this theory had long
since ceased to have the remotest correspondence with fact.
The Christian Republic had been broken up, or rather had
consolidated round certain historically determined nuclei into
a series of strong and independent national states.   The
Empire had become the shadow of a name, and its ruler exercised no effective authority beyond the borders of his own
ancestral domains.   It was, indeed, an utterly changed world
to which the Jesuit publicists had to accommodate the mediæval doctrines of law and sovereignty.   For the successful
accomplishment of the task there was needed a sure instinct for
what was of abiding value in the traditional doctrine and what
might be abandoned without essential loss or modified with
real gain.   It was just this instinct which Suarez brought to
the undertaking in a pre-eminent degree.

In his treatment of law he felt that it was necessary first of all
to reassert the reality of a universal natural right.   There had
always been a tendency to regard the *Jus Gentium*, *i.e.*, those
notions of right which were held in common by all or most
human societies, as part of the *Jus Naturale*, *i.e.*, of those eternal
principles of right which were rooted in human reason as such.
Now as the *Jus Naturale* was regarded as of Divine origin, this
meant that the mediæval jurists and theologians tended to
ascribe the character of Divine Law also to the prescriptions
arising out of the *Jus Gentium*.   On the other hand, this assimi-
lation of natural right and the customary rights common to
human societies was interpreted in an exactly opposite sense by

96

the positive thinkers of the Renaissance. Impressed by the slow growth of common right which their fuller knowledge of history revealed, they were inclined to regard the so-called Law of Nature as itself a result of social experience and custom. Suarez countered this tendency by distinguishing definitely between Natural Law and the *Jus Gentium*. According to him the *Jus Gentium* stood midway between Natural Law and the law of separate states, *i.e.*, between Divine and human law. The Law of Nature was imprinted in the hearts of all men alike. As creatures of reason they were immediately aware of its mandates and of their own obligation to obey them. Its commands and prohibitions were of the divinely ordered nature of things and could not be dispensed by any earthly authority whatsoever. Suarez recognised that the *Jus Gentium* was, on the contrary, of human origin, a product of human need and human will. Its principles and precepts had grown slowly out of social instincts and requirements. But on the other hand it was distinguishable from Civil Law first in that it represented the sense of customary right not of one nation or province, but of all—or, as Suarez is careful to add, almost all—nations, and secondly in that it had grown up and acquired its authority as unwritten usage, not like the Civil Law as written statute. But in one important passage Suarez recognises a much nearer approach to the Natural Law than to positive human law in the character of the Law of Nations. The passage deserves quotation in full not only for what it states, but for the fruitful implications involved in it. " The human race, however much divided into various realms and peoples, always preserves a certain political and moral unity, a unity pointed to by that natural precept of mutual love which extends to all, even foreigners of whatever nation. Wherefore though each sovereign city, republic, or kingdom is in itself a self-sufficient commonwealth [*communitas perfecta*], none the less each one of them is also in some wise a member of that *universum* which we call the human race. For never are those communities taken singly so self-sufficing that they can dispense with all mutual aid, fellowship, and communication whether for increase of their own well-being or by reason of some moral requirement and need. On this account they need also some law to guide and order aright this kind of communication and fellowship.

And though in great measure this may be provided by natural reason, yet it has not been in fact so provided in sufficient measure and with immediate application to all occasions. And therefore by the constant usage of these same nations certain laws adapted to this end [*specialia jura*] have been gradually introduced." There is the germ of an even greater idea than that of the mediæval Christian Republic, and also a foreshadowing both of the need and of the character of International Law.

V

We may now turn to Suarez' treatment of positive human law, *i.e.*, of law which has its origin in the will of a human legislator. Though under this head are included both ecclesiastical and civil law, it is with the latter only that we have now to deal. Suarez nobly proclaims as against Machiavelli, whom he expressly names, that the purpose of the Civil Law is to make good men, because otherwise it cannot make good citizens. " The end of the Civil Law," he says elsewhere, " is the true and natural happiness of the political society, and this cannot be obtained without the observance of all the moral virtues." But though he thus absolutely condemns the doctrine that State utility is the sole motive and measure of Civil Law and castigates the moral cynicism which professes to believe that the State can be preserved only by a clever hypocrisy, he is none the less quick to reject a merely puritan or theocratic conception of Civil Law. The civil legislator is always bound to command those things which are honourable, morally worthy, and never to command those things which are dishonourable. The positive precepts of human law must always conform to the Law of Nature, as the inferior to its superior. If such precepts should contravene that law, they thereby cease to be law, according to the well-known saying of St Augustine, *Lex injusta vel turpis non est lex*, and have no claim upon the obedience of the subject, who is on the contrary bound in the court of conscience to disobey them. But, says Suarez, it is one thing positively to command injustice ; it is another to permit it, or to refrain from punishing it, or even to fail to undo the evil that has been done. And Civil Laws may, he holds, thus permit or tolerate evils where to do so is clearly to avoid greater evils, even though they may never positively enjoin that which is in itself unjust.

Now it may well seem that such concessions are mere casuistical subtleties which explain away the rigour of his fundamental conception. But for Suarez they were a real part of that conception, and were established on a clear and definite ground of principle. The end of Civil Law was, as we have seen, the common good of men as members of a society. In that measure, but in that measure only, it must, in order to effect its purpose, aim at making men good. But that did not mean making them perfect. Human perfection could be attained only by an observance of the evangelical counsels. But not all, or not even many, were capable of such perfection. On the other hand, all men were in virtue of their rational nature strictly bound by the precepts of the Natural Law. But civil legislation must be for all and must therefore be confined, in its positive commands, to those acts which were possible for all. The Civil Law, for instance, could not enjoin virginity, which was a counsel of perfection, or frequent fasting, which was a difficult act of natural virtue. But still more Civil Law had no authority to prohibit private vices, *i.e.*, those vices which were not attended by open scandal or were not directly harmful to the public weal. It might not, for instance, prohibit fornication or the sale of goods at a higher price than their real value if the surcharge did not exceed 50 per cent. In short, Civil Laws were directed to the good of men in society, and were therefore limited in the matter of their commands and prohibitions to those acts which were absolutely necessary to the maintenance and promotion of the common good and were within the ordinary moral capacity of all its members.

VI

We are thus brought by a natural transition to consider Suarez' conception of the political society. Organised society, like property, had been regarded by many of the early Christian thinkers as an institution which had its origin in man's fallen state. It was a necessity imposed by man's sinful nature and yet, like property, served to resrain the evil results of that nature. Under the action of the Natural Law, unimpeded and undeflected by sin, organised society would have been unnecessary. Human society, like the angelic societies, would have been secured by the free action of the Natural Law in each individual will. Here Suarez, without abandoning altogether the native and deeply rooted individualism of Christianity, strikes a much more modern note. For him organised society, the distinctively political community, is a necessary expression and result of man's social nature. Without the voluntary act which constitutes society men are merely a multitude of unrelated or accidentally associated wills. From that state of primitive confusion they extricated themselves by the act of reason which recognised a common good to be sought and the act of will which constituted themselves into a society capable of achieving it. Thus the political society, the mystical body pledged to the pursuit of the common good, came into existence through the deliberate act of its members voluntarily sacrificing their individual liberty to this end. It is already the Social Contract theory of Rousseau.

Now the prime duty of the political society thus called into being is to frame the laws which are necessary for its due functioning, which will serve to promote and further its end. But to whom is this duty to be entrusted? Clearly it belongs of natural right to the whole body of citizens, to all those who by their common act created the society. They can therefore retain in their own hands the right to perform this duty and the responsibility for its due performance, or they can depute both to one or more of their own number. That is to say, the political society thus formed may be a sheer democracy, or a monarchy, or an aristocracy, or some composite form of these. Suarez, following Aristotle, regards monarchy or the authority of a single legislator as the best of these forms. But, whoever may be the chosen depositary of the legislative power, he regards the original delegation of it as definitive and incapable save under special circumstances of being withdrawn. Henceforward the will of the ruler, whether he be one or many, is law, in accordance with the ancient maxim *Quod principi placet habet legis vigorem*. But are there, then, no limitations to his power? It is, as we have seen, clearly limited in so far as it cannot contradict the precepts of the Natural Law. But it is still further limited by the express conditions under which it was originally conferred. As the original members of the society divested themselves of their natural right to make the laws necessary for the common good in order that that end might be more perfectly attained, it is clear that the person to whom that right had been delegated exercised it on condition that he really sought the common good. The ruler who consistently violated common right was a tyrant, and could and ought to be deprived of his sovereignty by the people who had conferred it. The case of tyranny, however, was one which Suarez was very slow to admit as sufficiently established in fact. He held, for instance, that the mere fact of ignorance or mistaken judgment on the part of the ruler was not sufficient to establish it. The ruler might promulgate a law which was in the general judgment prejudicial to the common good, and yet it might be the duty of the subject to obey that law in order to avoid the greater evil of division and turmoil in the State. Even in the case of a law which violated some precept of the Natural Law or of revealed Divine Law, it was incumbent on the subject only to refuse to obey it on the ground that it was not law and not because the ruler by imposing it had forfeited all competence to legislate or govern. But the right to depose the ruler still remained in the whole body of the citizens, and even the right if he resisted to put him to death. The justification of tyrannicide as a last necessity had been undertaken on grounds of natural right by many of the mediæval theologians and even civil jurists. At all times a perilous doctrine, it was so in a supreme degree at a moment when political passions were stirred to their depths by the religious wars which were being waged within and between so many European states. It is well, therefore, to scrutinise with more than usual care Suarez' declared opinions in the matter.

The tyrant may be either a usurper or a legitimate ruler whose rule has become an intolerable oppression and a permanent menace to the well-being of the State. In the first case there is no bond and never has been any between ruler and people. By the very fact of his usurping an authority which he could not legitimately possess otherwise than by grant from the sovereign people, he has declared war upon them and given them an occasion of the just war of self-defence against him. The people may not be able to wage effective warfare against the usurper, or if they find his rule beneficent they may give a tacit consent to it which will in the end in some sense regularise it. But if, on the other hand, his usurpation of the sovereign power does violence to the public weal and it seems hopeless for the people to resist him in open warfare, any private citizen who, intending the defence of the Republic, takes his life is acting in the name of the whole State and in the course of its just warfare. The case of the legitimate ruler is entirely different. Here there is no question of anything more than the resumption by the sovereign people of a power which was conferred by it on certain conditions and has now been abused by serious and prolonged breach of those conditions. The people may then through its authorised and competent representatives solemnly deprive the legitimate tyrant of the power which he has abused, with a view to conferring it upon some worthier instrument. But it must be added that even in the case of the legitimate prince whose tyranny threatens to destroy the State, Suarez held that it was lawful to kill him if the defence of the Republic could not be achieved in any other way.

VII

What, then, we may ask in conclusion, was most significant and of most permanent value in this elaborate treatment of the nature of law and political power which we owe to Suarez ? First of all I would say his clear reaffirmation, as against all the doubts and hesitations of the later mediæval writers and also as against the practical denial of the new school of rational jurists, of the Natural Law, i.e., of certain general principles of right inherent in the universal human reason, and having therefore the true character of law as directly willed by the Author of reason, as sufficiently promulgated in virtue of their rational character, and as therefore universally binding upon free rational beings. That these fundamental principles of justice universally known to men as men represented the actual nature of God and not merely His arbitrary will ; that they or immediate inferences from them appeared in the mass of customary right which had become accepted by all nations ; that the will of the human legislator, whether ecclesiastical or civil, might indeed add to but could not annul or violate them; that the obligation to obey them could not be dispensed by any earthly authority; finally, that they were prior to every particular Divine Revelation—these were affirmations which made law the sovereign and accepted arbiter of human destiny and not the chance product of human convenience or, on the other hand, the arbitrary decrees of a power whose will man had no means of understanding and yet must under penalty obey.

Again in the sphere of politics Suarez, it seems to me, rendered an inestimable service by reaffirming in a more modern form the mediæval doctrine of popular sovereignty. The verdict of history is no doubt conclusive against the fantastic fiction of an original social contract or of its corollary, an original contract between peoples and their rulers. But in the sixteenth century that verdict had not yet been given. Meanwhile, that century had to elaborate some theory which would meet the new fact of independent ecclesiastical and civil authorities, of Church and State as no longer different aspects of the same society, but as two independent and sovereign societies. And in the intellectual atmosphere of the sixteenth century it was inevitable that such a theory should provide for a practically equivalent sanction for both authorities. If the ecclesiastical society was of Divine origin and ordering, so also must the civil society be if its independence were to be sufficiently guaranteed. The secular publicists for the most part met the difficulty by claiming an immediate Divine appointment for the civil ruler. Suarez scouted the notion as a fantastic perversion of history. The Divine appointment of the Kings of Israel to which the theorists of Divine Right triumphantly pointed was a special instance which it was merely absurd in the face of history as a whole to invoke. No, the Divine mandate of the temporal ruler was a mediated mandate. And it was mediated exactly through the delegation of his power from the political community, whose very existence was a consequence of the Natural Law and therefore of Divine ordering and origin. Whatever judgment may be formed of the correspondence of either of these theories with historic fact, there is no doubt as to which of them has proved to have the greater measure of pragmatic truth. The total community whose well-being the State exists to preserve is the natural judge of what its well-being is, and, at least on Suarez' assumption of the existence and character of Natural Law, it is a competent judge. And to its judgment the temporary trustee of its sovereign power is always in the last resort responsible.

And finally Suarez did political theory a service in establishing on grounds of right and reason the complete independence of the secular state, its right as a *societas perfecta*, unhindered by the interference of any alien authority, to determine the requirements and conditions of its own continued existence. Here, indeed, exception may be taken to the use of the term ' secular state.' For Suarez, like Bellarmine, while denying absolutely the right of the Pope as supreme ecclesiastical ruler to interfere in the secular affairs of the civil state, yet reserved such a right where the interests of religion were concerned. And it is unnecessary to say that a right of this kind was capable of very wide interpretation, as it was in fact interpreted to include the deposition of a heretic king and the absolution of his subjects from their duty of obedience. Fortunately, however, the time-spirit made the exercise of this pretended right impolitic and its effective exercise impossible, so that Suarez' justification of the independence of the temporal authority in its own sphere prepared the way for the modern secular state, while his attempt to limit that independence may now safely be catalogued among the fossil remains of history.

A. L. Lilley

BIBLIOGRAPHY

Suarez, Franciscus : *Tractatus de Legibus ac Deo Legislatore.* 1613.
Hinrichs, H. F. W. : *Geschichte der Rechts- und Staatsprincipien.* 1848–52.
Holland, T. E. : *Studies in International Law.* 1898.
Krebs, R. : *Die politische Publizistik der Jesuiten und ihrer Gegner.* 1890.
Werner, K. : *Franz Suarez und die Scholastik.* 1861.

V

KING JAMES I

JUSTICE has seldom been done to James I, whether as a
statesman or as a thinker. As a monarch his reputation
has suffered by comparison with his Tudor predecessors, as
a theorist his merits have been obscured in part by his own
pedantry, in part by the biased judgments of later historians.
True, his advocacy of the Divine Right of Kings is familiar to
every student of English history ; but it is familiar mainly in
its bearing on the great constitutional conflict of the seventeenth century. In English tradition the theory of Divine
Right is inextricably associated with the despotic ambitions
of the Stuarts, and the political philosophy of the " British
Solomon" has too often been judged in accordance with exclusively English standards. In point of fact, the implications
of the doctrine, at least as it was developed by James himself,
are not solely or even mainly constitutional. As his latest
editor—Professor McIlwain of Harvard—is at pains to show,
James's theory of Divine Right was designed as much to
support the temporal against the ecclesiastical authority as to
defend the claims of absolutism against constitutionalism.
Only by placing James against his appropriate historical background is it possible to arrive at a just estimate of the value and
importance of his ideas.

The historical significance of the doctrine of the Divine
Right of Kings lies, as Dr Figgis pointed out, in its assertion,
as against the ecclesiastical authority, of the inherent and underived right of the secular power to exist. In this sense it
was one of the most potent factors in the development of the
modern theory of the State. Forged originally as a weapon of
the Empire in its struggle with the Papacy, it subsequently
became part of the armoury of the national kings who rose to
power at the close of the Middle Ages. The religious revolution of the sixteenth century shattered the old ecclesiastical

system of Europe and destroyed the international power of
the Papacy. Thus it removed the last effective check upon the
authority of the new national monarchs, and left them for the
first time fully ' sovereign.' But, paradoxically, it also set in
motion forces hostile to the monarchical absolutism it had helped
to create. Ecclesiastical pretensions were revived, although
under different forms. All over Europe religious minorities
struggled against odds for survival, and subjects strove
to maintain their doctrines against sovereigns whose beliefs
differed from their own. The result was a great outburst of
political speculation. " Every minority," as Mr Laski says,
" was driven by the logic of its situation to express its will to
live in terms of political right. It challenged the nature of the
authority that denied it a place within the categories of citizen-
ship." Questions as to the source, the nature, and the extent
of the royal power, and of the grounds and the limitations of
the obedience due from subject to sovereign, were mooted.
The Puritans in England, the Huguenots in France, the
Calvinists in Holland and in Scotland, developed doctrines of
popular sovereignty, and of the right of the people to judge,
depose, and even to kill their rulers ; and their example was
followed by Catholics who found themselves ruled by a heretic
prince. New theories of the relations of Church and State
were formulated. The Gelasian doctrine of the separation of
the spheres of temporal and ecclesiastical jurisdiction was revived. The Jesuits, the great champions in the sixteenth
century of the Church and the Papacy, adopted it as a necessary modification of the extreme mediæval theories of papal
sovereignty—as a concession to circumstances. The Calvinists adopted it as a vindication of their claim to immunity from
all secular interference. In both cases what was ostensibly an
assertion of the independence of the ecclesiastical authority
became in the last resort an assertion of its superiority. Jesuit
thinkers such as Bellarmine might deny to the Papacy the possession of any direct control over secular affairs, but they admitted that, when the salvation of souls was at stake, the Pope,
as spiritual head of Christendom, had the " indirect power "
to intervene in politics, and to punish and depose princes.
Similarly, the organised Calvinistic churches, and in particular the Presbyterian Kirk of Scotland, claimed the right, as

custodians of men's spiritual interests, to override in cases of conflict the division between the secular and the religious spheres, and to subordinate politics to spiritual ends.

It was against this recrudescence of ecclesiastical pretensions that James I contended. As King of Scotland he encountered the Presbyterian theories in their most uncompromising form ; as the foremost Protestant monarch of Europe he was brought into inevitable conflict with the papal claims as maintained by the Jesuits. In itself and in its origin his doctrine of the Divine Right of Kings was nothing more than a necessary defence of his own authority, as the embodiment of the secular power, against Catholics and Calvinists alike. His conflict with the English Parliament, viewed in its true perspective, is merely a sequel to the struggle to establish his independence of ecclesiastical control.

James's political doctrine was not the fruit of detached philosophical speculation. It was formulated with an intensely practical purpose, and can be properly appreciated only if considered in its relation to his career as King, first of Scotland, and later of Great Britain.

The son of Mary Stuart by her marriage with Darnley, James was born at Edinburgh on June 19, 1566. Thirteen months later he became, as a result of the enforced abdication of his mother, titular King of Scots. His accession marked the triumph of the Reformed Church, and of those theories of the limitations of obedience which had been adopted by Scottish Protestantism during its long struggle against the monarchy. John Knox, in his famous interview with Mary in 1561, had maintained the lawfulness of resistance to a prince who contemned the Divine Law and persecuted the children of God ; and the dethronement of the Queen six years later was the practical commentary on his teaching. Appropriately enough, he was chosen to preach the coronation sermon of the young King ; and he struck the keynote of the new *régime* by taking as his text the fall of Athalia and the coronation of Joash by Jehoiada the high priest.

James's childhood was passed under the domination of the triumphant Kirk. From 1567 to 1578 a series of regents ruled Scotland in his name ; while in 1570 a group of tutors, under the direction of the great scholar and publicist George

Buchanan, was appointed to educate him for the office which was being held in trust for him.

The ideal of scholarship for Buchanan, as for most of the sixteenth-century humanists, was that *pietas litterata* which Hume Brown defines as " true religion combined with a knowledge of the classics and the command in speech and writing of an elegant Latinity." It was in accordance with this ideal that the young King's studies were directed. He himself declared, " They gar me speik Latin ar I could speik Scotis " ; and the most impartial witnesses testify to his precocious mastery of the language which was still essentially the vehicle of European scholarship. His religious training was no less thorough. Under the guidance of Peter Young he was carefully instructed in the Calvinistic theology of the Scottish Reformed Church, and developed a skill in theological disputation that stood him in good stead in his later contests with both Catholics and Puritans. It was Buchanan's dictum " that a king ought to be the most learned clerk in his dominions." If James did not attain to that pre-eminent position, he at least owed to his early training the distinction of being, in Mark Pattison's words, " the only English prince who has carried to the throne knowledge derived from reading, or any considerable body of literature."

To Buchanan, however, the essential part of his duty in relation to his young charge was not the provision of a liberal education, but the inculcation of sound political doctrine. James was to be brought up as the ideal Protestant prince. On him were centred the hopes not only of the Scottish Calvinists, but of the whole Protestant world. The Scots hoped to see perpetuated in him the results of the revolution of 1567 ; the Continental reformers saw in him, as ruler of Scotland and probable successor to the throne of England and Ireland, the makings of a new Constantine, who, as Duplessis-Mornay wrote to Buchanan, should save the world. Himself one of the most radical thinkers of the day, Buchanan sedulously endeavoured to mould his pupil's ideals of government in conformity with his own. The three works in which he set forth his view of the true relations between king and subjects—the *Baptistes*, the *De Jure Regni apud Scotos*, and the *Rerum Scoticarum Historia*—were all dedicated to James in admonitory prefaces. The theory of monarchy they embodied was a theory of duties and responsibilities that left little room for rights. Kings, James was taught, exist by the will and for the good of the people. As the people are the authors of the kings, so they are, and ought to be, the authors of the law, which it is the king's duty to preserve, administer, and obey. The king, in his coronation oath, binds himself in a solemn compact with his people to discharge his office faithfully. If he breaks his oath and defies the law he constitutes himself a tyrant, and, as such, may be brought to account by his subjects and punished by deposition or even by death.

In 1578 the official regency of Morton was brought to an end, and James, at twelve years old, began his personal rule. His theoretical assumption of direct responsibility did not, however, entail his practical emancipation from control. Buchanan continued to supervise his moral and intellectual training until his death in 1582 ; while the Kirk displayed a marked disinclination to relinquish the political influence it had acquired during the King's minority. Knox had died in 1572, but his tradition was maintained by Andrew Melville, who succeeded him in the leadership of the Protestant party. In 1581, with the issue of the *Second Book of Discipline*, the organisation of the Reformed Church of Scotland assumed its definitive form. Episcopacy was rejected, and the Presbyterian form of government was fully established. The development of ecclesiastical pretensions kept pace with the development of ecclesiastical polity, and was fostered by a growing mistrust of James's intentions. The distinctive features of the new system were the appointment to ecclesiastical office by election and the inclusion in the Church assemblies of a strong lay element. The middle-class laymen who as deacons or elders sat in the Kirk sessions in the parishes, in the presbyteries, and in the general assemblies obtained there an ecclesiastico-political training and a means of political self-expression that were denied them in the aristocratically controlled Scottish Parliament. The clergy and the Kirk assemblies between them performed, it has been said, the functions of the modern Press and the modern House of Commons. The climax came when in 1596, in a sermon preached before the King, Melville definitely formulated the doctrine of the independence and ultimate superiority of the Church. "There are," he declared, in a well-known passage, "two kings and two kingdoms in Scotland, that is King James the head of the Commonwealth, and there is Christ Jesus the King of the Church, whose subject King James VI is, and of whose kingdom he is not a king, nor a lord, nor a head, but a member."

In the meantime James had been developing a theory of monarchy upon lines strangely different from those marked out for him by Buchanan. Constitutional kingship held no attractions for him, and Buchanan's very zeal as its advocate prejudiced his chances of success. Between master and pupil there was little sympathy. Buchanan was favourably impressed by his charge's intellectual ability, but he saw signs that, in character, James was a " true bird of the bloody nest to which he belonged," and he set himself with redoubled energy to eradicate these inherited defects. It was not without reason that James in later life used to say of a certain member of his Court that "he ever trembled at his approach, he minded him so of his pedagogue." Buchanan's stern *régime* produced its inevitable effect upon a nature in which the chief ingredient was, in Hume Brown's somewhat caustic phrase, "a pragmatical self-conceit." It bred in James a strong antagonism both to the person and to the principles of his tutor.

At this juncture a new influence was brought to bear upon the young King that completed his alienation from the teaching of Buchanan. In 1579 there arrived in Scotland as the emissary of France and the Counter-Reformation the King's cousin, Esmé Stuart, Seigneur d'Aubigny, who rapidly established over his young kinsman's mind an ascendancy such as Buchanan, with all his efforts, had never acquired. To the son of Mary Stuart the absolutist ideas current at the Court of Henry III were far more congenial than the constitutionalism preached by the Scottish Calvinists. It is not easy to determine the exact provenance of James's individual theories, for many of the arguments he employed were the common property of the European controversialists of the day, and it was inconsistent with his dignity to acknowledge his indebtedness to any authority that was not either Scriptural or classical. But among the many sources from which he derived inspira-

tion the writings of contemporary apologists of monarchy in
France may probably be assigned the foremost place. In
1576 Jean Bodin had elaborated his epoch-making doctrine
of sovereignty, and with the interests of his own distracted
country in mind had assigned to the monarchy, as to the only
power capable of evolving order out of chaos, the exercise of
the sovereign authority. A copy of his *Six Livres de la République* was included in the library of the young King of Scots
as early as 1577, and the influence which it exercised upon
him is attested by many similarities both of ideas and of
phraseology in James's own political writings. The parallel
is, indeed, so striking as to suggest that James took over bodily
from Bodin his conception of sovereignty and made it the basis
of his whole ideal of government.

Among later French writers James's cause found many
advocates. In 1581, for instance, the staunch Catholic and
Gallicised Scotsman Adam Blackwood dedicated to Mary
Stuart and her young son his *Apologia pro Regibus*. The
treatise was deliberately designed to refute the teachings of
Buchanan and the Monarchomachs in general, and developed
a theory of monarchy which, in its turn, appears to have owed
much to Bodin's inspiration. Subsequently another Catholic
and Gallicised Scot, William Barclay—the author of the *De
Regno et Regali Potestate*—stood to James in his conflict with
the doctrines of the Counter-Reformation in much the same
relation as that in which Blackwood stood to him in his conflict with Scottish Calvinism.

The influence upon James of the monarchist theories of
the Continent was soon reflected in his policy. In 1584 the
Scottish Parliament was induced to issue a formal condemnation of Buchanan's writings, and in the same year James
launched his first direct attack upon the Kirk in the famous
" Black Acts." Both the constitution and the claims of
Presbyterianism were incompatible with the conception of a
sovereign monarchy. The popular basis and representative
institutions of the Kirk made it peculiarly independent of
royal control. Presbytery, James found thus early in his career,
agreed with monarchy as well as God with the Devil, and from
1584 onward he made it the supreme object of his policy
to restore the monarchical principle in Church government

by the reinstitution of bishops. But it was the political doctrine inherent in Scottish Calvinism that constituted at once the most serious invasion of his sovereignty and the greatest menace to his personal security. In order to combat it he was driven to formulate his own claims and to marshal the arguments in their favour. To the Divine Right of the Kirk he opposed the Divine Right of Kings ; to the doctrines of popular sovereignty and the right of resistance preached by Knox and Buchanan he opposed the theory of monarchical sovereignty and the duty of passive obedience ; and over against the claim of the Kirk to be a *societas perfecta* he set his own claim to be *custos utriusque tabulæ*—or, as the English Act of Supremacy phrased it, " supreme in all things or causes as well spiritual as temporal."

His doctrine of Divine Right had its origin, therefore, in the necessity for defending his own authority, and with it the independence of the State, against the exorbitant claims of the Scottish Kirk. It was, however, an external consideration that gave to his theory its special direction. That consideration was the English succession, on which his ambitions had been set from childhood. James's claim to succeed Elizabeth was, from the hereditary standpoint, sound ; but legally his position was weak. Two Acts of the English Parliament barred his way to the throne ; and in common law his right to inherit was, at least, a doubtful one. Moreover, the Catholics, disappointed in their hope of James's conversion, regarded with disapproval the prospect of the union in his person of the two crowns. In 1594 the Jesuit Parsons published his *Conference about the Next Succession to the Crown of England*, in which he assailed the hereditary principle and maintained that a heretic was *ipso facto* incapacitated from the succession. It was for this reason that James made the principle of legitimism an integral part of his doctrine, and qualified the Divine Right of Kings by the adjective ' hereditary.'

His political ideas first found expression in the *Basilikon Doron*, written for the instruction of his eldest son Henry, some time before 1598. The book is, in form, one of those fashionable treatises on the duty of a Christian prince with which—to judge from the contents of his library—James in his own youth must have been depressingly familiar. It is arranged in three parts. The first deals with a king's duty toward God in religion; the second with the use of a king in administration of justice and politic government; the third with a king's outward behaviour, which, says James, is important, since subjects are naturally inclined " like apes to counterfaite their prince's manners." The treatise abounds in excellent advice as to the training—spiritual, mental, and physical, which is appropriate to a prince. The pursuit of manly sports James in general approves, but he warns his son against such rough and violent exercises as the football, which he stigmatises as " meeter for laming than making able the users thereof." Moral precepts, sage counsels, and shrewd observations such as these form the main content of the book, but among them can be distinguished in embryo form all the essentials of James's mature political thought.

Originally intended for circulation only among the members of the Court, the *Basilikon Doron* came, without the King's authorisation, to the notice of the public. It aroused, by its exaltation of the royal authority and its strictures upon Puritanism, such strong hostility that James found it advisable to issue an authorised edition in 1599, with an explanatory foreword. In the same year he published under the title of *The Trew Law of Free Monarchies* the first full and reasoned statement of his political doctrine.

In these two early treatises James's theory of the divine nature of kingship is already fully developed. In the *Basilikon Doron* he urges his son to love God " first for that He made you a man, and next for that He made you a little god to sit on His throne and rule over men." The king, he says elsewhere, is God's minister, the lieutenant of God upon earth, and monarchy the form of government which, as resembling the Divinity, approaches nearest to perfection. The power which God has thus conferred upon princes is, moreover, heritable according to a divinely ordained law of succession which proves to be none other than the familiar feudal law of primogeniture. The king is the heritable overlord of his people, and his right is inalienable and indefeasible. He comes to the Crown by right of birth and not by any right of coronation; and no objection, either of heresy or of any private law or statute, can impair his title.

As for the duties of kingship, they are defined in the Scriptures, in the fundamental laws of the kingdom, and in the Law of Nature. The good king, says James in the *Basilikon Doron*, in words that recall the teaching of Buchanan, acknowledges himself ordained for his people, while the tyrant thinks his people ordained for him. The godly prince is the father of his people, the tyrant their stepfather. In the *Trew Law of Free Monarchies* James draws an affecting picture of the paternal solicitude which the ideal monarch will display toward his subjects. "As the Fathers chiefe ioy," he says, " ought to be in procuring his children's welfare, reioycing at their weale, sorrowing and pitying at their evill, to hazard for their safetie, travell for their rest, wake for their sleepe; and, in a word, to thinke that his earthly felicitie and life standeth and liveth more in them, nor in himselfe; so ought a good Prince thinke of his people."

For the discharge of their duties kings must render account to God from whom their powers are derived. God, James declares, will be their stern and just judge—" the sorest and sharpest schoolemaster than can be deuised for them." Their lofty station and great privileges, so far from giving them license to sin, make their responsibilities all the heavier, for " Joves thunderclaps light oftener and sorer upon the high and stately oakes, then on the low and supple willow-trees : and the highest bench is sliddriest to sit upon."

But, if kings are responsible to God—and James certainly does not attempt to minimise their obligations in that direction—they are accountable to no earthly power. In the *Trew Law of Free Monarchies* James sets out to demolish the arguments of Buchanan and the rest of the Monarchomachs, and to develop a doctrine of sovereignty which, in its essentials, is that preached by Bodin. Buchanan had asserted that kings are created by the people and are subordinate to the laws made by the people. James admits that in the infancy of the world the origin of monarchy may have been by election; but in Scotland and in England, he argues, it originated by conquest, in the one case when Fergus came over from Ireland, in the other when William came over from Normandy. Thus he finds an historical as well as a theological basis for his claim to sovereign power. By conquest the king became absolute lord of both land and people. His power came into being before any forms of government or any laws ; and was, in fact, the source from which all laws and institutions took their rise. " By them [the kings] was the land distributed (which at the first was whole theirs), states erected and decerned, and formes of government devised and established : and so it followes of necessitie, that the kings were the authors and makers of the Lawes, and not the Lawes of the Kings." As for the Parliament, its existence does not impair the argument, since it is the creation of the royal will, and its part in legislation is entirely subordinate. In it the laws are " craved of the king " by his subjects, and made by him alone at their rogation and with their advice. This is proved by the fact that, while the king can legislate without Parliament, Parliament can make no law without the king. The royal assent only gives to any measure the force of law. The king, since he is thus the author of the law, is necessarily above the law. It is for him to interpret it in the interests of justice and equity ; and, although a good king will observe his own decrees " for a good example-giving to his subjects," yet " he is not bound thereto but of his goodwill." Thus we reach a definition of the king's power in relation to the law that is little different from Bodin's definition of sovereignty : " Unto sovereignty belongeth an absolute power not subject to any law. . . . The first and chief mark of the sovereign prince is to be of power to give laws to all his subjects in general, and to every one of them in particular, without consent of any other greater, equal or lesser than himself. . . . He that hath the sovereignty may bind all his subjects, but cannot bind himself. . . . The laws of a sovereign prince . . . depend on nothing but his mere and frank good-will." True, James recognises the existence of "fundamentall lawes," but they appear to consist, like the *leges imperii* of Bodin, merely of those rules " whereby confusion is avoided . . . and the heritage of the succession and monarchy maintained."

From his discussion of the relation of the monarch to the law James proceeds to refute the theories of resistance and tyrannicide advocated by the Calvinists, and to develop in their stead the doctrine of non-resistance and passive obedience. Resistance to a lawful monarch is, he declares, contrary both to the Law of God as revealed in the Scriptures, and to human reason. Children may not lift their hands against their parents nor scholars against their schoolmaster; how much less, therefore, are subjects justified in rebellion against the sovereign given them by God? As the head cannot be cut off without death to the natural body, so the king, who is the head of the body politic, cannot be destroyed without destruction to the whole Commonwealth. Resistance to a king is at once unlawful and inexpedient, since not only is the king appointed by God, but his is the binding force that holds the State together. In regard to their prince, subjects have duties, but no rights. They must love him as a father, obey his commands in all things as the commands of God's minister, and accept his judgment as that of a judge set over them by Heaven. Nor can any excesses on the part of the monarch absolve them from this duty. " A wicked king is sent by God for a curse to his people and a plague for their sinnes," and " Patience, earnest prayers to God and amendment of their lives are the only lawful means to move God to relieve them of their heavie curse."

As for the theory of a compact between king and people, such as Buchanan had postulated, James repudiates the idea that the king binds himself in any such form by his coronation oath. But allowing, for the sake of argument, that a contract exists, he inquires pertinently: Who is to be the judge between the contractors? To allow, as Buchanan would do, that one of the contracting parties may declare the other to have broken the contract is, says James, to outrage the fundamental principle that no man may be judge in his own cause. Between a king and his subjects God alone can decide. The attack is a shrewd one, and goes to the root of the matter, for the absence of a ' sanction ' is one of the weakest points of the contract theory. The credit belongs properly, however, not to James, but to Blackwood, from whose *Apologia* he appears to have borrowed the entire argument.

Thus James elaborates as against the opponents of monarchy his claim to an inalienable and indefeasible sovereign authority, deriving on the one hand from an historical, on the other from a theological source, and superior to all earthly control. Such a conception of the powers of royalty left no room in the State for an ecclesiastical *societas perfecta*. In the *Basilikon Doron* James expressly condemns as " an error to which the Puritans

incline over farre " the theory that the king is a " mere *laicus*."
His office is properly, he says, " mixed between the ecclesi-
asticall and the civill state " ; and he urges his son to study well
the Scriptures " as well for the knowledge of your owne salvation, as that ye may be able to containe your Church in their
calling as *custos utriusque tabulæ*. For the ruling them well is
no small part of your office." Above all he exhorts him : " If
ever ye would have peace in your land, suffer them not to
meddle in that place with the estate or policie : but punish
severely the first that presumeth it."

James's theory of monarchy was therefore full-blown before
his accession to the English throne. It was developed to meet
the exigencies of his position as King of Scots, and it must be
admitted that, as far as Scotland was concerned, it was justified
by success. If self-interest lay at the root of his political convictions it would appear that in this instance at least self-
interest and the national interest were coincident. North of
the Tweed James's early rule was marked by solid achievement. Between 1583 and 1603 he did for Scotland what the
Tudors did for England. He reduced the anarchical baronage
to obedience; he successfully combated the claims of the
Presbyterian Kirk; and he established a strong centralised
royal authority. It was no idle boast when he declared to the
English Parliament in 1607 : "This I must say for Scotland.
. . . Here I sit and governe it with my Pen ; I write and it is
done, and by a Clearke of the Councill I governe Scotland now,
which others could no doe by the sword."

But the very success of James in Scotland helps to explain
his failure in England. He came to this country with his
political convictions already firmly set, and his belief in his
own omniscience confirmed by twenty-five years of Scottish
rule. Although he governed England for over twenty years
he failed to the last to understand either the English Constitution or the temper of the English people. He looked at our
institutions through the eyes of Bodin and Blackwood and in
the light of his Scottish experience, and instead of adapting his
views to his new environment he endeavoured to mould his
environment in accordance with his own preconceived ideas.

His doctrine of monarchical sovereignty brought him into
conflict in particular with two great English institutions—the

Parliament and the Common Law. His low view of the status of Parliament was far from acceptable to the English Commons, accustomed as they had been by the Tudors to the idea of Parliamentary participation in government. In England sovereignty had already passed in practice, if not in theory, from the king to the composite body of ' king in Parliament.' To this fact James remained obstinately blind. He was fond of comparing the duties of a king with those of a schoolmaster, and there was certainly a strong element of the pedagogue in his own composition. With characteristic optimism he now set himself to teach the English Parliament its true function in the State. " Parliament," he declared in 1605, " is nothing but the King's great Councell," assembled by him for the interpretation of old laws or the making of new. Its duty is to advise the king in matters propounded to it by him, and to draw his attention to any disorders in the State that may have escaped his vigilant eye. It is not a place for " every rash and hare-brained fellow to propone newe lawes of his owne invention," " nor for particular men to utter their private conceipts, not for satisfaction of their curiosities, and least of all to make a show of eloquence by tyning the time with long-studied and eloquent orations." " Nay, rather," he added grimly, " I could wish these busie heads to remember the law of the Lacedemonians that whosoever came to prepare a new Law to the people, behoved publikely to present himselfe with a rope about his necke, that in case the Lawe were not allowed he should be hanged therewith." It is not for Parliament to " meddle with the maine points of governement " or attempt to teach the king his office. As for its privileges, they belong to it of grace and not of right. They are granted by the sovereign, who is the source of all privilege, and, as he declared in 1621, they continue only by his permission and " tolerance," since what the sovereign has granted he can also revoke.

Strongly as Parliament resented the King's attitude it was as yet neither sufficiently clear-sighted to realise fully the question at issue, nor sufficiently confident in its own strength to counter the King's claim to sovereign power by claiming sovereignty for itself. Instead it was content to deny the existence of sovereignty as defined by Bodin and understood by James I. To the theory that there must be somewhere in the State a power which is *legibus solutus*—a commander who cannot be commanded—it opposed the theory of a fundamental law, fixed and immutable, and binding upon kings and Parliaments alike. " Magna Carta," said Chief Justice Coke, " is such a fellow that he will have no sovereign in the land." Thus it has been said that in the last analysis the contest between the Stuarts and their Parliaments was a struggle of the common law against the king. To the claim of James to be above the law Coke and the common lawyers opposed the theory that there is a body of law above the king. To his claim to mitigate and suspend the laws at his discretion in the interests of equity Coke retorted that cases concerning the life and liberty of the subject were not to be decided by natural reason, but by the " artificial reason and judgment of the law " —the " golden metwand and measure " by which all causes should be tried.

The opposition which was thus encountered by James's doctrine inspired him to lay an ever-increasing emphasis upon the sacred nature of his office, in the hope of raising it above the questionings and criticisms of the mass of mankind. " The state of monarchy," he declared in 1609, " is the supremest thing on earth." Kings are justly called gods, for their powers are a replica of the Divine omnipotence. Like God they may " make and unmake their subiects . . . they have power of raising and casting downe : of life and of death. . . . They have power to exalt low things and abase high things, and make of their subiects like men at the chesse. . . . To Kings their subiects bodies and goods are due for their defence and maintenance." Here James goes farther than Bodin, who had asserted the principle that taxation should be by consent, and had allowed to the sovereign only a limited power of confiscation. We are reminded rather of the " mortal God " or " Great Leviathan " of Hobbes. " It is atheisme and blasphemie to dispute what God can doe," he told the Star Chamber Court in 1616 in a passage which has become classical ; " so it is presumption and high contempt in a subiect, to dispute what a King can doe, or say that a King cannot doe this, or that " ; and he added the warning : " Incroach not upon the prerogative of the Crowne : If there fall out a question that concerns my Prerogative or mystery of state, deale not with it . . . for they are transcendent matters, and must not be sliberely caried with over-rash wilfulnesse. . . . That which concernes the mysterie of the King's power is not lawful to be disputed."

Only on rare occasions do we find any signs of a relaxation of these extreme claims. In 1609 the unpopularity James had earned as a result of the incident of Cowell's Interpreter, combined with the desperate need of supplies, induced him to unbend to some extent in the hope of conciliating Parliamentary opinion. Salisbury, when delivering a message from the King to Parliament, reported him as acknowledging that " he had noe power to make lawes of himselfe, or to exact any subsidies without the consent of his 3 estates " ; and even that the common law had set the crown upon his head—an extremely doubtful statement, which moreover conflicts strangely with his doctrine of indefeasible hereditary right. James's own speech on March 31, 1609, strikes the same conciliatory note. True, he states the abstract rights of kingship with his usual emphasis ; but he then proceeds to draw an important distinction between the powers which the king possesses in theory, and those which he finds it judicious to exercise in practice. There is, he says, a difference between " the state of kings in their first originall," when their will served for law, and the state of settled kings and monarchie, when the laws have been formally set down in writing. The king in a settled kingdom is bound to observe the " fundamental laws " by a double obligation, tacit by the mere fact of being king, and express by his oath at his coronation. He who ceases to rule according to the laws becomes a tyrant. Here James seems to retract his earlier emphatic denial of a contract between king and people ; and even to modify his equally emphatic assertion of the sovereign's superiority to the law. It is noteworthy, however, that he makes no attempt to define the " fundamental law," and that the obligation he recognises is a purely moral one. He still insists that the right to judge of and punish its infringement belongs to God alone.

The speech of 1609 need not be regarded as representing a permanent modification of James's political convictions. It was merely a concession to the needs of the moment. On the whole, the history of his political thought in its relation to England testifies to his complete inability to unlearn the lessons of his youth. From the opinions formed in Scotland and justified by his Scottish experience no new situations or conditions could shake him, and his obstinate attachment to them must be regarded as one of the main causes of the constitutional revolution of the seventeenth century. James's career, as far as England is concerned, affords an outstanding example of the perils of consistency in politics.

So far we have examined James's theories against the familiar background of insular history. The part he played upon the wider stage of European politics is less familiar, but no less important. He was brought for the first time into direct and violent conflict with the political doctrines of the Counter-Reformation as a result of the Gunpowder Plot, which followed closely upon his accession to the English throne. A succession of Jesuit writers from Mariana to Bellarmine had developed theories of resistance and tyrannicide comparable to those advocated by the Calvinist Monarchomachs, but had associated with them the papal claim to judge and depose princes. These theories received their clearest expression in the works of Cardinal Bellarmine, one of the ablest of the Catholic controversialists. In his *De Controversiis,* as well as in later writings such as the *Tractatus de Potestate Summi Pontificis*, he asserted that while politic power and even monarchy were divinely sanctioned every particular sovereign derived his power not directly from God, but through the medium of popular election and consent. The Pope had no direct authority in temporal affairs, but as *Pastor gregis totius* it was his duty *politicum regimen dirigere et corrigere ad finem spiritualem*, and even, should the interests of Christendom require it, to decree the deposition of unworthy or heretical rulers. The enforcement of the decree rested not with the Pope, but with the people, who were the immediate source of the royal authority, and whom the Pope had power to absolve from their temporal allegiance; or alternatively its execution might be entrusted, in the name of the Church, to another prince. Bellarmine himself discountenanced assassination, and declared that it had never received the sanction of the Papacy; but it was openly advocated by Mariana, and contemporary

European history shows that it was not infrequently adopted in practice.

It is therefore scarcely surprising that Protestant opinion everywhere ascribed the attempt upon the life of James in 1605 to the direct influence of Jesuit propaganda. At the beginning of the seventeenth century Catholicism was steadily recovering much of the ground which had been lost a century before; and it was as a defensive measure against a very real danger, from his own and from the general Protestant standpoint, that James in 1606 imposed a new oath of allegiance upon his Catholic subjects. They were required, under heavy penalties, to recognise him as their lawful and rightful king, and to repudiate as impious and heretical " that damnable doctrine . . . that princes which be excommunicated by the Pope may be deposed or murdered by their subjects or any other whatsoever." The Pope replied by forbidding the English Catholics to take the oath, on the ground that it contained many things contrary to faith and salvation; and Bellarmine himself addressed a letter of exhortation and encouragement to the somewhat hesitant archpriest Blackwell. The result was to rouse James to action in defence of his policy. In 1607 he published anonymously his *Apologie for the Oath of Allegiance*. Its appearance was the signal for the outbreak of a paper warfare that embraced the whole of Europe and was the prelude to the Thirty Years War.

In the *Apologie* James defends himself warmly against the charge of religious persecution brought against him by his Catholic adversaries. He challenges them to prove that since his accession any Catholic has been put to death for cause of conscience. The intention of the oath he declares to be purely political. It has been framed to test the loyalty of his popish subjects, and, in particular, to distinguish between those who " though peradventure zealous in their religion " are yet " otherwise civilly honest and good subjects," and such " terrible firebrands of hell " as the Gunpowder conspirators. In defence of his measure he is driven to a tacit admission of the separation of the temporal and spiritual spheres. " Heaven and earth," he protests, " are no further asunder than the profession of a temporal obedience to a temporal king is different from anything belonging to the Catholic faith or supremacy of

St Peter." The Papalist attack had, indeed, touched James upon a tender spot. He piqued himself upon an intellectual tolerance in matters of religion—a tolerance which he was prepared to extend at least to all who, like himself, believed in the Scriptures, the creeds, and the first four General Councils. In the *Basilikon Doron* he had declared, apropos of Scottish Puritanism, his indifference to forms and ceremonies. Men might differ on questions of Church government and over the use of the surplice and the cornered cap; but, said James, " we all, God be praised, do agree in the grounds." Later, in his speech to the English Parliament in 1603, he declared: " I was never violent nor unreasonable in my profession. . . . But as I would be loathe to dispense in the least point of mine owne conscience for any worldly respect than the foolishest Precisian of them all . . . so would I be a sorry to straight the politique government of the bodies and minds of all my subiects to my private opinions." Persecution he deplored on the grounds both of humanity and of expediency. " I never found that blood and much severity did good in matters of religion," he said in 1609, " for besides it is a sure rule in Divinitie that God never loves to plant his church in violence and bloodshed; naturall reason may even perswade us, and dayly experience prooves it trew, That when men are severely persecuted for Religion, the gallantnesse of many men's spirits, and the wilfulnesse of their humours, rather then the iustnesse of the cause, makes them to take a pride boldly to endure any torments, or death it selfe, to gain thereby the reputation of martyrdome." There is no reason to doubt the sincerity of these professions. As Professor McIlwain says, it was as a king and not as a Christian that James feared and disliked the opinions of Puritan and Jesuit alike. His hatred was directed less against their religious beliefs than against the political implications of those beliefs. James's personal creed may be said without injustice to have been political rather than religious. He believed in the sovereign authority of the monarch, and all doctrines which challenged that belief were anathema. Hence Jesuit " popularity and Popery " were as repugnant to him as Puritan " popularity and parity." Jesuits, as he saw, were, as far as their political theories were concerned, " nothing but Puritan-Papists "; and it was the

anti-monarchical doctrine common to both parties that he persecuted. If the repression of the Catholics was more vigorous
and complete than that of the Puritans, the distinction in treatment is explained by the anti-national and anti-patriotic stigma
which had attached to the Catholic cause in the days of
Elizabeth.

In spite, however, of James's protestations of the purely
political significance of the Oath of Alliegance, it placed the
English Catholics upon the horns of a cruel dilemma. With
the majority the papal power of deposition was an article of belief; and the Act of 1606 made it more difficult than ever for
anyone to be at once a good Catholic and a good subject.

The *Apologie*, the true authorship of which was quickly
recognised, provoked a reply from Cardinal Bellarmine.
Under the name of one of his almoners, Matheus Tortus, the
Cardinal published a treatise, pointing out the fallacy of
James's arguments, and restating in full the claims of the
Papacy in relation to the deposing power. The King's re-
sponse was to carry the war into the enemy's camp. In 1609
he reissued the *Apologie*, this time under his own name,
adding a long preface addressed to " all most mightie monarchs, free princes and states of Christendom." Much of this
preface is devoted to the elaboration of the conventional, time-
worn arguments against the authority of the Papacy—the
negative argument that the temporal power has no basis in
history, and the positive argument that the Pope is Antichrist.
The main intention of James was, however, to advertise to the
princes of Europe the incompatibility of the papal claims with
their own sovereign authority. How, James inquires, can any
temporal ruler enjoy that sovereignty which is his right, if, as
Bellarmine asserts, the Pope can throne and dethrone princes
at his pleasure, and if the clergy are independent of secular
control ? Such doctrines are a challenge to all princes; but,
James argues, they concern in particular those who profess the
Romish religion, since they are of the Pope's fold, and in their
dominions his decrees are effective. He therefore exhorts the
Catholic sovereigns of Europe to awake, while there is yet time,
and to unite with their Protestant brethren in defence of their
common rights against the pretensions of the Papacy. Such
an alliance affords, he believes, the surest guarantee of religious

peace. A General Council, representing all the sovereign princes of Europe and " all the churchmen of Christian profession who believe and profess all the ancient grounds of the true ancient Catholick and apostolic faith," offers the only hope of the recovery of the lost unity of Christendom. As the basis of the settlement he suggests a religious compromise, which, while excluding " all incendiaries and novelist firebrands," whether Jesuit or Puritan, shall leave intact the traditional system of Church government and even the formal primacy of the Bishop of Rome. " Of Bishops and Church Hierarchie," he declares, " I very well allow, and likewise rankes and degrees amongst Bishops. Patriarchs I know were in the time of the Primitive Church, and I likewise reverence that Institution for order sake : . . . and for myselfe . . . I would with all my heart give my consent that the Bishop of Rome should have the first seate : I being a westerne King would goe with the Patriarch of the West. And for his temporall Principalitie over the Signory of Rome, I doe not quarrell it neither ; let him in God His name be *Primus Episcopus inter omnes Episcopos* and *Princeps Episcoporum*." " But," he adds in a significant parenthesis, " as I well allow of the Hierarchie of the Church for distinction of orders . . . so I utterly deny that there is an earthly monarch thereof whose word must be law, and who cannot erre in his sentence by an infallibilitie of spirit."

It is, of course, this project for a religious peace that underlies the much-criticised foreign policy of James, and in particular the ill-fated Spanish marriage scheme. James saw himself as the predestined mediator between the warring sects of Europe. He hoped to solve the religious problem by securing the co-operation of his fellow-sovereigns in extending to the whole of Christendom the Anglican principle of the *via media*. The project was foredoomed to failure, and has earned him the ridicule both of his own and of later ages. Characteristically, James underrated the strength of the forces he aspired to control as greatly as he overestimated his personal weight in the counsels of Europe. The extent of his miscalculation was proved when in 1620 the powers of Europe, ignoring his attempted mediation, referred the religious issue to the arbitrament of war. Yet James was actuated in his endeavours by a genuine love of peace, which is not the most ignoble of his characteristics, and his optimism was in some measure, at least, justified by existing conditions. The rise of the sovereign territorial state was the distinctive feature of the age, and contemporary history shows that Catholic sovereigns could, on occasion, treat the papal claims as unceremoniously as their Protestant *confrères*. Nor was it without significance that in his contest with the Jesuit doctrines James numbered among his supporters Catholic as well as Protestant controversialists. Apart from Bodin, whose religious convictions are open to doubt, Adam Blackwood, William and John Barclay, the English Benedictine Roger Widdrington, constituted themselves advocates of monarchy, and denied the right of the Papacy to intervene in temporal affairs even under spiritual pretexts. Considerations such as these may well have inspired James with the belief that the time was ripe for common action, on the basis of the common claims and interests of the temporal rulers of Christendom. As he said himself: "The cause is generall, and concerneth the authoritie and priviledge of kings in general, and all super-eminent Temporall powers."

The reception accorded to his appeal by the sovereigns to whom it was addressed was not, however, encouraging. The King of Spain declined to accept a copy of a treatise in which the claims of the Pope were assailed and his spiritual primacy denied. In France, although the third estate showed some sympathy with James, the cause of the Papacy found an able advocate in the Cardinal du Perron. In the assembly of the States-General in 1614 he reasserted the right of the Pope in certain instances to absolve subjects from their temporal allegiance, although he admitted the distinct and underived origin of the secular power, and deplored both the doctrine and the practice of tyrannicide. His able defence of the Catholic position called forth from James what is, in some respects, the most complete and systematic of his political works. In 1615 he published his *Remonstrance for the Right of Kings and the Independence of their Crownes*, a treatise which bears to his controversy with Catholicism the same relation as the *Trew Law of Free Monarchies* bears to his controversy with Scottish Calvinism. It is a formal restatement, as against the " popularity and Popery " of the Jesuits, of the arguments which had been

126

employed sixteen years earlier against the "popularity and parity" of the Presbyterians. Its theme recalls Bodin's dictum that "He only is to be called absolute sovereign who next unto God acknowledges none but himself." "I make no question," says James, "he is but a titular king that reigneth only at another's discretion, and whose princely head the Pope hath power to bare of his royall crowne." The old arguments against those doctrines of popular sovereignty, of contract, and of the right of resistance, which were common to both Jesuits and Puritans, are reaffirmed. Kings, James reiterates, rule by indefeasible hereditary right, and in their coronation oath they "make not their crowne to stoope to any power in the Pope or in the Church or in the people." They cannot, if they would, diminish their sovereign rights, since the sovereignty given them by God is in its very nature inalienable and indivisible. In his peroration he achieves a fine frenzy of eloquence. "How long then, how long," he asks, "shall Kings whom the Lord hath called His anointed, Kings the breathing images of God upon earth, Kings that with a wry or frowning look are able to crush these earth-worms in pieces; how long shall they suffer this viperous brood, scot-free and without punishment to spit in their faces? How long the majesty of God in their person and royal majesty to be so notoriously vilified, so dishonourably trampled underfoot?"

The *Remonstrance* was the last of James's formal political treatises. In the sixteen years which had elapsed since the publication of the *Trew Law of Free Monarchies* he had developed and expanded, without essentially altering, his original thesis. From first to last the main outline of his political creed was the doctrine of sovereignty which he had adopted from Bodin. To that doctrine the theory of Divine Hereditary Right was, in a sense, merely subsidiary. It provided a more adequate sanction for his sovereign claims than a mere appeal to history or to the principle of utility could do. In a theological age it afforded the only effective answer at once to the pretensions of his ecclesiastical opponents and to the revolutionary doctrines of the Monarchomachs. James, no less than Hobbes, was concerned "to rule out the right of the subject to rebel"; but while Hobbes achieved his end by a novel use of the pseudo-historical device of the contract, James was content to rely upon the traditional theological arguments and the sanction of Divine Law. Thus his theory is a curious blend of the old and the new. In so far as he admits the principle of sovereignty he looks toward the future, and is entitled to a place, however humble, among the exponents of the modern theory of the State; but in so far as he defends that principle by an appeal to the theory of Divine Right he looks back to the past, and his place is among the inheritors of the tradition established by the Imperialist advocates of the Middle Ages.

Finally the question arises : With what justification is James included among the great social and political thinkers of the seventeenth century ? Great in the sense of being profound or original he certainly was not. His genius was assimilative rather than creative, and his mind was cast in an essentially narrow mould. Political philosophy in the strict sense he had none. The mainspring of his theory of monarchy was an intense and slightly ludicrous egoism, and the intention of his political writings was polemical and propagandist rather than philosophical. As Professor McIlwain says, the eminent position he occupies in the history of political ideas must be ascribed rather to his kingly office than to the intrinsic value of his contribution to contemporary thought. Yet, if the defects of his mind and character forbid us to call him great, they should not wholly blind us to his merits. The very variety of the sources from which he derived inspiration testifies to his wide acquaintance with the literature of Europe ; and the skill with which the borrowed arguments are adapted to his purpose, and dovetailed together to form a complete and logical whole, is proof of an ability which, if second-rate, is at least not wholly negligible. Nor was his attention exclusively confined to politics. His writings include, apart from purely literary exercises, a treatise on *Dæmonology* and the famous *Counterblaste to Tobacco*, while his hand can be traced in the little tract entitled *The Peacemaker*, which was published in 1618. His gifts as a controversialist were undoubted, and were displayed to full advantage in his contests with his ecclesiastical adversaries, in which his by no means negligible theological knowledge stood him in good stead. In his dealings with his English subjects his theory of monarchy played him false, yet even here he frequently displayed a greater clarity and breadth of vision than his opponents. Thus in his grasp of the problem of sovereignty he was definitely in advance of Coke and the common lawyers; while his tolerance in religious matters, if not always consistently maintained, was in marked and pleasant contrast to the persecuting zeal of his Puritan Parliaments. Moreover, if he aimed at despotism it was at least at a benevolent despotism. Whatever the practical consequences of his policy, no man was ever less desirous than James of acting the tyrant. If, as we are so often told, he was a fool, at least we must admit that he was " the wisest fool in Christendom."

In conclusion, I cannot resist one more quotation—and that a singularly apposite one. In his speech to Parliament in 1607 James said, apropos of his own unpolished discourse: " Studied orations and much eloquence upon little matter is fit for the Universities, where not the subject which is spoken of, but the trial of his wit that speaketh is most commendable." I leave it to an indulgent audience to put upon this pronouncement what construction it will.

HELENA M. CHEW

BIBLIOGRAPHY

A. PRIMARY SOURCE

The Political Works of James I, edited by C. H. McIlwain. London, 1918.

B. SECONDARY SOURCES

FIGGIS, J. N.: " Political Thought in the Sixteenth Century," *Cambridge Modern History*, vol. iii, ch. xxii.
FIGGIS, J. N.: *The Divine Right of Kings*. Cambridge, 1914.
HARRIS, W.: *An Historical and Critical Account of the Life and Writings of James I.* London, 1772.

VI

HUGO GROTIUS

I

THE perennial conflict between ' direct action ' and constitutional procedure, which to-day agitates the world of Labour, in the sixteenth and seventeenth centuries rent in twain the world of Religion. Not trade-union leaders and academic syndicalists, but the heads of churches and dogmatic theologians were the persons who had to debate the question whether or not obedience should be paid to the civil authority, and whether or not opposition to policy should be carried to the length of privy conspiracy and rebellion. The particular form of direct action round which controversy raged was tyrannicide. At a time when autocracy was dominant, when individuality was resurgent, when personality counted more largely than it had done since the days of Cæsar, if not of Pericles, the short and simple way to change a government was to assassinate a king; the straight and effective device to frustrate a plan of campaign was to remove its leader by means of sedative or stiletto. The blow which slew Henry of Navarre in 1610 had a more profound and far-reaching effect on the destiny of Europe than a score of Parliamentary debates or a hundred political treatises. So obviously and immediately operative were accomplished tyrannicides that even wise and good men—blinded by the passion of the moment, and oblivious of the awful implications of such deeds—gloried in them, thanked God for them, and vindicated their perpetrators. The murder of Cardinal Beaton in 1546 was justified by John Knox; the assassination of Francis of Guise in 1563 was defended by Theodore Beza; the Spanish Jesuits maintained that the slaying of William of Orange in 1584 was a pious and praiseworthy deed; while Pope Sixtus V himself commended the monk who took the life of Henry III of France.

130

HUGO GROTIUS

Moreover, not only were isolated acts of homicide vindicated, but a general theory of tyrannicide was formulated in which with extreme precision the term ' tyrant ' was defined, and in which with elaborate care the proper agents of assassination were specified.   Perhaps the most advanced exponent of this appalling form of direct action was the Spanish Jesuit Juan de Mariana, to whom every heretical ruler was a tyrant, and by whom every devout heretic-slayer was justified.

The appearance of Mariana's *De Rege et Regis Institutione* in 1599 coincided with a formidable recrudescence of violence. The aggressive forces of the Counter-Reformation came into more and more ferocious conflict with the resistant but retreating forces of the Reformation.   In 1605 the Gunpowder Plot portended the murder of the Protestant James VI and I and the recovery of Scotland and England for Catholicism ; in 1608 a Catholic League was formed in Germany for the restoration of the Empire to the unity of the Faith ; in 1610 the great coalition of Henry IV of France against those main bulwarks of the Papacy, the Hapsburg rulers of Spain and Austria, was broken up by the dagger of Ravaillac.   For the next eight years the furies roused by plot and counterplot, by assassination and counter-assassination on the part of Catholic League and answering Calvinistic Confederation, seethed and raged until at last they found issue in the unparalleled horrors of the Thirty Years War.

Through the major portion of this period of battle, murder, and sudden death Grotius lived (1583–1645).   He was one year old when, in the country of his birth, William of Orange was shot by Balthazar ; he was six when the dagger of Clément extinguished the Valois house ; he was only thirty-five when the conflicts of religion reached their climax in the Thirty Years War, and he survived to witness all but three of the destructive campaigns of this last and worst of the sectarian struggles.   Grotius was a man of large and tolerant spirit. Sincerely pious, he had none of the fanaticism of the sectary or the fury of the partisan.   He felt that the great truths of Christianity which Catholic and Calvinist, Lutheran and Arminian, held in common were immeasurably more important than were the details concerning which they differed. His remarkable apologetic, *De Veritate Christianæ Religionis*

(1627), was devoted to the defence of a creed which was accepted by all the combatants in the suicidal wars of the sects. In many respects he resembled Bodin, *e.g.*, in his encyclopædic learning, in his legal outlook, in his desire for peace, in his belief in the principle of religious toleration. But he had none of Bodin's cynical indifference to religion, none of Bodin's fundamental scepticism. He desired tranquillity not merely in the political interest of his own state; he wished for it in the interest of both the Church Universal and also the whole family of the nations of Christendom. He had a wide cosmopolitan and catholic purview. It was to further the well-being of humanity as a whole that he composed and in 1625 issued his *magnum opus*, his famous *De Jure Belli et Pacis*, the basal treatise of modern International Law.

II

The early life of Grotius had well fitted him for the fulfilment of this supreme task of his life. Born on April 10, 1583, at Delft in the province of Holland, Huig van Groot (Hugo Grotius) was the son of an eminent and wealthy lawyer who had not only been four times burgomaster of the important town of Leyden, but was also curator of its famous university, the headquarters of the Arminian revolt against strict Calvinism, and a centre of Republican resistance to the ambitious house of Orange. The Groot family was of French origin; it claimed descent from the aristocratic Cornets, one of whom had migrated to the Netherlands in the fifteenth century. The family had become thoroughly naturalised in Holland, had prospered greatly, and had risen to a position of general esteem. Hugo was thus born in circumstances eminently favourable to the fostering of his talents, if he had any, and if he cared to foster them; or, alternatively, to the suffocation of his talents in *bourgeois* luxury and civic respectability. Fortunately, he was endowed with a quick and eager mind, avid for learning and tireless in industry. Hence he used his advantages to the full, and at a remarkably early age attained a wide reputation for scholarship. He was, in fact, an infant prodigy. When he was but eight years old his Latin verses were passed from hand to hand among schoolmasters and professors as

models of subtle thought and graceful style. At twelve he
entered the university, bringing with him an almost complete
mastery of the Greek and Roman classics. At sixteen he
emerged as a fully fledged Doctor of Law. During the period
of his pupillarity, moreover, he had published a critical edition
of Martianus Capella's famous pre-mediæval text-book of the
seven liberal arts, and had further been chosen to accompany
Olden Barneveldt on a diplomatic mission to Paris. At the
age of twenty (1603) he was appointed official Historiographer
of his native province; four years later he was made Advocate-
General of the Fisc for Holland and Zeeland; finally in 1613
he became Pensionary of Rotterdam. By that time he was
recognised as one of the ablest scholars and most learned
lawyers in Europe, and was looked upon as a leader in the
Arminian and Republican party which was struggling to check
the intolerance of Calvinism and to prevent the dangerous
aggrandisement of the house of Orange.

Soon after his appointment as Historiographer, Grotius had
been called upon to turn his attention to the problem of International Law. The Dutch East India Company had become
involved in a controversy with the Peninsular Powers arising
out of the seizure of a Portuguese galleon in the Straits of
Malacca by a captain in the employ of the Company. The
case was a complicated one because, first, Portugal had been
annexed by Spain, and Spain still nominally regarded the
Dutch as her own rebellious subjects; secondly, the East
India Company was a private mercantile organisation whose
right to engage in war was in the circumstances doubtful.
Grotius dealt with the whole matter in a masterly dissertation,
De Jure Prædæ, 1604. Not only did he solve, in the Dutch
interest, the specific problem raised; but he laid down general
principles of International Law substantially the same as those
which he afterward expanded and illustrated in his classical
De Jure Belli et Pacis. The treatise *De Jure Prædæ* was not
published at the time of its composition, and by some strange
freak of fortune it was completely forgotten for two and a half
centuries. Then, in the middle of the nineteenth century, it
was rediscovered, and first issued in 1868. Its publication
threw floods of light on the process of the formation of
Grotius's opinions, and it solved for ever the mystery of how

Grotius, a stranger in a strange land, had apparently been able to compose his great work on War and Peace, without previous preparation, in a little over a year (1624-5). A vast amount of preliminary work and preparatory thought had as a matter of fact been achieved in 1604. The critically important attitude of Grotius toward both the *Jus Naturæ* and the *Jus Gentium* had already been determined. Much of the material necessary for the construction of a systematic code of international morality and custom had been collected.

Although the *De Jure Prædæ* was not, as a whole, published during the lifetime of Grotius, nor for two centuries after his death, nevertheless one of its chapters (XII) found its way into print—probably without the consent or knowledge of Grotius —in connexion with another controversy which the Dutch were maintaining with their old Iberian enemies. This controversy related to the freedom of the seas. Could the high seas—the Indian Ocean, the Atlantic, the Pacific—become State property, in the same manner as islands and continents could become such ? Might the Spaniards and Portuguese, in virtue of prior discovery and first occupation, claim the right to exclude the Dutch, together with all other nations, from the great waters of the world? No, said Grotius in his *Mare Liberum* (1609). Twenty years later the same emphatic negative was presented to England's claim to exclusive control of the North Sea and the Channel. In vain did the English antiquary and lawyer John Selden attempt to rebut the arguments of Grotius in his *Mare Clausum* (1632). The issue had ultimately to be decided by the three Anglo-Dutch wars of the later seventeenth century.

Long, however, before the English and Dutch came to blows respecting the lordship of the narrow seas, the connexion between Grotius and his native land had been violently terminated. In 1618 the smouldering antagonism between the Republican party—*bourgeois*, commercial, maritime, Francophile, Arminian—and the Orange party—aristocratic, agrarian, military, Anglophile, Calvinistic—burst into open flame. Maurice of Nassau effected a successful *coup d'état* on July 31, routed the Republicans, and captured and executed their leader, Olden Barneveldt. Grotius was sufficiently important to become involved in his leader's fall, but not personally so obnoxious to Maurice as to incur the fate of Barneveldt.   He was condemned to lifelong incarceration, and in June 1619 was placed in the prison of Louvestein, near Gorcum, whence he expected never to emerge.   Fortunately, however, for himself and for the world he had in 1608 married a wife, Marie Reigersberg by name, who was a woman not only of complete devotion, but also of unusual resource.   Taking advantage of a concession which allowed books to be sent to her husband in his imprisonment, and taken away when read, she concealed the adventurous philosopher in a packing-case and had him conveyed from his cell as a cargo of Arminian theology.   After agonies not unlike those suffered by victims of premature burial, he was released by friends and enabled to escape, first to Antwerp and then to Paris, where he was welcomed by Louis XIII and provided with a pension (seldom actually paid).   This was in 1621.

It was soon after his arrival in France that he began seriously to turn his attention to the Law of War and of Peace.   The Thirty Years conflict had broken out in Bohemia during the course of 1618; the decisive battle of the White Mountain had been fought in 1620; the defeated Elector Palatine was in a flight that was destined to terminate only with his life; his territories were in process of devastation by exasperated and merciless enemies.   The spectacle horrified Grotius.   " I saw prevailing," he said, " throughout the Christian world a licence in making war of which even barbarous nations would have been ashamed; recourse being had to arms for slight reasons or for no reason; and when arms were once taken up, all reverence for divine and human law was thrown away, just as if men were thenceforth authorised to commit all crimes without restraint."   In these circumstances of unmitigated militancy some of the more extreme theorists, following the lead of Erasmus, tended toward an absolute pacificism.   Grotius entirely dissociated himself from them.   Some wars, he admitted, were just, were necessary, were divinely imperative. His problem was to find a law according to which righteous wars could be distinguished from unrighteous; a law potent enough to set a humane limit to the violence by belligerents; a law sufficiently evident and universal to be recognised as binding by men of all races, ranks, and religions.

135

III

Grotius, in setting himself to compose his great treatise *De Jure Belli et Pacis*, was faced by all the difficulties which naturally confront a man who is exiled from his home, cut off from his books, and in straitened circumstances.   He had, however, a copy of his earlier work *De Jure Prædæ* ;   he was assisted by a large collection of apposite quotations selected for him during the reading of many years by his laborious, if uninspired, brother, William ;   he was, moreover, endowed with a prodigious memory which enabled him to carry a dictionary of reference in his mind.   Finally, he was assisted by a number of French friends, one of whom lodged him comfortably in the Château de Balagni near Senlis, another of whom supplied him with books from an ample library.   So well, in fact, was he equipped that he was able to achieve his enormous and erudite work within the brief period already noted (1624–5).

What were the books which Grotius read ?   To what extent was he indebted to them for his ideas ?   How far was he original ?   As to his sources, he himself gives us a list in his Prolegomena, but the list is obviously incomplete.   He mentions Victoria, Ayala, and Gentilis, to all of whom his debt is evident.   But he does not name Suarez, with whose masterly treatment of the types and varieties of law he must have been familiar ;   nor does he refer to his Protestant forerunners, Oldendorf, Hemming, and Winckler, from whom even more conspicuously some of his leading conceptions were borrowed. Grotius, indeed, has little claim to originality.   Although he said of International Law, with some truth, that before him " no one had treated it as a whole and in an orderly manner," the novelty which he professes is to be found only in the completeness and orderliness of his work.   All its elements were preexistent.   He combined them, co-ordinated them, arranged them, harmonised them, displayed them with considerable lucidity and grace.   Hallam goes too far when, in his *Literary History*, he says that the *De Jure Belli* " may be considered as nearly original in its general platform as any work of man in an advanced state of civilisation and learning can be."   Hallam, with all his erudition, was insufficiently informed respecting

136

the fruitful labours of the forerunners of Grotius, and he suffered from the curious illusion (so soon to be dispelled by the writings of Darwin) that the limits of human knowledge had been almost reached.   Dr T. A. Walker in his careful and scholarly *History of the Law of Nations*[1] judges more accurately, when he says, "There was little novel in the legal system of Grotius, and there was equally but little original in either the arrangement or the matter of his work."   He proceeds to show in detail Grotius's indebtedness to Gentilis for arrangement and to Victoria, Ayala, Winckler, Bodin, and many others for his subject-matter.

If, however, the mind of Grotius was accumulative rather than creative; if it excelled in classifying and co-ordinating rather than in discovering and inventing; if it was more skilled in giving lucid expression to the old than in propounding the new, nevertheless the work of Grotius was of cardinal importance.   The very fact that it contained no startling novelties commended it to the conscience of the age.   It summed up the accepted wisdom of the ancients and applied it to the unprecedented conditions of the Renaissance and Reformation world; it epitomised all that had been written by Stoic philosophers, Roman lawyers, scholastic theologians, and Jesuitical casuists concerning the Law of Nature and the Law of Nations, and combined it into a solid foundation for an incalculably valuable superstructure of international morality and custom. The *De Jure Belli et Pacis* won instant recognition not only by reason of its vast learning, its methodical arrangement, and its admirable style, but also because of the European reputation of its author, and because of its own amazing appositeness to the circumstances of the age in which it appeared.   The urgent need of the day was the formulation of a code of laws of war which should be accepted as obligatory alike by Catholic and Protestant, by Christian and infidel, by theist and atheist. The conscience of mankind was in revolt against the limitless atrocities of the Wars of Religion—against, for example, the assassination of leaders, the slaying of prisoners, the violation of women, the massacre of children, the pillaging of defenceless towns, the poisoning of wells, the wanton spoliation of peaceful populations.   What principles could be found which should

[1] Vol. i, p. 333.

condemn these barbarities? On what basis could an authoritative body of rules be framed which the public opinion of the civilised world would require to be observed? On what foundation could be erected a stable structure of recognised international morality and custom?

The need of such a code had been felt as early as the Crusades, which had been a truceless war just because there had been no common authority to which the combatants could appeal for the consecration of oaths or the commendation to mercy. Still more had there been necessity for some universally established ethic of war when the supra-national authority of the Middle Ages—the Papacy—was itself engaged as a belligerent in the task of exterminating the Albigenses with fire and sword. The want had been emphasised when the New World was discovered, and when Christian adventurers, devoid of all compassion, went to conquer and to rule in regions east of Suez and west of Panama, where " there ain't no Ten Commandments."

Since we are not concerned with International Law, but are limited in our consideration to social and political ideas, we are exempted from the necessity of summarising the *De Jure Belli et Pacis* of Grotius. Those who wish to find such a summary will get what they want in Hallam's *Literary History*, or, better still, in Dr T. A. Walker's *History of the Law of Nations.* Best of all, however, would it be for them to read the abridged translation of the book—a masterpiece of selection and condensation—issued by Dr Whewell of Trinity College, Cambridge, in 1853. Suffice it here to say that the work consists of a Dedication to Louis XIII, a Prolegomena, and three Books. Book I treats of war in general, and particularly with the problem whether among so-called Christian nations war can ever be just. Grotius convincingly maintains, against the pacificists, that it can. That being his conclusion, in Book II he goes on to treat, at great length, of the possible just grounds of war—that is to say, he deals with rights which it is allowable to defend, and duties which it is imperative to perform. Book III, toward which the whole argument of the work majestically tends, discusses the laws of war—that is to say, the limits, moral and customary, beyond which belligerents must not go in maintaining even their just cause by armed force.

Books II and III are almost wholly legal; the Prolegomena and Book I, however, are rich in political ideas. Grotius is compelled to lay a foundation for his juristic system on a deep and wide basis of general theory. Incidentally, some of his tacit assumptions are as interesting as his explicit assertions. His political generalisations focus round two main themes, viz., (1) the State and (2) law. They do so because the aim and purpose of his work is, as we have already noted, to find some sort of law which is capable of binding and restraining that great Leviathan, the sovereign national state.

IV

(1) THE STATE

One of the most significant of the tacit assumptions of Grotius is that of the non-existence of the mediæval *Respublica Christiana*, which was the dominant conception of such papal theorists as St Thomas Aquinas, or such Imperial dreamers as Dante. The idea of a united Christendom has completely passed away, and has given place to that of a Family of Nations, or group of sovereign national states, who have no common superior, and acknowledge no allegiance to any extraneous authority whatsoever, whether civil or ecclesiastical. As to the origin of the State, Grotius is in accord with Aristotle, who regarded man as by nature social and political. " Man," says Grotius in his Prolegomena, " is an animal indeed, but an animal of an excellent kind, differing much more from all other tribes of animals than they differ from one another . . . and among those properties which are peculiar to man is a desire for society, that is, a desire for a life spent in common with fellowmen, and not merely spent somehow, but spent tranquilly and in a manner corresponding to the character of his intellect. This desire the Stoics call οἰκείωσις, the domestic instinct, or feeling of kindred." It may be remarked that Grotius is here much nearer to the truth as revealed by modern psychology than is Hobbes, who regarded society as a contractual arrangement made by men naturally solitary and antisocial, or even than is Bentham who conceived society as based merely on an intellectual recognition on the part of isolated

individuals that they would gain by association and co-opera
tion. Society, then, according to Grotius, comes into exist
ence naturally and instinctively as the result of the operation o
man's gregarious impulse. The State, however, is not quite
the same as society. It is both less and more. It is less
numerically: it consists of but a fragment of the whole com
munity of mankind, the great society. Functionally it is
more: it exists for defence against external foes, for the main
tenance of law and order against internal disorders, and for the
promotion of the general welfare of its constituent members
It is *cœtus perfectus liberorum hominum juris fruendi et communi.*
utilitatis causa sociatus, i.e., the perfect union of a body of free
men joined together for the purpose of enjoying the protection
of the law and of promoting the common interest. The State.
in short, is a section of society organised for a specific purpose
It is, therefore, not a product of nature in the same sense as is
society. It involves a perception of utility, and also an element
of mutual consent or even contract. Though Grotius clearly
recognises the existence of an agreement of wills beneath the
structure of the State, he does not emphasise or develop the
Contract Theory, as it is emphasised by his contemporaries, the
Monarchomachs, or by his successors, the Republicans. His
conception of the contract is derived from Roman Law rather
than from Old Testament Scripture or feudal practice. It is
the Social Contract of Hobbes and Rousseau which he en-
visages rather than the Governmental Contract of Duplessis-
Mornay, Hooker, and Locke.

Government he does not regard as based on a contract, but
as of the nature of a transfer of property. He looks upon it as
human in origin and legal in its character: he knows nothing
of any Divine Right of Kings. Neither, however, does he
know anything of any inalienable sovereignty of the people.
Even though primordially the source of sovereignty resided in
the peoples, yet when once they have formed their state and
established their government they have divested themselves for
ever of their pristine powers.[1] He seems to regard sovereignty
as a sort of dominion which, once having been alienated for
valuable consideration, cannot be revoked. Hence he takes a

---

[1] " Quidni ergo populo sui juris liceat se unicuipiam aut pluribus ita addicere ut
regendi sui jus in eum plane transcribat, nulla ejus parte retenta " (*De Jure Belli*, i, 3).

view of the relation between sovereign and subjects not unlike
that which Hobbes developed a quarter of a century later in his
Leviathan : a people having chosen its ruler and having conferred authority upon him has no right to rebel against him or
in any way to resist his will.   Republican though he had been
in Holland, at the time when he wrote the *De Jure Belli et
Pacis* his monarchic preferences were pronounced.   The dedication of the work to Louis XIII shows its strong inclination
and tendency.   When some years later his opinion was asked
concerning the quarrel which was developing in England between Charles I and his Parliament, he wrote without hesita-
tion, *Regi Angliæ opto prosperiora, tum quia est rex, tum quia bonus
rex.*[1]

Monarchy, however, to Grotius is by no means identical
with despotism.   He follows Bodin and many other of his contemporaries in distinguishing kings from tyrants.   The fourth
chapter of the first book of the *De Jure Belli* is full of subtle
discriminations between kings who may not be resisted and
tyrants who may not only be resisted, but even slain.   Pre-
eminently tyrants are those who have usurped a throne, and
those who, having acquired it legitimately, nevertheless govern
in violation of the fundamental laws of their realm.   For to
Grotius, as to Bodin, to Hooker, and to Suarez, the ultimate
supremacy in the world and in the universe at large resides in
Law.   Even sovereignty, to him, is a dominion held under
Law, and in especial the Law of Nature.   And since sovereignty
is of the nature of property he sees no difficulty in regarding
it as limited in several directions.   Just as an estate can be held
subject to any number of easements, so can the *summa potestas*
or *jus imperandi* be possessed under a large variety of restrictions—restrictions of time, as in the case of the Roman dicta-
tors ; restrictions due to pledges given at coronation ; restrictions established by immemorial constitutional connexions,
such as the Salic Law.   Grotius's conception of sovereignty is
not, as has sometimes been said, a confused and inconsistent
one.   But it is one so radically different from that of Hobbes,
Bentham, and Austin, that any attempt to state it in terms
of the more modern theory of these great jurists is bound
to generate confusion.   If it is realised that, to Grotius,

[1] *Grotii Epistolæ*, No. 946.

sovereignty is merely a limited right of property held under
Natural Law, all his reservations and restrictions fall into their
proper and logical places.

Among the possible and conceivable limitations of
sovereignty, however, is *not* limitation by another human will
The sovereign may and must obey Natural Law, Divine Law.
Constitutional Law, and even the Law of Nations, and he may
do so without any derogation from his sovereignty. For ever
God Himself is subject to the laws which He has instituted
But if any *civil* law can supersede the command of a ruler, if
any *human* will can override his will, then he is not sovereign
he does not hold the title-deeds which confer dominion
Hence Grotius defines sovereignty as " the supreme political
power vested in him whose acts cannot be rendered void by
any other human volition."

The principle of Grotius that—subject to the superiority of
Law Natural, Divine, Constitutional, and International, and
except in so far as bound by pledges given—the will of the
sovereign is supreme in the State enables him to set forth with
out any ambiguity both the duties and the rights of the indi
vidual in respect of the ruler. Active resistance is alway
wrong. " Even if we receive injury from the will of th
Supreme Power, we are to bear it rather than resist by force."
For " civil society being instituted to secure public tranquillity
the State acquires a superior right over us and ours, so far as i
necessary for that end." On the other hand, however, no
even the sovereign can require active obedience to fiats which
in the opinion of the subject, contravene the dictates of th
higher laws. " It is beyond controversy among all good men
that if the persons in authority command anything contrary t
Natural Law or the Divine Precepts, it is not to be done.
Those who thus passively resist the will of the sovereign mus
of course, be prepared to stand the racket. The sovereign ha
his duty to perform to society, and that duty involves the en
forcement of his authority. Here, then, is a real conflict of
loyalties—the clash of an irresistible force and an immovabl
obstacle. What will result? The passive resister and con
scientious objector must be prepared to perish from the com
munity—whether by death, or loss of liberty, or deprivation of
civil rights, as the sovereign may decree. He must, withou

demur, face the inconveniences of martyrdom. Then all will
be well. He will, on his part, have saved his soul alive,
and, on the other part, the sovereign will have vindicated
that authority which is both his proprietary right under
Natural Law and also his public duty under the Law of the
Constitution.

Grotius is concerned in describing the State and defining
its sovereignty not as a political philosopher, but as an international lawyer. His task is to frame a code of rules applic-
able to the relations between states and between the Governments of states. Therefore it is imperative for him to classify
his ideas and to give the precise connotation of his terms. All
his work of definition and classification is, however, preliminary in its nature. It is, for the most part, contained in his
Prolegomena and in the opening chapters of Book I. From
that he passes on to his real business—which, however, is *not*
our prime concern—the relation of states to one another in that
condition of masterless nature wherein the disintegration of
mediæval Christendom has left them. He postulates, first,
their complete independence, both of one another and of any
supra-national authority such as Empire or Papacy. Each and
every sovereign is within the territory under his control
supreme in all causes, whether temporal or ecclesiastical, and
over all persons. No extraneous power can interfere with any
claim to superior jurisdiction. A second postulate—one of
far-reaching significance and importance—is that of the formal
equality of states. The Law of Nature knows no distinction
between great and small in the Family of Nations. Legally
and for the purposes of diplomacy all are on a par, whether
strong or weak, whether rich or poor, whether monarchic or
republican, whether venerable with antiquity or newly admitted. In order, however, to share in the advantages of this
legal and diplomatic equality, membership of the Family of
Nations is essential. And membership is not without its qualifications. No community, however powerful and independent,
can be recognised as a full subject of International Law unless
it shows the marks of (1) a civilisation akin to that of the
Christian polities of the West ; (2) an organised Government
capable of entering into and observing treaties and conventions ; (3) a fixed territory within which its sovereignty is

complete; and (4) a stability which seems likely to offer a guarantee of permanence.

Among communities thus qualified for admission into the Family of Nations three different relations are possible. These are, first, *peace*, which includes both friendly intercourse of the active kind between specific states and also benevolent non-interference with similar friendly intercourse between other states; secondly, *war*, that is, armed conflict between states; and thirdly, intermediate betwixt the two and the most difficult to define and maintain, *neutrality*, a relation which arises when war breaks out between two states or groups of states, and non-belligerents wish to continue in peaceful intercourse with both the combatants. Although Grotius included *et pacis* in the title of his great work, he says, as a matter of fact, very little concerning the laws of peace. The most important matters that come under that head are the various pacific modes of acquiring property, the occasional deviations from the principle of territorial jurisdiction, the numerous formal rules for the conduct of legation and negotiation, and the general regulations for the making and the ratifying of treaties. Where Grotius discusses these questions at all, he does so not because they are sections of the laws of peace, but because they give rise to rights, the defence of which may become just occasion for the waging of wars. Concerning neutrality he says still less. International commerce was not very highly developed in his day, and consequently the problems of neutrality were not either so complex or so pressing as they became later. It was left to Bynkershoek in the eighteenth century—when trade had expanded, when chartered companies had established gigantic interests all over the world, and when colonies had been planted by all the leading European peoples—to formulate in detail the fundamental principles of a rational law of neutrality. In Grotius's day, as we have had occasion to notice more than once, the critical questions related to the laws of war. Grotius as official Historiographer of Holland had acquired an intimate knowledge of the limitless barbarities perpetrated by the Spaniards under Alva and his successors in their attempts to suppress the revolt of the Netherlands from 1572 onward. He lived and wrote amid the still more appalling horrors of the Thirty Years War. His main concern was to discover and formulate such principles of law as should appeal to the reason and the conscience of combatants, and should command such universal consent and such general obedience as to render a continuance or repetition of these abominations impossible.

The guiding motive of Grotius would seem to have been the determination to secure the recognition of the principle that war is an armed conflict carried on, under conditions fixed by morality and custom, between the *public* forces of responsible states, and not an unrestricted struggle of a whole people against a whole people, without any distinction between combatants and non-combatants, or between legitimate and illegitimate modes of violence. It marked an immense mitigation of the terrors of war when he and his successors secured the recognition of the existence of a non-combatant class among enemies, and established the rule that, in general, non-combatants should be exempt from injury in person and in property. It marked a still more notable advance when, largely through the influence of the *De Jure Belli et Pacis*, it came to be acknowledged, both in theory and in practice, that even as against combatant enemies there are certain forms of violence which cannot be allowed, and that, in general, no superfluous cruelty is permissible, but only such an amount of force as shall prove to be necessary to overcome the enemies' armed resistance.

These were great achievements. By what means was Grotius able to aid in their accomplishment? To what did he appeal as the sanction of his revised and meliorative law of war? He appealed to the Law of Nature and the Law of Nations. In doing so he had to define and explain these exalted and authoritative codes.

V

(2) LAW

The conception of 'law' is one which has been much canvassed by both philosophers and jurists from the days of the Stoics onward. It connotes the correlation of two distinct ideas, viz., on the one hand, a causal intelligence and will, and, on the other hand, a resultant conformity and uniformity of behaviour. The conception arose in primitive pre-scientific times, when the phenomena of human conduct and the phenomena of irrational and inanimate nature were regarded as of one and the same order; when the sun was looked upon as a chariot driven in a race, and when men were envisaged as automata moved in their predestined circles by inexorable fate. Hence no distinction was attempted between ' law ' in the scientific sense of the term and ' law ' in the juristic sense of the term. Thus Demosthenes spoke of " the whole world, and things divine, and what we call the seasons " as " regulated by law and order." So Cicero talked at large of law astronomical and law imperial as equally *ratio recta summi Jovis*. The confusion continued throughout the Middle Ages. St Thomas Aquinas, for instance, discoursed of a *lex æterna* which is *nihil aliud quam summa ratio divinæ sapientiæ, secundum quod est directiva omnium actuum et motionum*. From St Thomas the confusion between law scientific and law juristic entered the modern world; it is seen in the works of Suarez, Hooker, and many others. Becoming even less excusable, it reached the eighteenth century, and was glaringly exhibited in the opening sentences of Montesquieu's *Esprit des Lois* : " Les lois, dans la signification la plus étendue, sont les rapports nécessaires qui dérivent de la nature des choses ; et, dans ce sens, tous les êtres ont leurs lois ; la divinité a ses lois, le monde matériel a ses lois, les intelligences supérieures à l'homme ont leurs lois, les bêtes ont leurs lois, l'homme a ses lois." Quite unpardonably, Blackstone, the English lawyer, perpetuated the muddle when he advanced to his proper study, viz., the Laws of England, by way of (1) the laws of inanimate matter, (2) the laws of animal nutrition, (3) the laws of nature, and (4) the laws of Divine revelation. It was, indeed, left for Bentham in his *Fragment on Government* (1776) and Austin in his *Jurisprudence* (1832) to clear up the ambiguity of the term ' law,' and to render it impossible for any serious thinker any more, by reason of a twofold connotation, to " deluge the field of jurisprudence and morals with muddy speculation." [1] In spite of Austin, however, one still hears (especially from pulpits and platforms) such purely nonsensical expressions as

---

[1] J. Austin, *Jurisprudence*, fifth edition, p. 88.

"the violation of physical law" or "obedience to the laws of political economy."

The two original ideas included in the term ' law,' viz., (1) causal intelligence and will, and (2) resultant uniformity and order, have now been entirely separated from one another. ' Law' in the *scientific* sense of the word merely connotes an unvarying sequence of phenomena; it is a general statement in the indicative mood, an abstract idea of observed relations, a theoretical principle, a provisional hypothesis. For example, one of the ' laws of motion' runs : " Action and reaction are equal and opposite"; while Newton's famous ' law of gravitation' commences with the words " Every particle of matter in the universe attracts every other particle." Nothing here is said or implied respecting either the forces whose operation is described or the causes by whose impulse they operate. ' Law' in the *juristic* sense of the word, on the other hand, connotes command; its mood is imperative; it is a general rule of human conduct; it is addressed to the will of man by the will of superior authority. " Thou shalt not steal " : this law is intended to secure uniformity of behaviour on the part of all the members of the human race. But it remains ' law ' even if no member of the human race obeys it.

Grotius lived and wrote at a time when the confusion between law juristic and law scientific was at its height. Hence his work, like that of his contemporaries already mentioned, is to some extent vitiated by the ambiguity attaching to his fundamental term, viz., *jus*. It sometimes connotes a rule of conduct; but it also at other times connotes the necessary relation of things. For instance, Grotius, early in his first chapter, says, " Natural Law is so immutable that it cannot be changed by God Himself . . . thus God Himself cannot make twice two not to be four." Did he really suppose that it is owing to a Divine command that two and two make four? Can he indeed have imagined that a mere mathematical postulate, a provisional hypothesis, an assumption of logic—concerning the truth of which, by the way, Einstein has recently thrown grave doubt—has anything whatsoever in common with a command addressed to the human will ? Apparently he did in very fact suffer from this appalling confusion of ideas. Fortunately, however, it did not affect much of his writing. For he soon left the realm of science, in which he was an alien wanderer, and turned to the world of human behaviour, wherein he was at home and a master.

In treating of Grotius's conception of law, the first point to be noted is that he consistently prefers the term *jus* to the term *lex*. In other words, he selects a term which connotes ' right ' irrespective of its origin, and rejects a term which suggests statutory enactment. This choice was of special significance in respect of Natural Law; for whereas Suarez, who called it *Lex Naturalis*, had treated it as the unrevealed Law of God—as truly statutory as the law revealed in the Scriptures, or as the law promulgated by the canons of the Church—Grotius under the name of *Jus Naturale* regards it merely as the dictate of right reason, which would have weight even if (to quote the Prolegomena) " we were to grant that there is no God, or that He bestows no regard on human affairs." But perhaps I ought not to say " *merely* as the dictate of right reason " ; for the word ' merely ' suggests inferiority. So far, however, from regarding Natural Law as inferior to Divine Law—that is, to Law promulgated by the direct will and voice of God— Grotius regards it as the basis of that Law, and as determining the limits within which the Divine Will itself must move. " Natural Law," he says in Book I, Chapter I, "is so immutable that it cannot be changed by God Himself. For though the power of God be immense, there are some things to which it does not extend ; because if we speak of those things being done, the words are mere words, and have no meaning, being self-contradictory." Thus Natural Law stands in a class by itself. It is the δίκαιον φυσικόν of Aristotle. It is " the dictate of right reason, indicating that any act, from its agreement or disagreement with the rational nature, has its moral turpitude or moral necessity." [1] Hence it is of universal authority, supreme over angels and men alike, determining the modes and motions of all creatures both animate and inanimate, fixing the bounds of even the divine operations. As regards men, it existed in its pure form—*Jus Naturale Merum*— before the Fall. Since the Fall it has had to be somewhat

---

[1] " Jus Naturale est dictatum rectæ rationis, indicans actui alicui, ex ejus convenientia aut disconvenientia cum ipsa natura rationali, inesse moralem turpitudinem aut necessitatem moralem " (*De Jure Belli et Pacis*, i, 1).

modified, not in its principles but in its application, to suit the new circumstances: it is *Jus quod pro certo statu est Naturale*.

How may this sovereign Law of Nature be known and recognised? First, it is perceived instinctively by the conscience of the normal individual; secondly, it is proclaimed by general agreement among the best minds: thirdly, it is confirmed by the practice of all the most civilised peoples (*omnes moratiores populi*). But who shall decide what individuals are normal, what minds are best, what peoples are the most civilised? Grotius gives us no criterion; but it is obvious that he alone is normal; that minds which accord with his own mind are the best; and that the most civilised peoples are those who behave themselves as he thinks they ought to behave. In other words *Jus Naturale* is nothing more or less than the common dictates of conscience.

Similarly, *Jus Gentium* is nothing more than the precepts of common sense. Grotius, however, spends much time and energy in giving it an objective existence, and in placing it in its proper position in the category of laws. Over against the great body of *Jus Naturale*, consisting of the dictates of reason, he sets the *Jus Voluntarium*, or body of positive commands, which are the dictates of will. The whole of this class of laws is subordinate to the *Jus Naturale* and conditioned by it. It is subdivided into the *Jus Divinum*, or Law of God; the *Jus Civile*, or law of the State; and the *Jus Gentium*. But what is the *Jus Gentium*? The term is an expression of Roman Law, and in its original sense it meant law common to the peoples with whom the Romans had dealings. It was in Roman times private law, that is to say, law between subject and subject, a sort of highest common factor of the codes of the Italian tribes. It embodied dictates of common sense so obvious that, quite independently of one another, both the Romans and their neighbours had given expression to them in their legal systems. So closely did they in general accord with those dictates of conscience to which the name *Jus Naturale* had been given that some thinkers tended to identify the two entirely. The fact, however, that they differed on one or two matters—of which slavery was the most important—prevented their complete fusion.

The *Jus Gentium*, then, presented itself to Grotius as a code of precepts distinct from the *Jus Naturale* and of lower authority, yet immensely valuable. It provided a body of international custom which in a most serviceable way could supplement the universal morality of the Law of Nature. In order, however, that it might fulfil his purpose, he had to effect a complete change in the connotation of the term. He had to transmute it from private law, establishing relations between subject and subject; into public law, establishing relations between state and state. This was an immense and momentous transformation, and it has been warmly debated whether he effected it deliberately, or whether he perpetrated it by a happy accident out of sheer muddle-headedness and inability to distinguish between elementary differences. It may be admitted that the expression *Jus Gentium* is an ambiguous one; it may well stand for the law common to the peoples of all nations, or for the law which regulates the mutual relations of states. It may also be admitted that Grotius was not careful to indicate that he was using the expression in the second sense, whereas the Roman lawyers from whom he derived it had used it in the first sense. But it is incredible that a man of his erudition should have made a mistake which would to-day cause an undergraduate to be ploughed in a preliminary examination. It is possible that he did not wish to call attention to the fact that he was using the *Jus Gentium* in a manner unknown to the great civilians; it is probable that he considered that the validity of the principles of the *Jus Gentium* was not in the least affected by the fact that their application was extended from the sphere of private law to the sphere of public International Law. Be that as it may, he was not the first to make the extension: it had already been done by Benedict Winckler in his *Principiorum Juris Libri Quinque*, which had appeared in 1615. Thus, just as Grotius followed Bodin in regarding the *Jus Naturale* as the dictate of human reason rather than as the unrevealed Law of God, so did he follow Winckler in treating the *Jus Gentium* as a rudimentary code of International Law rather than as a body of private law. If, however, neither of these great conceptions was original to Grotius, it was his work which gave them currency and established them as the basis of modern international morality and custom.

How may the principles of the *Jus Gentium* be known and recognised? They are displayed, first, in the usages of the best nations, and secondly in the testimony of the wisest men. But which are the best nations, and who are the wisest men? There again, as in the case of the *Jus Naturale*, the best are those who act as Grotius himself thinks they should, and the wisest are such as agree with his opinions. Hence the distinction between *Jus Naturale* and *Jus Gentium* tends to vanish away. The standard of international morality and the criterion of international custom become one and the same, viz., the conscience and the common sense of Grotius himself. Thus the *De Jure Belli et Pacis* is essentially the judgment of Grotius concerning what is allowable in war and proper in peace. The numerous opinions quoted are those of which Grotius approved; the rest he rejects. The frequent examples cited are those which support his plea for mercy and moderation; those which do not support it are either ignored or are condemned as the barbarities of nations other than the best. Thus the argument travels in a circle, and it ultimately returns to the point whence it started, viz., the conscience and common sense of Grotius.

The weakness of so-called International Law has always been the absence of any extraneous standard. The *Jus Naturale* has no objective existence, and the *Jus Gentium* is a mere code of custom devoid of moral quality. Thus International Law lacks determinate source, lacks precise formulation, lacks sanction, lacks effective tribunals. Hence in times of severe stress, as for example in the autumn of 1914 and increasingly during the course of the Great War, it breaks down, and shows itself powerless to prevent a recurrence of precisely those barbarities which stirred Grotius to attempt his great task. To say that, however, is not to say that Grotius and his successors laboured in vain. It is not for nothing that a general set of rules has been framed, even though the force necessary to ensure their observance has hitherto been wanting. For gradually but certainly there is coming into being an International Authority—a Concert of Europe; a Council of Great Powers; a Hague Tribunal; a Geneva Court; a League of Nations—which in due time will give to the moral precepts and the customary practices which the conscience and the common sense of the great jurists have formulated, the force and the majesty of a genuine and operative International Law.

THE EDITOR.

BIBLIOGRAPHY

A. PRIMARY SOURCE

GROTIUS, HUGO: *De Jure Belli et Pacis Libri Tres*, accompanied by an abridged translation by William Whewell. 3 vols. 1853.

B. SECONDARY SOURCES

CARMICHAEL, C. H. E.: "Grotius and the Literary History of the Law of Nations" (*Transactions of the Royal Society of Literature*, Second Series, vol. xiv).

FRANCK, A.: *Réformateurs et publicistes de l'Europe.* 1864.

HÉLY, D.: *Étude sur le droit de la guerre de Grotius.* 1875.

HOLLAND, T. E.: *Studies in International Law.* 1898.

KALKENBORN, K.: *Die Vorläufer des Hugo Grotius.* 1848.

PRADIER-FODÉRÉ, P. L. E.: *Essai sur Grotius et son temps.* 1865.

VREELAND, H.: *Hugo Grotius.* 1917.

WALKER, T. A.: *History of the Law of Nations.* 1899.

WHITE, A. D.: *Seven Great Statesmen.* 1910.

VII

THOMAS HOBBES

I CAN give you no better introduction to the way of thought, the method, and the temper of Thomas Hobbes than the brief life of him by his friend John Aubrey. Aubrey did not think of him as a man of immense learning. " He had very few books . . . he had read much if one considers his long life "—Hobbes was born in 1588 at Malmesbury, a *plebeius homo* who talked broad Wiltshire; he died in 1679— " but his contemplation was much more than his reading. He was wont to say that if he had read as much as other men he would have known no more than other men." " He thought much, and with excellent method and stedinesse, which made him seldom make a false step." As he thought, so he lived. " He was (generally) temperate, both as to wine and women— *et hæc tamen omnia mediocriter*," says Aubrey in a whimsical sentence. During his long old age he kept to a careful *régime* which included singing prick-song in his bed for his lungs' sake, and playing tennis three times a year. The simple worldliness of his ways is shown by an odd note on the fly-leaf of an early copy of his *De Corpore Politico* in All Souls Library. " I have heard of Mr Hobbs that when amongst those that weer strangers to him, he ever applyed himselfe to him that wore most clothes on taking him to be the wisest man." For a great part of his life he chose the unheroic but comfortable career of companion tutor to noblemen's sons; but he lived in an age when, if ever, the English upper class had both a sense of noble living and a care for knowledge. It was in this great country-house society that in middle life he made the discovery of the new mathematics. Aubrey says, " He was 40 yeares old before he looked on geometry; which happened accidentally. Being in a gentleman's library . . . Euclid's *Elements* lay open, and 'twas the 47 El. libri I. He read the proposition. ' By G——,' sayd he, ' this is impossible.' So he reads the demonstration of it, which referred him back to such a proposition; which proposition he read. That referred him back to another which he also read. *Et sic deinceps*, that at last he was demonstratively convinced of that truth. This made him in love with geometry." Once discovered, geometrical reasoning became his pattern of sound thinking. He took a certain pride in his own knowledge, and met, at some time during his life, the greatest scientists of his day—Bacon, Descartes, Gassendi, Galileo. But though the experts generally found his theories ingenious, he was never so learned as he took himself to be, and in old age made himself ridiculous by thinking he had squared the circle. The bent of his mind lay rather in the application of scientific principles to the study of man in society. Man in society was interesting enough in the sixteen-thirties and sixteen-forties, and Hobbes might well forget his mathematics. In Aubrey's words, " After he began to reflect on the interest of the King of England as touching his affaires between him and the Parliament, for ten yeares together his thoughts were much, or almost altogether, unhinged from the mathematiques; but chiefly intent on his *De Cive* [published in 1642], and after that on his *Leviathan* [published in 1651—the fullest exposition of his views]: which was a great putt-back to his mathematicall improvement—*quod N.B.*—for in ten yeares (or better) discontinuance of that study one's mathematiques will become very rusty."

Hobbes might well reflect on the affairs between the King of England and his Parliament. His was no abstract interest. He thought, without sufficient grounds it would seem, but, as he said, " he and fear were born twins "—that he had endangered his head by rash frankness in controversy, and " went over into France, the first of all that fled." By this flight an end was put to his commodious living in great houses; his exile was "to his damage, some thousands of pounds deep." For eleven years Hobbes stayed in Paris, while his countrymen were engaged in civil war and political experiment which must have seemed more destructive of peace to the exiles in France than to the inhabitants of Malmesbury. Hobbes' ideas had developed before the outbreak of the war. In 1640 it was twelve years since he had fallen in love with geometry. At some time, probably during these years, he had suddenly (after dinner, it is said) come to the conclusion that the principle of motion gives a sufficient solution of the cause of all human activity. Beginning from this principle, and employing the method of reasoning he had found so cogent in mathematics, Hobbes thought he could reduce to a few simple formulæ the complicated turmoil of living, and build up again upon certain, simple, and infallible rules a reasonable way of life. If men but knew these rules they would heed them, and if they heeded them the incommodities of civil war, " the seditious roaring of a troubled nation," would be avoided.

The circumstances of the civil war did not then originate Hobbes' principles, but provided a wondrous confirmation of them. These principles are laid down, these deductions are made most clearly in the *Leviathan*. Aubrey was told by Hobbes how the *Leviathan* was written. " He walked much " (in the good hours of the day between seven and ten of the morning) "and contemplated, and he had in the head of his staffe a pen and inke-horne, carried always a note-booke in his pocket, and as soon as a thought darted, he presently entred it into his booke, or otherwise he might perhaps have lost it. He had drawne the designe of the booke into chapters, etc., so he knew whereabout it would come in. Thus that booke was made." So Hobbes' first principles are taken from what he took to be the reasoned conclusions of positive science—science being the knowledge of consequences—and are justified in their application to men by the observation of the nature and behaviour of mankind. Hobbes begins by assuming that all man's conscious life is built up from sensations, and that all sensation is a form of motion. From this he concludes that man is determined by God, the first cause of all motion, to respond in a certain way to the excitements from without. Man therefore is not free in the sense of being himself a first cause ; such freedom as he has is nothing but absence of opposition—" by opposition, I mean external Impediments of motion." This freedom may belong " no lesse to Irrationall and Inanimate creatures, than to Rationall." It is the freedom of water to run downhill if it be not checked. "Liberty, and Necessity are Consistent ; As in the water, that hath not onely liberty, but a necessity of descending by the Channel ; so likewise in the actions which

men voluntarily doe : which, because they proceed from their
will, proceed from liberty ; and yet, because every act of mans
will, and every desire, and inclination proceedeth from some
cause, and that from another cause, in a continuall chaine,
(whose first link is in the hand of God the first of all causes,)
proceed from necessity. And therefore God, that seeth, and
disposeth all things, seeth also that the liberty of man in doing
what he will, is accompanied with the necessity of doing that
which God will, and no more, nor lesse."

In what way has God predisposed men so ineluctably to
act? As well as the "vitall motions," such as the "course of
the Bloud," there are in men "voluntary motions," "small
beginnings of Motion, commonly called Endeavour . . .
Appetite, or Desire, . . . and Aversion. . . . Whatsoever is
the object of any mans Appetite or Desire ; that is it, which he
for his part calleth Good : And the object of his Hate and
Aversion, Evill." Now the greatest good is life, the greatest
evil death, " the terrible Enemy of Nature, Death, from whom
we expect both the loss of all Power, and also the greatest of
bodily pains in the Losing." All men therefore seek life and
the goods which it brings. No emotion or action of man is
unselfish ; " necessity of nature maketh men to will and desire
Bonum sibi." Even laughter and pity are intellectualised to
become wholly self-regarding. " Sudden Glory, is the passion
which maketh those grimaces called Laughter, and is caused
[in men] either by some act of their own, that pleaseth them ;
or by the apprehension of some deformed thing in another,
by comparison whereof they suddenly applaud themselves."
"Grief for the calamity of another is Pitty, and ariseth [in a
man] from the imagination that the like calamity may befall
himselfe." Now it follows that happiness must consist solely
in the satisfaction of these appetites or desires. How far is
prolonged happiness possible? It must be remembered that
Hobbes did not limit himself to gross pleasures ; he included
intellectual curiosity, " the love of the knowledge of causes,"
as one of the lusts of the mind, " that by a perseverance of
delight in the continuall and indefatigable generation of knowledge exceedeth the short vehemence of any carnall Pleasure."
But even so Hobbes never thought complete happiness possible. " Continuall successe in obtaining those things which

a man from time to time desireth, that is to say, continuall prospering is that men call Felicity; I mean the Felicity of this Life. For there is no such thing as perpetual tranquillity of mind, while we live here, because Life itself is but Motion, and can never be without Desire, nor without Feare, no more than without Sense." "Felicity is a continuall progress of the desire from one object to another, the attaining of the former being still but the way to the latter." Of mankind in general Hobbes is therefore led to conclude: "In the first place, I put for a generall inclination of all mankind, a perpetuall and restlesse desire of Power after power, that ceaseth onely in Death. And the cause of this, is not alwayes that a man hopes for a more intensive delight, than he has already attained to; or that he cannot be content with a moderate power: but because he cannot assure the power and means to live well, which he hath present, without the acquisition of more." Now with these desires that will never have rest must be taken into reckoning the equality of men. "Nature hath made men so equal, in the faculties of body, and mind; as that though there be found one man sometimes manifestly stronger in body, or of quicker mind than another; yet when all is reckoned together, the difference between man, and man, is not so considerable as that one man can thereupon claim to himself any benefit, to which another may not pretend, as well as he. For as to strength of body, the weakest has strength enough to kill the strongest, either by secret machination, or by confederacy with others, that are in the same danger with himself." "From this equality of ability, ariseth equality of hope in the attaining of our ends." At once we are led by our nature to disaster. (Remember that we have no free will. We are predetermined to feel the sting of desire, and the hope of attainment.) For "if any two men desire the same thing, which neverthelesse they cannot both enjoy, they become enemies; and in the way to their End, (which is principally their owne conservation, and sometimes their delectation only,) endeavour to destroy and subdue one another." So we are driven to a continual "diffidence" and overreaching (πλεονεξία, "incroaching") of other men, and they to a like diffidence and overreaching of us. Unless there is a common power to keep us all in awe (Hobbes hints here at his sovereign), we are all in "that condition which is called Warre; and such a warre, as is of every man, against every man."[1] This is, according to Hobbes, the State of Nature; the condition before civil society comes into being. There is nothing of the pleasant Golden Age about it. A magnificent paragraph in the *Leviathan* describes the barrenness of such a life, which has "no place for Industry, . . . no Culture of the Earth; no Navigation, . . . no commodious building; no account of Time; no Arts; no Letters; no Society"; but only "continuall feare, and danger of violent death." Justice and injustice have no meaning in this "irregular justling and hewing one another," for "they are qualities that relate to man in society, not in solitude."

How, then, can we escape from this nastiness? The way out, as well as the way into the State of Nature, is predetermined for us. Those same passions, the "notable multiplying glasses," of self-love, which were directing us to self-destruction, must as inevitably lead us to give up our illusory claim upon all things, for a smaller but an assured gain. "The Passions that incline men to peace, are Feare of Death; Desire of such things as are necessary to commodious living; and a Hope by their Industry to obtain them. And Reason suggesteth convenient Articles of Peace, upon which men may be drawn to agreement." These "Articles" are the "Laws of Nature." Hobbes distinguishes between the Right of Nature and the Law of Nature, between *jus* and *lex*. "Right, consisteth in liberty to do, or to forbeare; Whereas Law determineth, and bindeth to one of them: so that Law, and Right, differ as much, as Obligation, and Liberty." The Right of Nature is, then, that treacherous and phantom liberty of the State of Nature from which we are glad to escape; the Laws of Nature are, for Hobbes, the dictates of reason showing us the way of escape from the State of Nature; as such, they are not laws properly speaking: "for they are but Conclusions, or Theoremes concerning what conduceth to the conservation and defence 'of men,' whereas Law, properly is the word of him, that by right hath command over others." Yet in a real sense they can be regarded as laws, because God has so ordered our being that we must keep these laws or perish. "If we

---

[1] The "state of war" does not necessarily imply continual fighting, "but in the known disposition thereto."

consider the same Theoremes, as delivered in the Word of God, that by right commandeth all things, then are they properly called Lawes." Law, then, is a restraint, and the Laws of Nature are " those restraints by which we agree mutually to abridge one anothers liberty." This abridgment is in the hope of some good. We give up our right, our *jus*, to all things as in the interest of our defence ; a man must be " contented with so much liberty against other men, as he would allow other men against himself." All the Laws of Nature have been " contracted into one easie sum, intelligible even to the meanest capacity ; and that is, Do not that to another, which thou wouldest not have done to thy selfe."

But there are things which we cannot give up. If the purpose of renunciation is " the security of a mans person in his life, and in the means of so preserving life as not to be weary of it," it follows that we cannot give up the defence of our lives or means of living ; water can never flow uphill. Yet if self-interest is our law of living, shall we not cheat in our very agreement of renunciation ? I shall break my own promise, and hope that other men will keep to theirs ; other men will break their promises, and try to " incroach " upon me, hoping that I shall be "modest and tractable." Se we shall all break our word and at once we shall find ourselves back again in the State of Nature, " that dissolute condition of masterless men without subjection to Lawes." Reason and passion must devise some stronger bond. " The force of Words," says Hobbes, " being too weak to hold men to the performance of their Covenants " (" words," he writes elsewhere, " are wise mens counters, but they are the money of fools ") " there are in mans nature but two imaginable helps to strengthen it. And those are either a Feare of the consequences of breaking their word ; or a Glory, or Pride in appearing not to need to break it." Hobbes has already defined " the exaltation of the mind called Glorying " as " arising from imagination of a mans own power and ability." He now says that this kind of generosity, which is in itself a form of selfishness, is " too rarely found to be presumed on, especially in the pursuers of Wealth, Command, or sensuall Pleasure : which are the greatest part of Mankind." Most men are never sure of themselves ; no man is always sure of himself. Therefore " the Passion to be reckoned upon is

Fear." " There must be some coercive Power to compell men equally to the performance of their Covenants, by the terrour of some punishment greater than the benefit they expect by the breach of their Covenant." " Such power there is none before the erection of a Common-wealth." " The Validity of Covenants begins not but with the Constitution of a Civill Power sufficient to compell men to keep them."

How is this " Civill Power" created? Here I must put before you not a sentence or two, but a whole paragraph of the *Leviathan*, for we have reached the centre of Hobbes' doctrine. " The only way to erect such a Common Power, as may be able to defend them [*i.e.*, men] from the invasion of Forreigners, and the injuries of one another . . . is, to conferr all their power and strength upon one Man, or upon one Assembly of men that may reduce all their Wills, by plurality of voices unto one Will: which is as much as to say, to appoint one Man, or Assembly of men, to bear their Person; and every one to own, and acknowledge himself to be Author of whatsoever he that so beareth their Person, shall act, or cause to be acted, in those things which concern the Common Peace and Safety; and therein to submit their Wills, every one to his Will, and their Judgments, to his Judgment. This is more than Consent, or Concord; it is a real Unity of them all, in one and the same Person, made by Covenant of every man with every man, in such manner as if every man should say to every man, I Authorise and give my Right of Governing my selfe, to this Man, or to this Assembly of Men, on this condition, that thou give up thy right to him, and Authorise all his Actions in like manner. This done, the Multitude so united in one Person, is called a COMMON-WEALTH. . . . This is the Generation of that great LEVIATHAN, or rather (to speak more reverently) of that Mortal God, to which we owe under the Immortal God, our peace and defence. . . . And he that carrieth this Person is called SOVERAIGN, and said to have Soveraign Power; and every one besides, his SUBJECT."

Consider now man in his new condition. What are the rights of the sovereign? What are the liberties of subjects? It matters little in practice whether the sovereign has gained his power by institution, that is, by the contract of man with man we have been describing, or by conquest. In the first case men choose the sovereign " for fear of one another, and not of him whom they institute "—that is, the sovereign is to constrain us to keep a promise which, as individuals, we might wish to break if we had the security that others would keep it. In the second case men "subject themselves to him they are afraid of. In both cases they do it for fear." It matters little whether the sovereign be one man or an assembly. Hobbes prefers monarchy, and always speaks of Leviathan as one person, as indeed he has made him to be. One man or many, established by the subjects, or self-imposed, the sovereign has the plenitude of power and is absolute. For other men have agreed with one another to transfer their rights to him. The transfer is but fictitious ; for, in fact, other men have renounced their rights, but the sovereign has renounced nothing ; he is no party to the contract. Other men have abandoned the State of Nature, the Right of Nature ; the sovereign is in the State of Nature ; he still possesses the unlimited Right of Nature. He holds that sword which makes covenants " something more than words and breath." He holds it for us, even when he may seem to hold it against us, for he stands between us and violent death brought near to us by the unchecked rapacity of other men who are like ourselves. This is what Hobbes means by saying that the acts of the sovereign are acts " done in the person and by the right of every one of the subjects in particular." Reason and passion—fear of death—have led us to see that we must have this sovereign, and that the sovereign must, in our interest, have absolute power. If the subject is the author of all the actions and judgments of the sovereign instituted, it follows that the sovereign cannot commit injustice, though he may commit iniquity. He cannot "justly" be put to death (there is an obvious reference to Charles I) " or otherwise in any manner by his subjects [be] punished." " He that complaineth of injury from his Soveraign, complaineth of that whereof he himself is Author ; and therefore ought not to accuse any man but himself ; no, nor himself of injury, because to do injury to oneself is impossible." He who wills the end, wills the means. It follows that the subject must allow to the sovereign, if the sovereign is to exercise his function as protector, the right of making war and peace, the right of judging the means of peace and defence, of choosing all counsellors, ministers, magistrates, and officers, of rewarding and punishing, of prescribing the laws under which property is to be held, of judging what opinions and doctrines are averse from and what conducive to peace; "for the Actions of men proceed from their Opinions, and in the well governing of Opinions, consisteth the well governing of mens Actions." To which Hobbes adds ingeniously, "Though in matter of doctrine nothing ought to be regarded but the Truth; yet this is not repugnant to regulating the same by Peace. For Doctrine repugnant to Peace can no more be true than Peace and Concord can be against the Law of Nature." (Here, again, the reference to contemporary happenings is clear enough.)

What, then, of subjects? Remember that on Hobbes' principles liberty means the absence of opposition, and that men have surrendered themselves to certain constraints in order to avoid the anarchy arising from the uncontrolled liberty of every one. As men have made "this Artificiall Man, which we call a Commonwealth, so also have they made Artificial Chains, called Civill Lawes, which they themselves, by mutuall covenants, have fastned at one end, to the lips of that Man or Assembly, to whom they have given the Soveraign Power; and at the other end to their own Ears. These Bonds, in their own nature but weak, may neverthelesse be made to hold, by the danger, though not by the difficulty of breaking them." "The danger of breaking them"; here again we come to the ultimate sanction of law. If liberty is the absence of opposition, of external impediments to motion, then the subject is free only where he is not bound for his own good. "The Liberty of a Subject lyeth therefore only in those things which in regulating their actions the Soveraign hath prætermitted"—and here follows an interesting list of liberties—"such as is the Liberty to buy and sell, and otherwise contract with one another, to choose their own aboad, their own diet, their own trade of life, and institute their children as they themselves think fit, and the like." There is indeed liberty more than appears. The commonwealth is founded, the sovereign is set up, by men acting as God has made them to act, "for the attaining of peace, and the conservation of themselves"; therefore they only give up their liberty "in so far forth." They cannot give up

THOMAS HOBBES

the right of self-defence, for the nature of man will not allow
such a surrender. So every subject has liberty " in all things
the right whereof cannot by Covenant be transferred." From
this curious consequences follow. No man need fight in war
if he can find a suitable substitute ; " allowance is to be made
for naturall timorousnesse, not onely to women . . . but also
to men of feminine courage." Even so, " when the defence
of the Common-wealth, requireth the help of all that are able to
bear arms, every one is obliged, because otherwise the institution of the Common-wealth which they have not the purpose, or
courage to preserve, was in vain." They will be back in the
State of Nature, which is worse than organised war. Finally,
all obligation to obedience is " understood to last as long as,
and no longer, than the Power lasteth by which he [the
sovereign] is able to protect them." Otherwise men would be
giving up the right to protect themselves. Thus there is no
Divine Right of Kings. " The end of obedience is protection,
which, wheresoever a man seeth it, either in his own or
anothers sword, nature applieth his obedience to it." The
dissolution of commonwealths where protection has failed is no
rare thing. " Soveraignty is in its own nature, not only subject to violent death, by forreign war ; but also through the
ignorance, and passions of men, it hath in it, from the very institution, many seeds of a natural mortality, by Intestine Dis-
cord." In all these things it is clear that Hobbes is thinking
of England.

Such, then, is Hobbes' theory of evil society and of
sovereignty. He sums it up in a few words : " That the condition of meer nature, that is to say, of absolute Liberty, such as
is theirs that neither are Soveraigns nor Subjects is Anarchy
and the condition of Warre ; that the Precepts by which men
are guided to avoid that condition are the Lawes of Nature ;
that a Common-wealth without Soveraign Power is but a word,
without substance, and cannot stand ; that Subjects owe to
Soveraigns simple Obedience in all things wherein their
Obedience is not repugnant to the Laws of God." There
follows in the *Leviathan* a long and sophistical attempt to show
that this theory of obedience to the civil power cannot be repugnant to the Christian religion. Hobbes was afraid not of
the resistance of individuals to the State, but of the great

bodies corporate, which based their power upon " the fear men have of spirits invisible." He does not hide his malice against the Church (" The mysteries of religion are like pills to be swallowed whole "); he shows that the control of religious doctrine in all well-ordered states has been in the hands of the sovereign, and ends his book by comparing the Church of Rome to " the kingdom of the fairies." But Hobbes knew well enough that a disbelief in free will and a mechanical theory of the universe were hard indeed to combine with the Christian revelation. No one was caught in his fine-spun webs, and the clergy returned with interest Hobbes' remarks that all changes of religion in all parts of the world could be attributed " to one and the same cause, and that is, unpleasing priests ; and those not only amongst Catholics, but even in that Church that hath presumed most of reformation."

Hobbes touched many subjects which I should like to discuss with you. There is, for example, his theory of punishment. He found it difficult to explain " by what door the Right, or Authority of Punishing in any case, came in. For no man is supposed bound by Covenant, not to resist violence; and consequently it cannot be intended, that he gave any right to another to lay violent hands upon his person." The only foundation of the right of punishment is that the sovereign is left in possession of the rights against others which subjects have renounced as against one another and the sovereign. "The aym of punishment is not a revenge, but terror." " We are forbidden to inflict punishment with any other design than for correction of the offender, or direction of others."

Again, I should like to discuss Hobbes' classification of government. Democracy, he says, " is no more than an Aristocracy of Orators, interrupted sometimes with the temporary Monarchy of one Orator." There is great interest also in Hobbes' attacks upon the universities of his time, and upon the pernicious influence of classical learning, because men take the liberty praised in antiquity to be, not a liberty of the commonwealth, but a fancied liberty of private citizens. " I think I may truly say, there was never anything so deerly bought, as these Western parts have bought the learning of the Greek and Latine tongues." Aristotle is singled out for par-ticular blame, partly because the unscientific schoolmen took

164

him as their master. " I know that Aristotle, in the first book
of his *Politics*, for a foundation of his doctrine, maketh men by
Nature some more worthy to command, meaning the wiser sort
such as he thought himself to be for his Philosophy, others to
serve, meaning those that had strong bodies but were not
Philosophers as he."

But I must turn from these byways to a larger question.
Does Hobbes help us to comprehend the nature of the State,
and the limits of our obedience to it? What truth is there in
his seemingly outrageous philosophy? In the first place, we
must remember that Hobbes did not believe in the " contract "
as an historical fact. (I need not trouble you with the origin
and history of the contractual theory of the State.[1] You have
studied Hooker, and will have understood how Hobbes twisted
the received theory, or theories, to fit his new psychology and
made a commonplace of democratic thinkers into a weapon of
defence for absolutists.) Hobbes denied that the state of war
existed everywhere. "It may peradventure be thought, there
was never such a time, nor condition of warre as this ; and I believe it was never generally so, over all the world, but there are
many places, where they live so now. For the savage people in
many places of America . . . have no government at all, and live
at this day in that brutish manner, as I said before." In the *De
Corpore Politico* Hobbes has already spoken of the " Experience
of Salvage Nations, that live at this day," and had mentioned
" the Histories of our Ancestors, the old inhabitants of Germany, and other now civill Countreys, where we find the people
few and short-lived, and without the Ornaments and Comforts
of Life, which by Peace and Society are usually invented and
procured." But there is no need to appeal to history for
evidence of a contract which would not necessarily bind us in
the present unless it were to our interest. The contract is
therefore implicit ; the State of Nature is a logical alternative
which may or may not have existed in fact for any people or
race. The justification of civil society and absolute sovereignty
lies in the conclusion to which all reasoning men come when
they reflect upon their own nature and environment. It is true
that most men do not reflect : " Men for the most part are too

[1] For an account of the earlier history of the contract theory see R. W. Lee, *The
Social Compact* (1898).

busy in getting food, and the rest too negligent to understand."
But Hobbes would have them reflect, for if they reflected they
would acquiesce positively in the society which they now accept
through indolent habit. In other words, that would be an end
of civil war. The contract therefore is a process of reasoning
why we live in society and obey laws; a state of mind which men
may reach in stages separated by long periods of time, or may
never reach at all, or to which they may attain by a connected
chain of thought unbroken in time. To Hobbes civil society
should be based upon a knowledge of the nature, and therefore
of the powers and limitations, of man, and sustained by a
positive will—" Will," he says, " is the last appetite in de-
liberation." The State does not exist because its members
happen to be there, chance ' to have turned up ' in some folk-
migration long ago, but because they will to make themselves
into civil society. Imitation and habit may keep most men in
the State, but habits must be formed, and imitation implies a
pattern. The foundation of society is " passion agreeing to
the dictates of reason." But what passion is predominant?
It is true that Hobbes makes fear to be the strongest bond.
But fear of what? Fear not merely of losing life, but of losing
the commodities, the commodiousness, of living. Be it remembered that Aristotle had found a certain noble element in
mere life. For Hobbes the will that sustains the State goes
far beyond mere life. Even so, for the generality of men,
until they are better taught, fear of the consequences of disobedience is of more avail than a reasoned view of the advantages
of obedience. There is no doubt that Hobbes both exaggerated the importance of fear, and misunderstood its nature.
Fear, as Dr Graham Wallas has well pointed out,[1] is " too
clumsy and uncertain, too imperfectly adapted to the conditions
of civilised life to make it a general basis for modern government." Russia, Prussia, and Turkey have tried it without
lasting success. Dr Graham Wallas is thinking of the history
of fear, and treating fear as one among a number of emotional
dispositions evolved to meet an environment which for us has
long passed away. If Hobbes had known anything of the
history of fear he would never have made the mistake of intel-
lectualising emotional states of a widely different origin to make

[1] *The Great Society*, Chapter VI.

them look like forms of fear.   And here we come near to the
root of the matter.   Hobbes proceeds step by step with great
care and few faults from a number of physical and psychological postulates.   These postulates are either wrong or non-
proven.   He begins by denying human freedom.   He may
be right; but the case cannot be proved.   He then assumes
that men are determined as atoms, in isolation, desiring the
unsocial acquisition of private delights, further from the gods
than ants or bees.   Oddly enough, it would be easier to accept
Hobbes' second postulate if we could be sure that in the last
analysis of conduct there lurked no free acts

> like hares and mice and conies
> That run before the reaping hook and lie
> In the last ridge of the barley.

For free acts may mean many actors, each one of whom, by
definition of his freedom, might be finally, tragically, separate
and self-enclosed.   But the determinist has not to defend what
we call personality, " the hold that falls not when the town is
got," and can deny without any such afterthought the islanding
of men.

Whatever our view of freedom, and of the impossibility of a
true science of ' man in isolation,' we need not accept Hobbes'
next assumption.   The absence of final tranquillity, the continual progress of desire (in what different context does Hobbes
use almost the words of St Augustine !) have not as their cause
or consequence an unlimited appetite for power, for greater
external displacement or satisfaction at the expense of others.
The desire to know causes, the passing of time, and " the
falling of the petals of the rose," awake a deeper disquiet than
Alexander knew.   Even the desire for external goods and
satisfactions has limits.   The ' beastliness ' of Hobbes' State
of Nature is due to the absence of ' limits '; but the limits
are reached most easily in the primitive societies upon which
Hobbes speculated without much knowledge.   The " old inhabitants of Germany, our ancestors," to whom Hobbes refers,
would divide up their lands, yet they would have land to spare :
Et superest ager, says Tacitus.   Hobbes would have been on
surer ground if he had thought of the pressure of numbers
upon food-supply and not of the greed of individuals as a cause

of war between men. Above all (granted that man is only free to seek a greater and more secure satisfaction from external goods), in his study of man in isolation Hobbes forgot that mutual aid is as old a weapon as mutual distrust in the struggle of man against the over-fecundity of life. Long use has made men care for this weapon or shield of mutual aid for its own sake. The argument can be pushed farther. If the instincts or impulses—let the psychologists choose the word—which have grown up round this ' mutual aid ' are thwarted, checked, ignored, there will burn up in a man a resentment no fear can quench. By these instincts or impulses I mean the desire to ' give a lead,'[1] to play a part in the decisions of the group to which we belong, to accept as one who has had choice of refusal, in short, all those Protean desires and emotions which we know best under the name of a love of liberty. Call them by this simpler name, and who would balance them against fear, or dare to say that men are only led by sophistries of speech to rebel against tyrants? In the light of history, then, the right of self-defence is almost the least of the great things that a man cannot, of his nature, surrender by covenant, and there are comfortable ways of living which a brave man fears more than death.

If Hobbes has failed to observe rightly the nature of man, he cannot be right in his conclusions; if the principles are wrong, the deductions must be wrong. If I do not want an ever-increasing share in the goods of the world at the expense of others, if at times I desire to help my neighbour as much as at other times I desire to ' incroach ' upon him, I cannot be said to have any right to all things. If I have not this right, I can neither renounce it nor transfer it. If I cannot transfer to the sovereign this absolute right, he can never acquire it; for in a State of Nature—historical or hypothetical—he has no more absolute right than I. Nor shall I allow him to assume absolute power in my own interest, and in the belief that covenants without force are but words and that civil society is only kept together by fear. For if I need to work with my neighbour, to play a part in society, to give as well as to receive, I shall not want ' external terror ' to keep me from an anti-social life.

But what of the unreasoning many? Surely I must see that

---

[1] *Cf.* Graham Wallas, *Our Social Heritage*, Chapter VII.

they are as I am, though they may not have gone through the full process of reasoning, and may talk prose, as it were, without knowing it. The desire for liberty, like those other instruments of our nature which have helped us through the centuries too distant to be recorded, is deep beyond all reason; it is, by definition, one of the constructive forces in society. It leads to social action, not individual isolation. This desire, and not fear, is " the passion most to be reckoned on." Yet action must be regulated, and regulation means some form of coercion. Have not the unreasoning many and the reasoning few certain bad hours when stark coercion is needed? But this coercion covers only a small field of the work of the sovereign, of the area of political government; it cannot be the one foundation of authority. More than this, we are beginning to doubt the final, ' long-period ' value of any external coercion, and to regard the need for constraint as the symptom of a disease in men or states. From this doubt we are led to ask: what of the seemingly irreducible minimum, of the few whose minds would appear to have no good hours? How are we to deal with them, unless we reckon chiefly upon fear? How do we deal with them? In the first place we have always remembered that there is honour among thieves; we have a precedent of terrible illustriousness. To this memory has been added in our own time an uneasy knowledge that the crimes of society weigh too heavily upon one class; that those whom we punish do but show us our own acts in a tarnished mirror. In short, we are beginning to dissociate punishment from what we call the administration of justice in the same tentative way in which men gave up physical torture and religious persecution. We can say, then, that coercion plays so small a part in our own lives, that it plays so small a creative part in the lives of those who, in the grim injustice of things, are most coerced, that we can speak less reverently of that mortal God who was to frighten us into salvation.

Can we even hope, one day, to close His temple? Is any form of sovereignty, in the sense of an absolute coercive authority dominating all other forms of association, ultimately necessary to society?

Let us see what has happened to the field of activity of the sovereigns who were Hobbes' contemporaries. These sovereigns were preoccupied with war, religion, and the keeping of public order. Coercion was their chosen instrument. War between states I must leave for a moment. I turn to the coercion of subjects within the boundaries of their states. Hobbes, as we have seen, was most concerned with the dangers to society from the differences of religious opinion. But we have dethroned fear from heaven. No man need walk, as Hobbes walked, a mile to church for fear of the bishops; and yet we are at peace; religion is not dead; nor is society destroyed by factions. After religion came the danger to the tranquillity of the State from private men's opinions in affairs secular. But the peace of modern states has grown steadily with the increase in the liberty of the Press and of public opinion. Conversely, public order at the moment is most precarious and uncertain precisely in those societies wherein the sovereign claims and exercises a censorship of opinion. Of punishment I have already spoken; of our doubts about the value of prison doors, and our graver doubt upon which side of the doors we shall find the most guilty. Where then is Leviathan? How are the mighty fallen! Look now at the other side. What of the liberties which the sovereigns of Hobbes' time allowed, by their silence, to their subjects? Hobbes left almost the whole field of economic life to the private judgment to which we leave religion. His preoccupation with public order was one of the consequences of the closeness with which he observed the affairs of his age, an age which became out of date even more quickly than the age of the French Revolution. The problems seemed of a simpler order; one man's intelligence and resolution could settle them. Even religion appeared capable of settlement in a book of instructions and Thirty-nine Articles. But in modern societies the mere increase in numbers, and the accumulation of external goods and powers, make the character of government new, and preclude government by one man. In St Simon's words, government has ceased to be " power over men " and has become " the administration of things." In the manifold and interwoven operations of men in modern societies the once-coercive sovereign State is become a coordinating, a regulating authority.

We are left, then, with the stark coercion of the bad

(remembering again our doubts), and that coercion which is only arrangement. The former is only a small part of the action of our sovereign authority : society has not come into being merely to provide prisons ; the latter is a limited power rendered necessary by the unwieldiness of large masses—one might compare it to the power of the marshals over those who wish to take part in a procession.

But here I must leave the sovereign in his own State, with this enormously increased activity (there was relatively little skilled administration in Hobbes' day outside the domain of war and taxation) and correspondingly diminished power. I wish I could deal with the interesting question raised by those who distrust the State even as a co-ordinating and regulating body, and prefer forms of organisation which have long been abandoned as insufficient for the needs of a complicated society, or as serving too easily the more selfish ends of their members. This distrust of the State is due not so much to any strong views about the plurality or indivisibility of sovereignty, but to the "pathology of the modern State"; by which I mean the concentration of interest and ability upon political "power over men," and a forgetfulness that, as Harrington saw in the lifetime of Hobbes, political power follows the distribution of property, and that a greater care for "the administration of things" is therefore a surer way to good social ends, to "commodious living."

But I must end with a question I cannot answer. If, like Hobbes, we regard society as based upon, and continually sustained by will ; if, unlike Hobbes, we think that fear has played always a subordinate part, and in our time is playing a diminishing part in the determination of this will, in the maintenance of a commonwealth—what are we to say of war? I find war between states a difficulty. I can hear one of Hobbes' more splendid periods : "But though there had never been any time, wherein particular men were in a condition of warre one against another; yet in all times, Kings and persons of Soveraigne authority, because of their Independency, are in continuall jealousies, and in the state and posture of Gladiators; having their weapons pointing, and their eyes fixed on one another; that is, their Forts, Garrisons, and Guns upon the Frontiers of their Kingdomes; and continuall Spyes upon their neighbours; which is a posture of War. But because they uphold thereby, the Industry of their Subjects; there does not follow from it, that misery, which accompanies the Liberty of particular men." In this last sentence is the greatest difficulty. For in war there is more than fear; there is mutual aid in one of its oldest and deepest forms. No one who has seen war can forget the sense of companionship which takes the sting out of terror. It is hard not to give a hollow answer to the question what is to take the place of the songs men sing as they go into battle. I will not say that we shall lose nothing by the disappearance of war; I will say that the best men in society will lose most, and only the best will understand what they are losing. But if history has taught anything about war in the past it is that victory does not belong to despots, and that free men uncoerced make the best soldiers. As for the future, war will not be ended, because men are become more fearful of death—through their very fearlessness is the spring gone out of the year for our time—but because of the desire for a more " commodious " life and because the force of things, the accidents of economic need, the blind destructiveness of our weapons, have made victory scarcely less a calamity than defeat. The forts of which Hobbes wrote are becoming cumbersome ruins, and the frontiers old boundary-marks. There can be no longer a song of the sword.

So remote, then, and so antique is become the scheme of Thomas Hobbes that I can end with the thought of men going out to find fear which has been lost from the world.

E. L. WOODWARD

BIBLIOGRAPHY

A. PRIMARY SOURCES

THOMAS HOBBES: *Collected Works*, edited by Sir W. Molesworth. Latin 5 vols., English 11 vols. 1839–1845. (The only collected edition of Hobbes' works.)

Leviathan. Introduction by W. G. Pogson Smith. Oxford, 1909.

Leviathan. Introduction (and bibliography) by A. D. Lindsay (" Everyman's Library ").

THOMAS HOBBES

B. Secondary Sources

Cambridge History of English Literature, vol. viii, chapter xii (W. R. Sorley), and bibliography at end of volume.

JANET, P. : *Histoire de la science politique dans ses rapports avec la morale*, vol. ii.

SETH, J. : *English Philosophers and Schools of Philosophy.*

STEPHEN, Sir LESLIE : *Hobbes* (" English Men of Letters " Series).

VIII

JAMES HARRINGTON

THE seventeenth century in England is an age which neither historians nor the general reader have scorned. It is never termed dull, nor material, nor futile, nor immoral. Its warfares are rarely denounced, even by the most pacific of historians. Individuals still contest its problems, with a vivid intensity of interest commonly reserved for their own concerns. Perhaps, then, it really was the epic period of English history. There are few of its great men who brought anything common or mean into those memorable scenes—few of whom we can complain that

> 'Tis ye, 'tis your estrangèd faces
> That miss the many-splendoured thing.

Some of them found it, indeed, in strange places—in legal subtleties, in defence of Magna Carta, in personal loyalties, in gloomy penitence, or arrogant beliefs; in trifling bits of ceremonial or even more trifling hatred of ceremonial in Church or in Commonwealth. But they followed, however feebly, after what was great; when they missed it they did not miss it because their faces were estrangèd, but because they were rather feeble, inadequate mortals.

This is peculiarly true of James Harrington. He seems to have missed greatness of thought, just as he missed vigour of action; to have missed beauty of character, just as he missed that many-splendoured tongue, the English prose of the seventeenth century; to have missed power while he sought wisdom. He did not consciously turn away his face; perhaps he followed only too conscientiously. Yet he missed all through the note of inspiration and of sympathy, the understanding of what lies at the root of all true political thought. He is dull—not only because he cannot write save in shrewd pedestrian fashion, but also because he does not really understand his fellow-men.

174

JAMES HARRINGTON

Why, then, should we stop to consider him and his political thought? Partly, I suppose, because his book is extremely unreadable, and therefore well adapted to a single lecture; and partly because it contains very unusual ideas, hardly to be paralleled in any English writer till the nineteenth century, which ideas have nevertheless had a considerable practical influence, both in England and America.

Harrington first wrote his unmanageable work, the *Oceana*, and launched it upon the world; then he wrote it again and again in different forms. All these forms are collected in the folio edition of his *Works*, edited by Toland. His verse, consisting largely of translations of Virgil, was judged by Toland to be worthy neither of him nor of the light. From Aubrey we gather the impression that the reader has cause for gratitude.

Harrington himself made excuse for one of his pamphlets with the twofold reason that something must be conceded to the spirit of the times, and that it had at least provided him with occupation for some hours on a rainy day! One of his biographers remarks that one must needs love so ingenuous an author. Yet it would be hard to adduce two worse reasons for writing on politics.

Having gone thus far in alienating sympathy, let me look back to examine Harrington's life—very briefly—before going on to consider his ideas, and to endeavour to justify my opinion that Harrington missed life all through.

His youth was evidently a quiet and well-ordered affair. The qualities for which he is most commended to us by his biographer have in them a slight flavour of *The Fairchild Family*. His own family are said to have been ' awed ' by his natural gravity and love of learning while he was still a boy. Left fatherless at an early age, he was privileged, as a soccage tenant, to choose his own guardian; he chose his grandmother, who managed his estates most admirably. When he made the ' Grand Tour,' he was not content with charming the Electress Elizabeth and her entourage; he was careful also to learn the language of each country that he visited. Yet he must have had real charm; he took special pains with the education of his sisters (not always a grateful task), making large discourses to them on religion, on benevolence, on the reading of useful books, and the constant practice of virtue, teaching them the true rules of humanity and decency, and warning them not to confuse good manners with a fashionable carriage. Nevertheless, his sisters declared that he was " in a special manner, the darling of his Relations."

Little seems to be known of his career at Oxford, though we have sketches of his personality from both Aubrey and Anthony Wood. One point, which has been noted by most of his biographers, seems to be very insecurely based. Harrington entered Trinity College in 1629, and became the pupil of Dr Chillingworth, afterward a famous Latitudinarian. To his influence Harrington's love of toleration is often traced. Yet Chillingworth left Oxford a few months later to become a Roman Catholic " with an incredible satisfaction of mind," as Anthony Wood tells us. It was not till several years later that he returned to the Church of England, with a somewhat ' broad ' interpretation of her teaching. He is therefore hardly likely to have been in a position to influence Harrington toward Latitudinarian views during his undergraduate days. Harrington's ' Grand Tour,' for which he had prepared himself by a study of modern languages, took him through Holland, to the Court of the Prince of Orange, and also of the exiled Electress and Queen of Bohemia ; to Denmark, Flanders, France, and Italy, and home through Germany. It was the usual education of a young man of good birth. Harrington differed only from other young men in the zeal with which he collected the works of Italian writers on politics, the undying admiration which he conceived for the constitution of Venice, usually quoted in England as an awful example, and the fervent yet discriminating enthusiasm for Machiavelli which runs through the whole of his work.

Once at home again, Harrington gave himself to a quiet life of study and benevolence, apparently on his own estates, though the evidence is not very clear. To this a not too exacting appointment at Court was added later, when he was made one of the King's Privy Chamber Extraordinary. Harrington would seem to have had a pretty wit and a courtly tongue, joined to a somewhat militant Protestant feeling. He is said to have been disgusted with the ceremonies of Candlemas Day in Rome, and to have refused to kiss the Pope's toe. Yet when the King expostulated with him for refusing a mere act of courtesy, he neatly extricated himself from criticism by replying that, having had the honour to kiss the King's hand, he could not bring himself to kiss the foot of any other prince. At this Charles dropped the argument.

It is not very clear when or why he became a republican. Something was due, no doubt, to what Hobbes considered the dangerous influence of Plato and Aristotle as taught in the universities; something again to that ever-fruitful source of republican opinion, Plutarch's *Lives*, much more to the actual example of Holland and of Venice, or Genoa. He understood Machiavelli well enough to know that when he writes ' Prince,' it is wise to read ' State,' thereby saving oneself some degree of moral indignation. Nothing evidently is due to any personal dislike for or grudge against Charles, whom he accompanied to Scotland in 1639. Indeed, he writes, " Nor shall any man show a reason that will be holding in prudence why the people of Oceana have blown up their king, but that their kings did not first blow up them." And again, " The Laws were so ambiguous that they might have been eternally disputed."

But Harrington was evidently already opposed to monarchy when the war broke out, for, after an unsuccessful attempt to enter Parliament in 1642, he retired again into obscurity, and is heard of no more till 1647, when he was appointed by the Commissioners of the Parliament as Groom of the Bedchamber to the captive King—doubtless because he had maintained a neutral position, and was known and liked by Charles.

The years 1644–47 had seen an immense increase in republicanism, as opposed to the earlier demand for limited monarchy. For real republicanism was the result rather than the cause of the struggle against the King. Harrington's views, though of earlier date, had doubtless sharpened and crystallised during this critical period; an academic dream had become practical politics. Yet Harrington maintained the conciliatory tenor of his way, developing close personal relations with the King whom he loved while he belittled his office. Wood says that his Majesty conversed with him rather than with others of his Chamber, and " that they had often discoursed concerning Government, but when they happened to talk of a Commonwealth, the King seemed not to endure it." Aubrey,

from whom Wood's information is probably derived, gives a
more probable, if less attractive, version : " The King loved
his company ; only he would not endure to hear of a Commonwealth."

Harrington was once, possibly twice, removed from his
office because he vindicated and defended the King's arguments too strongly for Parliamentarian taste. He found
means to see the King again at St James's and is said to have
accompanied him upon the scaffold together with Juxon,
William Levett, and Herbert. The King's death was evidently an immense shock and personal loss to Harrington ; he
retired into complete seclusion in his library, and was accused
by his friends of melancholy and discontent. When he
deigned to satisfy them, he brought forth to them his first-
born, the *Oceana*. Surely there are few stranger scenes in the
history of politics than this man, the beloved companion of

> The saddest of all kings
> Crowned, and again discrowned,

sitting down to reason with his grief and stifle his regrets by
writing the most thoroughgoing and fantastic of republican
Utopias.

The story of the publication of the *Oceana* is well known,
and pleasant enough, perhaps, to be repeated once more.
Cromwell had apparently had the manuscript of *Oceana* con-
fiscated while it was being printed. Harrington went to
intercede for it with Lady Claypole, the Protector's favourite
daughter. While waiting in her antechamber he fell into con-
versation with her little daughter, aged three. " He enter-
tained the Child so divertingly, that she suffered him to take
her up in his arms till her Mother came ; whereupon he,
stepping towards her and setting the Child down at her feet,
said, Madam, 'tis well you are come at this nick of time, or I
had certainly stolen this pretty lady. Stolen her, reply'd the
Mother ! pray what to do with her ? for she is yet too young
to becom your mistress. Madam, said he, tho her Charms
assure her of a more considerable Conquest, yet I must confess
it is not love but revenge that promted me to commit this theft.
Lord, answer'd the Lady again, what injury have I don you
that you should steal my Child? None at all, reply'd he, but

178

that you might be induc'd to prevail with your Father to do me justice, by restoring my Child that he has stolen." Eventually Cromwell gave up the manuscript, disdaining to be moved " by a little paper shot " to give up what he had won by his sword. The detail of the story seems to bear some guarantee of its truth. Yet it is hard to believe that Harrington really loved the *Oceana* as More may have loved *Utopia* or Lady Claypole loved her little daughter. However, it was a prodigious piece of work, and he may well have been thankful to be spared the pain of reproducing it.

The most important period of Harrington's life falls within the years 1656–60, when through a group and a club he really exercised considerable influence on public affairs, and when there was a brief chance that his type of republicanism might have won its way, if not to supremacy, at least to the position of a strong party. For republicanism by 1656 had reached the turning of the ways. There were at least three distinct types. There were the orthodox republicans, looking back to the Long Parliament, and the anomalous Government which existed between 1649 and 1653 ; these men believed that a republic could be made by merely cutting off the King and the House of Lords. Secondly, there were the ' Saints ' of various kinds, fanatics, sectaries, Fifth Monarchy Men—all those, in fact, who wanted " dominion founded in grace." Lastly, there were the speculative republicans, comparable perhaps with the philosophic radicals of the nineteenth century, desiring a Commonwealth with a Constitution derived from Greek or Italian models, and having a touching faith in the efficacy of ' dodges '—if I may so irreverently describe such expedients as ballots, equal electoral divisions, vetoes, and referenda.

Harrington stands out among the speculative thinkers as a man who had a definite plan, and was prepared to carry it out even if it involved ' scrapping ' the House of Commons and starting afresh with a clean slate on which Cromwell, as sole Legislator, might write the prescriptions of the theoretic republicans. Harrington had the courage of his opinions to a very unusual extent. His Oceana was a practical Utopia, planned on such lines that it might have been carried out, defined, and limited in every particular. " There be many things in Utopia," said More, " which I rather wish than hope to see." Harrington has no such modesty. Nor would Lamartine's inimitable words, when the Constitution of 1848 had been agreed, have appealed to him. "*Alea jacta est*," cried Lamartine; "something must be left to God and the People." Harrington would not have cared to make even this concession.

It is instructive to compare him with Cromwell, the man of action. "No man," said Cromwell, "goes so far as he who knows not whither he is going." Yet when Cromwell was confronted by the Army with a ready-made scheme for a Constitution he could only answer: "If we could leap out of one condition into another that had so many precious things in it as this hath, I suppose there would not be much dispute; though perhaps some of these things may be well disputed; and how do we know if, whilst we are disputing these things, another company of men shall gather together, and they shall put out a paper as plausible as this." Cromwell for himself was content not to know whither he was going, but for the State he preferred the well-trodden ways. The faith that would take all risks he was apt to describe as "carnal imagination." There was never any real chance while Cromwell lived that Harrington's ideas would receive a practical trial. If Harrington ever expected what he demanded of the "Lord Archon," it is but another proof of his ignorance of human nature.

Yet Harrington's one characteristic activity, the Rota Club, was certainly based on a knowledge of some types of human nature, and it was remarkably successful in interesting the 'man about town.' All that is known of the famous club is derived from Aubrey, himself a member, and from Harrington's own pamphlet, the *Rota*; from Pepys, and from one or two satirical songs or pamphlets. Aubrey's description of the meetings in Miles' Coffee House is well known. Pepys is not as illuminating as might have been expected; he takes the meetings which he attended quite seriously, and his description merely shows how very like a modern debating society Harrington's Rota was—with its minutes, its chairman, its rotating ballot-box for elections, its members, and its visitors. These casual visitors were perhaps the most important feature of the club. Harrington had hit upon the one really

JAMES HARRINGTON

effective method of building up a new party—by constituting
a close inner circle, which is able to achieve publicity.
Shaftesbury's Green Ribbon Club, of which so much has been
made in the history of party organisation, was only a more
dramatic disciple of Harrington's Rota. The mechanical
working of the Rota and of the ballot was Harrington's best
advertisement. Yet it is clear that he could only have converted a certain definite class, of professional men, of speculative politicians, of embryo economists, or broadminded
merchants. As Harrington himself realised, these pretty
devices met with a ribald reception from the people. Like
proportional representation at the present day, Harrington's
scheme demanded a considerable initial education, and a peace-
able willingness to rest content with inexplicable and unwel-
come results. The Rota came to a hasty and unforeseen end
after February 1660, when Monk marched down to London.
Apparently Miles' Coffee House became an impossible ren-
dezvous, and although there was some talk of moving elsewhere, it is evident that the members were turning their
energies in other directions—to the readmission of the
" Secluded and Excluded Members " of the Long Parliament,
and to the gathering cry for a freely elected Parliament after
the old models. By March 26 the Rota was no more.

The later part of Harrington's life seems to have been one
long struggle with adversity—political, physical, and mental.
In 1661 he was arrested and accused of conspiracy and im-
prisoned in the Tower. Under the unreformed methods of
granting *habeas corpus* he was kept in the Tower five months,
and then carried to an island off Plymouth to avoid the
action of the writ. His health gave way, and he was moved
to Plymouth and there suffered from kindly meant quack
remedies—which injured both body and mind. Eventually
he became insane, or at least subject to curious delusions, from
which he never quite recovered. Nevertheless in these days
he married an old friend, and after successive maladies died in
1677.

It is difficult to see quite what lay behind these troubles.
Henry Morley, in a brief biography, ascribed them to the
" low-minded Charles II." But it does not seem like Charles
to persecute a quiet scholar and his father's favourite—even

though a republican. Some private enmity or misguided zeal such as Lauderdale's may be a more probable explanation. Harrington is buried in St Margaret's Church, Westminster, where a marble memorial tablet, said to have been beautiful, lies obscurely beneath the organ.

Harrington's work falls roughly into three parts : it is philosophic and speculative ; it is voluminously historical—a treatise on comparative politics ; it is Utopian, with a multitude of fantastic details checked by considerable lack of originality, or perhaps lack of any desire to get away from the traditional institutions of England.

The historical sections I propose to ignore ; the philosophic introduction is the most important in estimating Harrington's political ideas, but it is perhaps wisest to begin with his Utopia, in order to possess ourselves of the tangible illustrations of his philosophy. It is this part of Harrington's work, too, which has had the most definite influence, mainly in America. Harrington's *Oceana* is the picture of an ideal commonwealth as it might and ought to be established in the British Isles. The book requires a short 'key' to make it intelligible. Oceana is England, Marpesia Scotland, and Panopæa Ireland. London is Emporium and Westminster Hiera. Henry VII, his great hero, is Panurgus, and Elizabeth Parthenia ; Cromwell is Olphæus Megaletor. Leviathan and Verulamius explain themselves—as designations of his model, Bacon, and his *bête noire*, Hobbes. Harrington describes an ideal state in which there shall be an attempt to maintain an equal division of landed property, and a republican government based on a system of rotation of office, separation of powers, and election by ballot.

To put it as briefly as possible, for Harrington writes hundreds of pages of detail, England was to be divided into twenty thousand parishes by a thousand surveyors, charged to make an approximately equal division, and to teach the people the use of the ballot. Above the parishes come the hundreds, a thousand in number, which are again grouped into fifty tribes. The deputies from the parishes bear the time-honoured names of overseers, constables, and churchwardens. Harrington's inventive powers always failed him when he came to the lower ranks. " The mountain in Labour produced only the ridiculous Mouse. Out comes a constable, an over-seer, and a churchwarden: Mr Speaker, I am amazed," said a scoffing critic within the *Oceana* itself.

As regards status, the people were classified as freemen or servants, youths and elders, horse and foot—the latter group according to a property qualification.

The Constitution itself had been made by the Lord Archon with a Council of fifty Legislators; below them a Council of Prytans, which met in public, endeavoured to keep in contact with popular demands and to pass them on to the Legislators, so that the constituent body had the opportunity of leisure and retirement in making decisions while they were kept in touch at second-hand with the people. The wisdom of this pro-vision has been demonstrated again and again during revolu-tions, in Paris and elsewhere.

The Central Government, when the constituent body was dis-solved, consisted of (*a*) the Senate, composed of elected knights, and (*b*) "the People," or Prerogative Tribe, composed of elected deputies; the two together constitute the sovereign power, the Parliament of Oceana. The elected represen-tatives hold office for fixed periods by rotation. The Senate alone was to debate, while the People decided the broad questions put to them after preparation by the Senate or the Councils. Harrington laid great stress upon this separation of function; it is comparable, though Harrington does not make the comparison, to the famous passage in Tacitus, or to the constitution of the Landsgemeinde in the primitive cantons of Switzerland. It might conceivably be successful among a people who had never known a House of Commons endowed with full freedom of debate.

The executive power in Oceana was committed to four Councils—which somewhat curiously foreshadowed future developments. There is to be a Council of State, a Council of War, a Council of Trade, and a Council of Religion. The Council of State fulfils the functions of a Committee on Foreign Affairs to some extent; it also supervises provincial councils, and prepares business for the Senate.

The Council of War also conducts much of the business of a Foreign Office, and is permitted to do so with great secrecy and without communicating its proceedings to the Senate.

" Secret diplomacy," in Harrington's eyes, was still essential. No war, however, could be proclaimed without the consent of People and Senate. The Council of War had also something of the function of a Supreme Court; it could employ martial law against all such as tried to change the Constitution, and it could sentence to death without appeal. In a striking afterthought toward the end of the book Harrington speaks of the relationship between the General or Commander-in-Chief and the Council of War. It is impossible for a Council to direct a General. " The hours that have painted Wings and of different colours, are his Council; he must be like the eye that makes not the scene, but has it so soon as it changes." To the soldier, in the multitude of counsellors there is weakness.

The Council of Trade was to receive later instructions; at first it was merely to advise or instruct the Senate. Harrington never really faced the question of trade.

Further provision is made for an emergency power in times requiring great haste, to be committed to a junta of nine knights extraordinary added to the Council of War. All Councillors were to receive reasonably liberal salaries. Economy in this matter was to be ' penny wise.' " If a poor man (as such a one may save a city) gives his sweat to the public, with what conscience can you suffer his family in the meantime to starve! "

The Council for Religion was to take special care in manning the universities and in encouraging learning. All benefices were to be improved to the value of £100 a year. A Directory of Public Worship was to be prepared by separate appeals to the two universities begging them to consult all their divines above the age of forty, and to return answers to the Council.

There was to be a National Church, but no coercive power; both teachers or divines and their audiences were to be purely voluntary. Freedom was permitted to any congregation that was not Popish, Jewish, nor idolatrous. (Harrington seems to have thought poorly of the Jews; he considered them worthy settlers for Ireland, but not for his own country.) The officers of any congregation might appeal to the Council and the Council to the Senate, but as no one had any coercive power whatever it is difficult to see what would follow these consultations.

Harrington is specially concerned with the universities as the vehicle of religious truth—not that the water from these fountains is nourishment or religion in itself, but it is the means without which a man cannot be nourished. Religion cannot stand without learned education in its upper ranks. "The Holy Scriptures are written in Hebrew and Greek. They that have neither of these languages may think light of both." The whole passage in defence of universities and the study of classical languages looks as if it were directed against the doctrine of the "inner light." Winstanley the Digger and some of the early Friends were never weary of inveighing against the idea that a man from Oxford or Cambridge necessarily understood the Scriptures. Harrington admits the possibility of a greater light, but argues that this greater light does not extinguish the sun, nor does any light of God's giving extinguish that of Nature, but increases and sanctifies it. The Commonwealth is not to presume upon that which is supernatural! Hence if the universities are the seminaries of a national religion it shall be safe for all other men to follow the liberty of their own conscience, insensibly checked by the centres of wisdom and moderation. The ministry of the national religion is to have no synods nor assemblies, to avoid the danger of debate. How this was to be secured without coercive power Harrington does not tell us. Ministers are not to meddle with politics in any way, for "an ounce of wisdom is worth a pound of clergy."

The choice of a parson or vicar of a parish is very carefully provided for. On the death of such a parson the congregation is to send one or two elders, duly provided with a certificate from the overseers, to the Vice-Chancellor of one of the universities, notifying him of the vacant benefice and of its value. He shall thereupon call a congregation which shall make choice of a fit person, who shall go to the parish and there do duty as a probationer for a year. He is to pray, preach, and administer the sacraments according to the Directory. If unacceptable by a majority of a ballot vote at the end of the year he is returned to his university, and the process of choice starts again. It is not at first clear what constitutes a "fit person," but as Harrington later explains that this order "restores the power of ordination to the people," it seems that a knowledge of classical languages and a popular vote were the only defined qualifications.

Harrington evidently hoped and believed that his " national religion " would satisfy the great majority of the people ; he makes provision for independent congregations and denies the State any coercive power in dealing with them.   But he makes no attempt whatever to define their place within the State, and does not face the possible difficulties.   He does not, like Hobbes, think that the question of Church and State of necessity causes men to see double, nor, like Bishop Stubbs, does he believe that the problem will remain unsolved while the world shall last " as a trial of our faith."   He merely presents us with the incompatible ideals of a State Church, and a principle of Independency or Congregationalism existing side by side, and thereupon leaves us to reconcile them as best we may.

Harrington's treatment of education is so closely akin to his plan of government that a brief note on it may perhaps be inserted at this point.   Education is the plastic art of government, and it must be deliberately adapted to the type of government which it is hoped to perpetuate.   There were to be sufficient free endowed schools for the whole population, controlled by the " censors of the tribe," but staffed apparently by the clergy, whose " honest vocation " is to teach and thus by occupation to be hindered from tampering with the government.   If a parent has only one son, he may determine at choice the education of that son.   If he has more, the State will step in and insist upon his going to school and definitely choosing his way of life at the age of fifteen.   Education at school is from the ages of nine to fifteen—a very reasonable period when one could postulate parental discipline at home. Education is not to be prolonged beyond the age of fifteen, except for those who have chosen one of the learned professions.   This limitation is in the interests of military service. Harrington, as was natural, was anxious to promote foreign travel.   " Home-keeping youth," he believed, " have ever homely wits "—even when educated in Emporium.   Hence he arranges for almost unlimited passes and recommendations (not, I think, travelling scholarships) for young men who wished to make the ' Grand Tour.'   On their return they were to hand in a written report on the countries they had visited, and these reports, if good, were to be published at the expense of Government. "No man can be a politician except he be first an historian or a traveller; for, except he can see what must be, or what may be, he is no politician. Now if he has no knowledge in history, he cannot tell what has been, and if he has not been a traveller, he cannot tell what is; but he that neither knows what has been, nor what is, can never tell what must be, nor what may be."

Both the Commonwealth and the school must aim at a common end—courage and wisdom, "which he who has attained is arrived at the perfection of human nature. . . . It is true that these virtues must have some material root in him that is capable of them; but this amounts not to so great a matter as some will have it. . . . Education is the scale without which no man or nation can truly know his or her own weight or value."

In addition to this broad Utopian outline Harrington describes at immense length the working of his favourite ballot system, which is literally a dropping of little balls into urns with varying degrees of ceremony. He duly reports the mockery with which his scheme was received. Sometimes he was accused of inconsistency for his "puking at Popery," and yet undertaking to govern a nation with a set of little billiard-balls or nine holes like beads. Harrington is at no loss for an answer to such gibes. "And so may your lordships, unless your ribs be so strong that you think better of football." Harrington has a habit, rather annoying for posterity, of anticipating every minor criticism and supplying an answer—often not very adequate, but always shrewd and to the point. This is particularly true of his concrete and detailed proposals. Criticism of the fundamentals he does not seem to have anticipated.

This description of the machinery of Oceana occupies very many pages of the book, but it has here been reduced to the most rudimentary form in order to spare time for discussion and criticism of the philosophic implications of Harrington's ideal state.

Harrington defines government as "an art whereby a civil society of men is instituted and preserved upon the foundation of common right or interest; or, to follow Aristotle and Livy,

it is the empire of Laws, and not of men." He follows
Aristotle in the orthodox fashion in his division of governments into three main types with their corruptions, but draw-
ing apparently from Plato's *Laws* he goes on to explain that
the principles of government are twofold—internal, or the
goods of the mind, and external, or the goods of fortune. The
former are such virtues as wisdom, prudence, courage; the
latter are riches. The goods of the body—health, beauty,
strength—he proposes to neglect, since apparently they do not
conduce to victory or empire, which are won rather by discipline, arms, and courage—a reflection perhaps natural to an
observer who had watched the fortunes of the Great Civil War.

A legislator who can unite in one government the goods of
the mind with the goods of fortune comes nearest to the work
of God, whose government consists of heaven and earth, or to
that ideal commonwealth of which Plato speaks, where princes
should be philosophers and philosophers princes.

Harrington draws a sharp distinction between authority and
power. Power alone is his concern. Empire, he declared, is
founded upon dominion, and dominion upon property, real
or personal. It is possible that he has in mind Wycliffe's
formula, " Dominion founded in Grace," for there were few
things Harrington hated more sincerely than the " rule of the
Saints." His language is not so vivid as that of Hobbes, but
he evidently believes that to pretend a covenant with God is
not only a lie, but the act of a vile and unmanly nature. His
argument is really the familiar cry, less familiar then, that
government is founded upon force; he mocks at Leviathan for
speaking of the public sword, yet he only elaborates Hobbes'
metaphor when he says: " An army is a beast that has a great
belly and must be fed; wherefore this will come to what
pastures you have. Wherefore . . . he that can graze this
beast with the great belly . . . may well deride him that
imagines he received his power by covenant. . . . If the
property of the nobility . . . be the pastures of that beast, the
ox knows his master's crib." The argument has often enough
in history proved its truth, but Harrington does not see that
visibly in a democracy, invisibly in any other form of government, the great beast must be pastured by the whole people,
and that when this becomes clear the people may turn upon

188

the beast, asking, not always silently, " And what good came of it at last ? " And when the people seriously repudiate the great beast, and not merely change his shape, then they are ready to believe that will, not force, is the foundation of the State. A modern reader, perhaps, will criticise Harrington chiefly for his reliance upon an army, and for the inordinate amount of space he spends on the detailed organisation of a citizen army. Hobbes himself based the power and authority of Leviathan less exclusively upon external causes.

It was a revolutionary, Godwin, who declared that " Truth is not made more true by the number of its votaries." Harrington, republican though he was, never attained this discovery as regards politics, though he uses it as the basis of tolerance in religion.

Turning from the external to the internal goods, Harrington is obliged to stop and define the soul of man as the mistress of two potent rivals—reason and passion, and according as she gives up her will to either of these is the felicity or misery of which man partakes in this mortal life. This is a point to which we must return.

Government, then, is the soul of a nation or city ; her virtue is law, and liberty for the State consists in the rule of law, just as liberty for the man consists in the rule of reason.

Such is Harrington's philosophic introduction. Since I am here dealing only with the political thought of Harrington himself, it is not necessary to follow his influence into America, or trace his contribution to the separate state Constitutions, as Mr Theodore Dwight and Mr Russell Smith have done with admirable precision.[1] The seventeenth-century builders of America knew Harrington's work, and borrowed very freely from it, thereby enhancing the republican character of their institutions. The American statesmen of the eighteenth century knew his work and found in it many of the expedients in which their souls delighted for securing stability and continuity and the balance of power. Mr Russell Smith writes : " Again and again one is tempted to substitute the name America for Oceana, and spell his new England with a capital N. The written constitution, the unlimited extension of the elective principle, and the separation of the three functions of

[1] See Bibliography.

government lie at the root of American political theory; the equal division of property among children is one of the most far-reaching social and political factors in the United States; the principle of indirect election, though now discredited, has been employed since the formation of the Union. Short tenure of power, the multiplication of offices, the system of checks and balances, rotation, the ballot, the use of petitions, the popular ratification of constitutional legislation, the special machinery for guarding the constitution, religious liberty, popular education—all these things play their part in America."

But on one point Mr Russell Smith seems to have done Harrington less, or perhaps more, than justice. Harrington to his biographer was an American before there were Americans. Now a good American may not talk of empire. Hence Mr Russell Smith practically ignores Harrington's imperial ideas. Yet they are worthy of note. It is possible for a republican to value the conception and the fact of empire. Sir Charles Dilke is the outstanding example of the combination of opinions in modern times. He would have been in the closest sympathy with some of Harrington's ideas on this subject.

A Commonwealth, says Harrington, may be " for increase " or for " preservation "; the latter type is narrow, frail, and apt to grow top-heavy. Oceana is to be a " Commonwealth for increase," definitely claiming *imperium*; but always an *imperium* rooted and grounded in equality. " If the whole earth falls into your scales, it must fall equally, and so you may be a greater people, yet not swerve from your principles one hair. . . . A Commonwealth of this make is a minister of God upon earth, to the end that the world may be governed with righteousness. . . . To ask whether it be lawful for a Commonwealth to aspire to the empire of the world, it is to ask whether it be lawful for it to do its duty, or to put the world into better condition than it was before." And again, " If, while there is no stock of liberty, no sanctuary of the afflicted, it be a common object to behold a people casting themselves out of the pan of one prince into the fire of another, what can you think, but if the world should see the Roman Eagle again, she would renew her age and her flight? . . . If the cause of mankind be the cause of God, the Lord of Hosts will be your captain . . . [though] if setting up for liberty, you impose yokes, He will infallibly destroy you. . . . If you have subdued a nation that is capable of Liberty, you shall make them a present of it. . . . Now if you add to the propagation of civil liberty . . . the propagation of the liberty of conscience, this Empire, this patronage of the world, is the kingdom of Christ. . . . The first of these nations (which if you stay her leisure, will in my mind be France) that recovers the health of ancient prudence, shall certainly govern the world. . . . Here is that empire whence justice shall run down like a river, and judgment like a mighty stream. . . . The growth of Oceana gives law to the sea."

Mr Russell Smith suggests that Harrington is uncertain and uncomfortable in the presence of the idea of empire. If this is to be uncertain what shall we say but " May Heaven preserve us from the confident "! A consistent republic, it appeared to Harrington, had a right and a duty to govern the world, and to obtain its subjection by force, even though it should make a gift of liberty to the conquered. There is a certain *naïveté* in the idea of going round the world imposing liberty at the point of the sword upon unwilling but capable peoples. We are gradually escaping the bondage of this idea. But to omit this conviction of Harrington's is to omit a very vital point in his conception of the future of Oceana. The constitution he so ingeniously constructed was to be capable of expansion until it might embrace the world in a kind of federation of liberty. These pages on empire are among the few passages in which Harrington reaches eloquence.

Before definitely attempting to criticise Harrington's political ideas the question arises, What did he owe to his predecessors? He quotes a very large number of authorities, but follows them very little, or very inconsistently. It seems undeniable that he had Plato's *Laws* continually in mind. He writes in the spirit of the *Laws* rather than of the *Republic* ; there are frequent parallels, often in small matters which cannot be accidental, though he never mentions the *Laws* and rarely speaks of Plato. Yet he tends to adopt the form of Plato's suggestions, and to throw over just those points which bespeak a genuine knowledge of human nature. For example, Plato sees, clearly enough, that equal partition of land must involve, if it is to be maintained, not only some kind of primogeniture, or inheritance by one, but also some kind of control by the State over the numbers and disposition of the family; Harrington objects to primogeniture ("treating men like puppies," as he describes it) and aims at equal partition of land, with a blind faith, unjustified by history, that subdivision would not go too far. Harrington decides to ignore health, beauty, strength—the goods of the body. Plato could hardly even have argued with a disciple who began thus. Probably Harrington was well aware of the divergence, and recognised that he could not claim Plato as his master, but merely as the suggester of isolated points in his political thought.

Harrington's debt to Machiavelli is of another kind. Harrington and Sir Walter Raleigh were perhaps almost the only Englishmen of their day who were not shocked by Machiavelli. It may be that they regarded him as primarily an historian and not as a political theorist nor a writer on ethics. Harrington certainly treats Machiavelli as an historian rather than as a political philosopher, although he describes him as the " greatest artist in the modern world," " the prince of politicians." Consequently he quotes his opinion constantly, but never on the fundamentals of the art of politics. It is significant that he quotes mainly, I believe, from the *Discourses on Livy* rather than from *The Prince*. Harrington thinks that no man would lightly oppose his opinion to that of Machiavelli, but he himself does not scruple to criticise. He writes, " Of the whole stable Machiavelli seems to me to have saddled the wrong horse " when he ascribed the peace of Venice to good luck rather than to prudence. He differs sharply from him as to the value of "gentlemen" whom Machiavelli, he thinks, underrates ; on the other hand, he quotes with full sympathy Machiavelli's opinion that "the people" are less ungrateful than other classes, and his love of a "legislator" makes him endorse the dictum that constitutions which would be immortal must ever be turning back to their foundations. One of Harrington's great grudges against Hobbes is that he seems to think of Machiavelli as " a beardless boy that has newly read Livy." Nevertheless, Harrington's acknowledged debt to Machiavelli is not very significant, though their positions are roughly identical. He never quotes his master on an issue of first importance.

Aristotle and Livy and Moses appear again and again to point a moral or adorn a tale, but they are only used as historians, to prove a point in his comparative study of constitutions. Bacon, however, is one of the great formative influences on Harrington's mind. From Bacon he adopted bodily the theory of Tudor development which is the base of all his agrarian ideas. How far his guide led him safely I have tried to discuss in connexion with the land problems.

Hobbes affected Harrington very vividly and roused in him the greatest hostility. Perhaps Harrington hated Hobbes the more because their systems of thought had a common outcome—the rule of force; it was only in the choice between monarchy and republic that the divergence became acute. It is in their conception of the Legislator and of the Prince that they show their fundamentally different readings of human nature. Harrington postulates a man who could really make the supreme sacrifice and relinquish the power he had built up. He has classical legend on his side. Hobbes says in effect, " There's not a man alive who would do it." Countless examples in history support his side. But Harrington does not seriously meet Hobbes' contentions.

Harrington's originality, or perhaps his close dependence on classical models, shows itself in his absolute ignoring of the Social Contract. Save in one phrase, " him that imagines that he received his power by covenant," there is nothing in the *Oceana* to show that he had ever heard of the theory that filled the pages of all his contemporaries. Harrington indeed is curiously aloof from his contemporaries; he will not fit into any category, nor adopt any known label of his own day. Consequently he appears more original than he really was.

Midway perhaps between the philosophic and the Utopian side of Harrington's thought is his treatment of the land problem. His theory of the agrarian foundation of government has been much praised for its essential truth; it has rarely, if ever, been criticised from the point of view of facts. As a land reformer, Harrington suffers from the dangers of his position as well as from an incurable spirit of caution and compromise. Hobbes' incisive mind could never discover what was meant by a " fundamental law." Harrington knew, though his definition was peculiarly his own. Fundamental laws are such as state what it is that a man may call his own—that is to say, property ; and what the means be whereby a man may enjoy his own—that is to say, protection. Hence the fundamental laws of Oceana are the Agrarian and the Ballot. Possibly he owes something here to the Army debates on Property, in which most speakers treat it as a " fundamental."

By the " Agrarian " Harrington means a law requiring either equal division of lands among a man's children or the limitation of bequest to not more than £2000 in land. No woman was to receive more than £1500, either by bequest or as a marriage portion. This was to improve the physique of the race by preventing mercenary marriages.

Now Harrington was living and writing in the midst of a silent revolution in the land distribution of his country, yet he hardly gives a hint that he has ever heard of contemporary problems. The wholesale confiscation of the lands of the Royalists, together with the proceedings of the Committee for Compositions, had produced a situation very like chaos. Estates were being subdivided, rents refused, the manorial courts were in rebellion, the local committees were incompetent and overworked. The abolition of the special courts, e.g., the Court of Wards and the Court of Augmentations, had begun the confusion which was only ended by the abolition of the feudal tenures in 1661.

Yet only in a few and rather obscure passages does Harrington hint at his disapproval of confiscation, or show any sign that he was cognisant of what was going on around him. Nevertheless, he was a country gentleman himself, and his estates in Rutland must have brought him in close contact with the prevalent disorder.[1] Probably it was caution that kept him silent after a few wise words on the folly of trampling upon a conquered foe. " Men that have equal possessions and the same security for their estates and their liberties that you have, have the same cause with you to defend both ; but if you will be trampling they fight for liberty, though for monarchy and you for tyranny, though under the name of Commonwealth."

[1] The mention of his name among the reports of the Committee for Compositions appears always to refer to his cousin, Sir James Harrington.

In place of contemporary conditions he goes back to Bacon and to the sixteenth century for his authority and his illustrations of the agrarian revolution.   Bacon's *Essays* and the *Life of Henry VII* provide him with his text, from which he proves the inevitability of the recent uprising against the King. Power and government follow the balance of property—in England chiefly of property in land.   It is this part of Harrington's work that has been most admired and approved.

He argues that Henry VII by his legislation against ' engrossing ' and by his laws against livery and maintenance, Henry VIII by the Statutes of Alienations and by the dissolution of the monasteries and the break-up of the great monastic estates, had effected a remarkable redistribution of land, throwing it more and more into the hands of the gentry rather than of the nobility, strengthening the middle class and destroying the last remains of a feudal baronage.   It is characteristic of Harrington that he never once mentions the sixteenth-century revolution which strikes the modern reader as all-important—the revolution among the smaller manorial tenants, the disappearance and ruin of large numbers of copyholders, and the disappearance of a smaller but more significant number of freeholders—forty-shilling freeholders and therefore full citizens with a vote.   All this is as nothing to Harrington.   An estate of less than £500 per annum in Ireland, or of under £2000 in England, is to him politically negligible.   Not that he would deny these smaller men their indirect vote, but that their influence struck him as quite unimportant.   " That the politics can be mastered without study, or that the people can have leisure to study, is a vain imagination. . . . Take the common sort in a private capacity, and except they be injured, you shall find them to have a bashfulness in the presence of the better sort, or wiser men, acknowledging their abilities by attention."   Harrington, though a republican, was no democrat.

Yet without further considering the small landholder Harrington's argument rests on a mere assumption.   If the tendency to break up estates and the tendency to ' engross ' were balanced, about the year 1600, it is probable that the actual number of landholders might well prove to be smaller than in 1500.   It is, of course, true enough that there had been a levelling both up and down, and there was now less contrast, for example, between the estates of the Duchy of Lancaster on the one hand and the little plot of a " ferling man " on a Taunton manor, working his field with pick and mattock, than there had been in the fourteenth century. So far Harrington's assumption of a much wider distribution of land may be defended, but no farther. Nevertheless, his argument might reasonably lead to a Whig oligarchy, if not to a democracy, and thus far history justified him.

But the actual redistribution cut both ways. ' Engrossing ' balances the break-up of great monastic estates. The backbone of the Parliamentary armies may have been the small freeholder of the eastern counties, where sheep-farming was not very much developed, but it was precisely this class whose numbers in other districts had been lessened by the economic changes of the sixteenth century. Moreover, Harrington entirely ignores the industrial and mercantile elements, which had played a more important part in the struggle against the King than had the middle-class landowner, who was to be found, fairly well balanced, on both sides. He admits that the industrial and mercantile interest may be of paramount importance elsewhere—for example, in an Italian port such as Genoa—but he stoutly and blindly denies its importance for the England of the Great Rebellion. On this point he is either ignorant or purely doctrinaire—certainly far less enlightened than Charles II.

For a man who had ever lived upon his own estates in the country, Harrington is extraordinarily vague in his treatment of the land. I think he once mentions " cocks and ricks of hay." He never mentions methods of cultivation, the dawn of scientific advance in agriculture, nor the practical effects of enclosure. He once speaks of the confusion of tenures as complicating the work of redistribution (for nothing had been done to simplify the tenure of land within the manor), but he merely remarks rather airily that what William I had accomplished in Domesday Book could be done again, with the resources of civilisation and progress at the disposal of the statesman. It is an argument that has been heard in the twentieth century. It was precisely the lack of what we call civilisation that enabled William to value the land. Moreover, the land

196

has always presented a certain silent and solid resistance to the reformer; even William I learned this. Harrington's "Agrarian" remains a "castle in Spain."

Leaving aside much that is interesting, some general criticism must be attempted, though it is difficult to criticise a thinker so unsystematic as this lover of mechanical devices. Harrington fails as a writer on politics because he makes no adequate definition of the end toward which the State should strive. To him, as to Machiavelli, the mere existence of the State appears to be its own justification. Conservatism stands upon its own merits—regardless of the quality of the thing conserved. And this is strange, because almost alone among English political thinkers before Bentham, Harrington is willing to allow a single Legislator to remodel the Commonwealth. Yet his inconsistency is tolerably well explained by the times in which he lived. The more a political thinker strives to make his mind a *tabula rasa*, to think in abstract terms for men of all countries and of all ages, the more clearly his thought seems to become historical and autobiographical. Hobbes and Harrington have the same background, the same inspiration, "Give peace in our time, O Lord," and for the sake of that peace they would bear with Leviathan, or with the Legislator, the Lord Archon, Cromwell. "Peace and no more revolutions" takes the place of any definition, however slight, of virtue, of felicity, of the public interest which is the interest of all mankind. Harrington leaves the "public interest" hanging, as it were, in the air, because he does not know what "all men" ought to want. Or rather, he assumes that he knows. He has the weakness of most 'moderate' men. He cannot believe that anyone really wants anything which does not seem to him right and reasonable. Hence he cannot believe that the people will rebel at the division of the land into £2000 units; it would not seem wise to him to subdivide again into forty-shilling freeholds all round, and he assumes that no one will wish to do it. The argument is familiar: "The whole rent or revenue of the nation if divided equally comes to but £10 per annum per head. But he that has a cow upon the common, and earns his shilling by the day at his labour, has twice as much already as this would come to for his share." Compared with the discussions on Property in the Army in 1647, Harrington's assumptions are what we should call mid-Victorian—to be compared only to the ostrich. Again, Harrington assumes that trade is relatively unimportant in England, although he recognises that it may be as weighty a factor as land in other states. He assumes that religion is always and only a matter of "sweetness and tranquillity." The language of St Paul, of Bunyan, or of Cromwell would have seemed to him almost silly! He assumes that a scholar of the university chosen by the congregation will be regarded by almost every one as adequately ordained, and that almost every one will be willing to accept his ministrations.

These are the assumptions of a man who has little or no intuition—little or no psychology. They are like many liberal assumptions. The only possible objection to them is that they are not true. Men's minds do not work like that. If they did, the world would be a singularly drab place, but a much easier place to live in! Actually, passion and reason cannot be balanced as Harrington wished. The metaphor is all wrong. They must be fused, and the result is no longer appetite or passion, but desire, love, will—passion so fused with reason that it becomes fruitful. Now no political philosophy is worth the paper on which it is written unless it is prepared to discuss the desires of men, the nature of happiness, the final purpose of man's life. All this is outside Harrington's purview.

If I may digress for a short space I should like to compare Harrington with a contemporary writer, who has never, to my knowledge, been quoted as a political thinker—partly because his works were only rediscovered some twenty years ago, and partly because he writes a magnificent prose, mainly religious in subject-matter, and has therefore not found his way into text-books on political thought, but rather into literature. I refer to Thomas Traherne, a scholar of Oxford, who came from a shoemaker's poor home, and went on to an obscure chaplaincy—a writer who in the all-embracing sweep of his thought was more akin to Hooker than to Harrington, and who has certain affinities with Spinoza, in his treatment of ethics. His view of politics is to be found in two works—the *Centuries of Meditations*, discovered and printed for the first time in 1908, and the *Christian Ethicks*, printed during the author's lifetime

(1675), but apparently stillborn, in spite of many fine and striking passages. In the *Centuries of Meditations* Traherne writes: " He that studies polity, men, and manners merely that he may know how to behave himself and get honour in this world, has not that delight in his studies as he that contemplates these things that he might see the ways of God among them, and walk in communion with Him. The attainments of the one are narrow, the other grows a celestial King of all Kingdoms. Kings minister unto him, temples are his own, thrones are his peculiar treasure. Governments, officers, magistrates, and courts of judicature are his delights in a way ineffable, and in a manner inconceivable to the other's imagination. . . . By humanity we search into the powers and faculties of the Soul, inquire into the excellencies of human nature, consider its wants, survey its inclinations, propensities, and desires, ponder its principles, proposals and ends, examine the causes and fitness of all, the worth of all, the excellency of all. Whereby we come to know what man is in this world, what his sovereign end and happiness, and what is the best means by which he may attain it. And by this we come to see what wisdom is: which namely is a knowledge exercised in finding out the way to perfect happiness by discerning man's real wants and sovereign desires." Hence Traherne rightly begins by considering the desires and not the possessions of men, and, by defining the nature of true felicity, he is led on to refine somewhat further and more subtly upon that idea of self-interest on which Hobbes had based his political philosophy. Hobbes had simply denied altruistic feeling, and most idealistic behaviour he derived from desire for the deferred pleasures of heaven, and so reduced it to nothing more than long-sighted self-interest.[1] Traherne, besides advancing instinct as a cause of behaviour, inquires *why* a man loves life—a point which never apparently struck Harrington and which Hobbes

---

[1] I cannot find it in my heart to " refute Hobbes," even by proxy, without quoting that one sentence of his which is to me the most significant he ever wrote: " That which gives to humane Actions the relish of Justice, is a certain Noblenesse or Gallantnesse of courage (rarely found), by which a man scorns to be beholding for the contentment of his life, to fraud, or breach of promise." The man who could write thus, in a casual aside, where his natural self crops out, may be a cynic, but it is useless for him to label himself a sound utilitarian or materialist.

explains only negatively by his fear of death. Hence in his *Christian Ethicks* Traherne supplies perhaps the soundest answer to Hobbes that was ever made. " I make it a great question, would men sink into the depth of the business, whether all Self-love be not founded on the love of other things? . . . It is a surprise to an Atheistical fool that it should be one's interest to love another better than one's self, and yet Bears, Dogs, Hens, Bees, Lions, Ants do it. . . . Preservation is the first, but the weakest and the low'st principle in Nature. We feel it first and must preserve ourselves that we may continue to enjoy other things, but at the bottom it is the love of other things that is the ground of this principle of Self-preservation. . . . We desire to live that we may do something else ; without doing which life would be a burden." With direct reference to Hobbes he goes on : " It is a great mistake in that arrogant Leviathan, so far to imprison our love to ourselves as to make it inconsistent with Charity towards others. . . . There is a kind of sympathy that runs through the Universe by virtue of which all men are fed in the feeding of one ; even the Angels are cloathed in the Poor and Needy." Or, as he puts it elsewhere in a word : " Love has a marvellous property of feeling in another." Self-love is only a round in the ladder, and that the lowest, but " they that remove it had as good take away all. . . . Self-love is the cause of our Gratitude, and the only principle that gives us power to do what we ought."

Traherne's definitions and descriptions of felicity, and the goods for which men ought to strive, fill almost the whole of his *Centuries of Meditations* and most of his poems. Here and there he makes a striking summing up of his thought. In a little devotional work, published anonymously, he wrote that he thanked God chiefly for His mercy " in giving me the Beauty of the World, the Land in which I live, the Records of all Ages, Thyself in all for evermore." That one touch " the Records of all Ages " ought to endear Traherne to all historians. There are many yet finer words in *Christian Ethicks* in praise of history as one great source of felicity.

Elsewhere, in passages often quoted for the splendour and vigour of their language, he writes of enjoyment. " You never enjoy the world aright, till the Sea itself floweth in your veins, till you are clothed with the heavens, and crowned with the stars. . . . Yet further, you never enjoy the world aright, till you so love the beauty of enjoying it, that you are covetous and earnest to persuade others to enjoy it. And so perfectly hate the abominable corruption of men in despising it, that you had rather suffer the flames of Hell than willingly be guilty of their error. There is so much blindness and ingratitude and damned folly in it." [1] This is the flood-tide. of the reaction against Puritanism—cynicism was not inevitable. The link between Traherne's discussion of happiness and the function of the State lies in his conception of justice. " Justice is a severe vertue and will keep up all the Faculties of the Soul upon hard duty. For otherwise it would not pay to Felicity its due"—that is, since felicity is impossible without justice, the State is necessitated by the very nature of man.

This is a long digression. I will not apologise for it, because it illustrates precisely what is lacking in Harrington. To him the mover of the will, whether in a commonwealth or a monarchy, is interest, private or public. Public interest is in some ways more reputable than private interest. Harrington does not examine why. We are left to surmise that it is in some ways better to satisfy a large number than a few. In one passage alone, so far as I have discovered, Harrington explains that the State should aim at courage and wisdom, but whether in disregard of self-preservation, or in addition to it, he does not make clear. The remark occurs rather casually in defining the purpose of education in a passage already quoted, and Harrington lays no stress upon it.

Professor Holdsworth says of Harrington that he is not primarily concerned with political theory, as were Hobbes or Locke, but merely propounds a practicable scheme under a disguise of fantasy. But in point of fact Harrington does attempt political theory, and it is for this reason that I have endeavoured to treat him rather as a political philosopher than as merely the composer of another Utopia. It is precisely the lack of clear-cut philosophic thought that places Harrington emphatically in the second rank of writers on politics. Again, it is precisely his lack of human vigour and sympathy, his *dilettante* life, his would-be ignoring of health, beauty, strength,

---

[1] *Centuries of Meditations.*

that makes his Utopia a cold and bloodless affair, in spite of his efforts to preserve some of the amenities of life, such as cathedrals, theatres, picturesque costumes, and country houses for every one! Man is a political animal, no doubt. Happily he is sometimes something more and something better. Utopia was built by More's love of beauty rather than by his love of politics. In Harrington we miss this serener air, and have to content ourselves with honesty, homely wit and shrewdness, and great ingenuity and curious foresight.

Wordsworth did all that could be done for Harrington when he wrote:

> Great men have been among us; hands that penned
> And tongues that uttered wisdom—better none!
> The later Sidney, Marvell, Harrington,
> Young Vane and others who called Milton friend.

I would not say so much. I can make of Harrington neither a hero nor a villain, neither a guide nor a satisfactory heretic. Montesquieu pronounced, " Of him indeed it may be said that for want of knowing the nature of real liberty, he busied himself in the pursuit of an imaginary one." Indeed, he busied himself so much that I am conscious only of all that I have left unnoticed of what might reasonably, with the help of rainy days, have been said of Harrington and his vision of Oceana. The well is wide rather than deep, and one bucket is only too inadequate.

A. E. LEVETT

BIBLIOGRAPHY

A. PRIMARY SOURCES

HARRINGTON, JAMES: *The Oceana and Other Works*, collected by John Toland. 1737.

HARRINGTON, JAMES: *The Commonwealth of Oceana*. Introduction by H. Morley. 1887.

AUBREY, JOHN: *Lives of Eminent Men*. 1813.

WOOD, ANTHONY: *Athenæ Oxonienses*. 1692.

B. SECONDARY SOURCES

BAXTER, RICHARD: *A Holy Commonwealth*. 1659.

DOW, JOHN G.: " The Political Ideal of the English Commonwealth," in *English Historical Review*. 1891.

JAMES HARRINGTON

DWIGHT, T. W.: " Harrington," in *Political Science Quarterly* (Columbia University). 1887.

FIRTH, SIR C. H.: *The Last Years of the Protectorate, 1656–58.* 1909.

FRANCK, A.: *Réformateurs et publicistes de l'Europe.* 1864.

GOOCH, G. P.: *English Democratic Ideas in the Seventeenth Century.* 1898.

HALLAM, H.: *Introduction to the Literature of Europe.* 1839.

LECKY, W. E. H.: *History of Rationalism in Europe.* 1865.

MAITLAND, F. W.: *Collected Papers*, vol. i, " A Historical Sketch of Liberty and Equality." 1911.

MASSON, DAVID: *The Life of John Milton.* 1859–94.

RUSSELL SMITH, H. F.: *Harrington and his Oceana.* 1914.

TRAHERNE, THOMAS: *Centuries of Meditations; . . . now first printed from the Author's manuscript*, edited by Bertram Dobell. 1908.

[TRAHERNE, THOMAS:] *A Serious and Pathetical Contemplation of the Mercies of God, etc.* 1699.

TRAHERNE, THOMAS: *Christian Ethicks.* 1675.

BENEDICT SPINOZA

SPINOZA was born at Amsterdam in 1632. His parents belonged to a community of Jews from Portugal and Spain who had settled in the Netherlands a generation before, a small and closely knit people, who kept up their use of Portuguese and Spanish, but were full of gratitude for the liberty they had found in Holland. They were a learned community, and the young Spinoza was brought up both in Jewish learning and in the ordinary secular studies of the time. He was taught Latin by a certain Van der Ende, a doctor. He it was probably who introduced him to Descartes and to the science of the time. His community had learnt the lesson of toleration as ill as persecuted minorities usually learn it, and when Spinoza showed signs of unorthodoxy he was expelled and excommunicated in 1656, when he was twenty-three. He left Amsterdam and settled outside the city with a family of Remonstrants. He removed with them to near Leyden in 1661 and then moved to Voorburg, a suburb of The Hague, in 1664, and finally to The Hague itself, where he lived till his death in 1677. He maintained himself by the trade of making and polishing lenses for optical instruments, the practical side of the great sciences of the day, and gained great repute among the scientists of the time as an optician. In 1663 he published an exposition of Descartes' philosophy, and in 1670 not under his own name, the *Tractatus Theologico-Politicus*. The book was prohibited by the States-General. He published nothing else in his lifetime, but his other writings and particularly the *Ethic* were circulated in manuscript to such friends as were thought trustworthy.

Though Spinoza led a singularly quiet and retired life, he was yet in touch with the philosophical and scientific speculations of the time. Oldenburg, the first Secretary of the Royal Society, knew him well and corresponded with him regularly.

Huygens and Leibnitz became acquainted with him and sought his advice on optical questions.

Spinoza's system is sometimes thought of as the glorification of an impersonal abstraction: yet there is no philosopher whose personality shines out so commandingly in his works. Many readers who have neither the patience nor the ability to master much of the argumentation of parts of the *Ethic* are nevertheless mastered by the serenity, strength, and beauty of the personality which shines through a rather repellent form. No one can read the fourth and fifth books of the *Ethic* without feeling that he is being brought into contact with a singularly great and good man. All that we learn of him from his letters and from his biography confirms that impression. He lived simply and frugally, supporting himself by his craft, and devoting all his spare time to study and philosophic discussion. All who knew him seem to have been devoted to him. He was uniformly kind, cheerful, and without thought of personal advantage or resentment. The impression that his letters and his biography give is not merely that he was a good man, but that he was a saint.

Yet this man raised against himself a greater storm of abuse than perhaps any other seventeenth-century writer. It became a commonplace that his works were " blasphemous, atheistic, deceitful, soul-destroying." Sir Frederick Pollock relates that a certain Dr Bontekoe, writing two years after Spinoza's death, replied to the charge of atheism by saying: " I will one day show the world what sort of an atheist I am, when I refute the godless works of Spinoza, and likewise those of Hobbes and Machiavelli, three of the most cursed villains that ever walked the earth." The eighteenth century was no better than the seventeenth in this regard. Hume refers to Spinoza's " hideous hypothesis " and " the sentiments for which Spinoza is so universally infamous." Universally infamous he was—his religious seriousness disgusted the French rationalists as much as his apparent materialism disgusted the orthodox, and universally infamous he remained for rather over a hundred years, when there were suddenly found persons who could understand the depth and greatness of his teaching, and the ordinary estimate of Spinoza changed completely. The German Romantics discovered Spinoza: first Lessing, then

Jacobi, Herder, and above all Goethe. The atheist of the early eighteenth century became the God-intoxicated philosopher to the early nineteenth. Ever since that time Spinoza's reputation has steadily grown, and he has been recognised more and more as the most religious of philosophers.

That is a strange reversal of reputation, and I mention it at once, for if we understand the reason for it, we shall understand the greatness of Spinoza's achievement and the relation in which it stood to the thought of the seventeenth century.

This philosopher-saint was in his century more execrated and abused than even Hobbes. The reason is not far to seek, paradoxical as the fact may seem. For no one can read the *Leviathan* without being at once aware that the doctrines he finds there are immoral, and aware also that the author knows that they are. The reader may not be able to answer Hobbes, but his moral sense, being directly and honestly assailed, will encourage him to resist or to refuse to take seriously the speculations which he cannot refute. He will find in Hobbes' respectful if curious references to religion the homage which vice pays to virtue, and the tone of the author will make him feel that he has to do with ingenious speculations, which need not be taken seriously. Hobbes on the whole, like most genuine sceptics of the time, leaves theology alone. He encourages the general attitude by which the science of the seventeenth century found room to continue its work undisturbed—an attitude which kept science and theology as far as possible in two distinct worlds. "The truths of our religion," says Hobbes in one of his inimitable sentences, "are like wholesome pills for the sick, which if swallowed whole do oft effect a cure, but if chewed, are cast up again without effect." That sentence respects the informal truce between philosophy and theology which both sides on the whole respected. If the philosopher and the scientist left theology alone, however much their works might undermine its fundamental presuppositions, they might hope that the theologians would leave them alone. With this working arrangement Spinoza will have nothing to do. His first original published work, the only original work of his published in his lifetime, is called the *Tractatus Theologico-Politicus*. It laid the foundations of nineteenth-century Biblical criticism by calmly announcing that the Scriptures are to be interpreted by precisely the same scientific methods as any secular books. It categorically refuted the possibility of miracles and of everything which was ordinarily thought of as supernatural. Above all, Spinoza did all this with immense seriousness, was clearly a man who cared intensely for religion and the affairs of the spirit. The ordinary religious man was bound to feel that he had been wounded in the house of his friends: he could not dismiss Spinoza lightly as an ingenious sophist or a light-hearted scoffer. It was inevitable that he should treat him as a traitor. The philosophers and the scientists for their part felt that Spinoza had let the cat out of the bag. With the religious significance of the consequences he had deduced from their assumptions they were not concerned. They could only too well see the trouble into which those consequences would get them. They saw that their only hope of being allowed to carry on their work in peace and to maintain the truce with theology which was of so much importance to them, was to dissociate themselves from Spinoza's conclusions and join in the hue and cry to make him " universally infamous."

The qualities which made Spinoza execrated by his generation were just the qualities which make his philosophy so profound and far-reaching. They were the qualities which made Socrates a martyr and the true originator of philosophy. Spinoza combined in a peculiar degree the scientific and the religious temper. He was a rationalist through and through and he was also a mystic. He felt, as no one else of his generation did, the immense significance of the new view of the world which the sciences of the seventeenth century introduced. Because he was a saint, who believed that man's happiness lay only in the knowledge and love of God, he was concerned above all to ask how this new view of the world affected the assumptions of conduct and religion. He was determined to hold on to both science and religion, and the nature of his scientific and of his religious temper alike made it impossible for him to escape the difficulties with which he was faced by any theory of separate spheres or watertight compartments. God was One. That was the great message of his race to religion, and no one ever believed that more earnestly than Spinoza: and because God was One, He was to be found in science as well as in religion, and science was bound to be religious and religion scientific. Both his science and his religion were to be uncompromising, and in their uncompromising form they were to be brought together.

This bringing together of science and religion in a form which was to be faithful to both was Spinoza's problem, and what a problem it was we shall understand better if we consider for a little how revolutionary and far-reaching the implications of the new sciences were.

The scheme of the world which had been built up by Greek thought in the fourth century B.C.—which, unaltered in its essential features, had furnished ever since a background for men's thought about themselves and the world in which they lived, was essentially pluralistic. It thought of the world as consisting of a number of separate individual substances. No doubt these substances were in relation with one another. But their relations were accidental to their nature. Their natures or essences were peculiar to themselves, and their properties and behaviour were deducible from their essences. They were explainable from themselves alone. Further, the key to the relations between these separate entities or substances was purpose or final cause. The relations of man and other substances to one another were thought of in terms of human action. When this general scheme found expression in theology, God was necessarily thought of as separate and distinct from the other substances in the world—infinitely greater and more perfect than these, but a substance distinct, and the relations which governed the world were the relations determined by God's purposes; and because the world and all that it contained was thought of as having been set there and created to serve the purpose of God—a purpose conceived of as being like a human purpose—the world was pictured as finite, with earth, man's dwelling-place, the centre of it. This conception of the world when applied to physics had assumed that motion was to be explained in terms of the specific properties or qualities of bodies that moved. Bodies fell to the earth because of some essential kinship between their nature and that of the earth. If the moon controlled the tides, its nature must have some peculiar affinity with water.

Now the result of the physical discoveries of Galileo and

Descartes was that the motion of bodies was now explained in
virtue of their position in the one physical system.   Temporal
and spatial relations assumed an importance in scientific investigation which they had never had before.   Science began
now with the system as a whole and explained the motion
of bodies in terms of their relations.   Final causes were abandoned, and proximity in time and space became the leading
principle of causal explanation.   Further, the astronomical
discoveries of the time destroyed the picture of the finite
world set round the earth as its centre and put in its place a
world of infinite extension.   Things were now what they
were and behaved as they did because of their place in this vast
infinite system : they were constituted by their external relations—mere links in chains of connexions infinitely prolonged ; and they came thus to be thought of as nothing but
their external relations, mere points or meeting-places of
relations.

Descartes, who first thought out the implications of the
new physics, had taught that everything which happened in
the world, except man's actions—even the behaviour of
animals—had a mechanical explanation and that the essence
of matter, which formed this infinite physical system, was
extension.   In the physical world everything was determined
by what was external to it, and the ultimate nature of everything physical was quantitative.   Final purposes and individual
qualities had both disappeared.

The mind of man was not, according to Descartes, a part of
this system, but was known directly as a quite independent
substance, not determined but free, and so entirely different in
its whole nature from the outside world and from its own body
that no rational or natural explanation could be given of the
relation between mind and body or between mind and the
external bodies which it perceived.

This absolute distinction between mind and body had the
curious effect on the prevailing philosophy of the seventeenth
century that its scheme of the world demanded perpetual
miracles, and miracles of a foolish and perverse kind.   The
general upshot of the rejection of final causes and of the acceptance of the principles of mechanical explanation had been to
give a picture of the physical world from which the notion of

God's direct intervention and therefore of miracle was de-barred.   God had made the physical world so that it could run of itself.   But the dualism of body and mind implied that this machine was of such a nature that God had continuously to intervene to establish any connexion between that world and mind.   Miracle was banished from nature to reappear in a most capricious and arbitrary form in the connexion between body and mind.   For mind in its essence was conceived of as rational and therefore, like the external world, ruled by order and necessity.   But all connexion between the two worlds and all that depends upon that connexion, perception and qualities, was the region of perpetual miracle.   On the one side was a world of pure thought, on the other a world of pure extension, and in a miracle-sustained limbo between them—perception, action, qualities—in short, life.   The central thought in Spinoza is the denial of this dualism : the demonstration that there can be only one substance, that that substance has infinite attributes—two of which are mind and extension ; that every attribute is, so to speak, self-contained, *i.e.*, has its own necessary order and sequence, so that there is no passage from a mode in one attribute to a mode in another—no passage from a thought to a body, but that there is no such passage because there is no need for it.   The thought is just the thought side of the body, and the body is just the extension side of the thought.   The *ordo et connexio idearum* and the *ordo et connexio rerum* are one and the same.   God is One and His attri-butes are infinite, and God is His attributes and all the modes which they imply ; and the attributes and all their modes flow from the nature of God as the properties of a triangle flow from its nature—by the necessity of reason.

It follows that all theories or doctrines which describe God as standing apart from nature—whether as creating it or con-trolling it from outside to His purposes—or standing toward it as a man stands toward the things on which he acts, are figura-tive and strictly speaking unmeaning.   All things are in God and must be in God : they are all alike manifestations or con-sequences of His nature.

That is Spinoza's central doctrine.   Whether it is a blas-phemous and soul-destroying atheism, as most of his contem-poraries thought it, or an uplifting and elevating pantheism, as

Goethe found it, depends on how it is interpreted. But in any case it makes unmeaning most theological language which was thought out under the ruling conception of a pluralistic world of substances. It may be that the only difference is that that conception started with diversity and sought unity, while this starts with unity and seeks diversity, but the imaginative difference between the two conceptions is very great. It may be that the vital truths which the old theology was trying to express can be restated in the new scheme—but they would have to be restated. However true it may be that Spinoza's central doctrine denies, not the vital truths of Christian theology, but the intellectual framework in which they were stated, nevertheless he did, by his unfaltering acceptance of the new view of the universe implied in the new sciences, entirely destroy that intellectual framework. Most of his contemporaries had never realised how the new scientific theories which they had accepted involved the destruction of that earlier framework. To them Spinoza's system seemed gratuitous destruction. By the beginning of the nineteenth century the implications of the new sciences had become common property and changed the background of men's minds. Thus men were ready to notice, not that Spinoza had a conception of the world fitted to modern thought, but that he found God in it.

The greatness of Spinoza's intention must be clear enough. To be true both to the discoveries of science and the facts of religious experience, to insist that somehow these apparently different worlds were one world, was a great conception. But the value of such an attempt will largely depend on how the unity is actually achieved.   On the assumptions of the case the philosopher will start with a science and a religion which have been kept sharply separate and are therefore each defective. So when he tries to bring them together, will the scientific narrowness of his science pervert his view of religion or the religious narrowness of his religion pervert his view of science, or will he be great enough to divine just how each suffered from abstraction and will gain from being brought together? As we have seen, Cartesianism had worked out a dualistic view of the world with an abstract physical world which was nothing but extension on the one side and an abstract mental world which was nothing but reasoning on the other, with perceptions and qualities in an unexplained and miraculous limbo between. When Spinoza took these two abstract worlds of mind and extension and put them together, did he put them together as they were and leave out the limbo in the middle— which was no doubt full of irrational miracle but was also full of life—or did he conceive the attributes of mind and extension differently because he conceived them both as attributes of one substance—God?

The answer to that question, I think, is that he partly did both of those things—that there are two tendencies struggling in Spinoza, neither of which is completely dominant, and it is this division in his thought which makes the difficulty not only of his metaphysics, but of his politics.

The question the answering of which is vital for the understanding of Spinoza is how he worked out his doctrine that the order and connexion of ideas is the same as the order and connexion of things. The doctrine is manifestly not true. To take even Spinoza's favourite example of the connexion between the definition of a triangle and its properties, the necessity seems to be the same in the thinking and in what is thought : but in the thinking there is a succession in time, and in the properties of a triangle there is not.

Actually Spinoza has in mind three kinds of connexion— the mathematical relation of implication we have referred to ; physical causation, the determination of one event or, as Spinoza says, one mode by another in an infinite chain ; and a third and quite different connexion which he never so clearly distinguishes, but which inspires all his finest work, the relation by which a mind somehow expresses or is conscious of its unity with itself and with the whole of which it is a part. Man's universal nature flows from the nature of God with the universal necessity of geometrical implication. Had we adequate knowledge we could so deduce it. The particular nature and existence of this or that man is on the other hand determined by his relation to external causes—determined as part of the infinite chain of physical causation. These are both forms of necessary relation, and between them the nature and character of all men are determined inexorably through and through, and determined though in different ways by the nature of God; and yet the central thought in Spinoza's *Ethic* is the difference between human bondage and human freedom, or between the extent to which man is determined by his passions—*i.e.*, by the working of external causes upon him— or by his own inner nature. Spinoza in his account of human action is trying to hold together three truths: (1) that man is part of the external world, and cannot escape from the conditions which that fact imposes or act save through external means; (2) that man's powers and man's good and evil are determined by his general nature—a man has to be a man, and humanity has its definite conditions and its limits; and (3) that yet consistently with that double necessity man may let himself be dominated by his passions so that his individuality is destroyed and he becomes a mere concourse of external relations, or he may act more and more completely from his own individual nature until he becomes more and more like God, whose essence it is to be entirely determined by His own nature.

There is already a contradiction between the two first forms of necessity as Spinoza states them. For if the nexus of physical causation is absolute and all-embracing, then the individual is unreal—only a concourse of relations with nothing to relate. The physical system which Spinoza took over from Descartes was a purely quantitative system which left no room for individuality because it left no room for qualitative differences. If that part of Spinoza's system is taken literally, it is atheism and it is in the most literal sense soul-destroying. But the central thought of Spinoza's ethics is the individual, who necessarily seeks to preserve his own nature and who can preserve it only by freeing himself from passions, his dependence on the external world, and finding himself by the knowledge of God. Knowledge is for Spinoza the key to liberty. For man can come to know God. By pursuing knowledge he will come to union with his fellows and so to greater power. If men would be led by reason, they would all attain blessedness. The distinction between human bondage and human freedom is for Spinoza the distinction between a man's being determined by the passions—that is, by the influence of external things upon him—and being determined by his own nature; and a man's own nature is to know God. No man can entirely escape the domination of the passions, for man is necessarily a part of an external nature which is greater than him ; but blessedness consists in such freedom from passions and such self-determination as is possible to man.

It would be idle to maintain that Spinoza manages to reconcile satisfactorily the different points of view to which he seeks to do justice. Nevertheless, much of his strength comes from his combining a high degree of moral insight with a resolute determination to take men as he finds them : he is consistently idealist and matter-of-fact at the same time.

This combination of the matter-of-fact and the ideal is the distinguishing feature of his political theory. " Philosophers," he says in the first paragraph of his *Tractatus Politicus*, " regard the passions from which we suffer as vices into which men fall through their own fault. They are therefore accustomed to laugh at them, lament or blame them, or, if they desire a reputation for more than usual piety, to detest them. They think therefore that their action is divine and that they attain the height of wisdom when they praise in all kinds of ways a human nature which nowhere exists and pour reproaches on human nature as it actually is. For they conceive men not as they are, but as they would like them to be. Whence it has come about that they mostly write satire instead of ethics and have never conceived a politics which could be of any practical use. Their politics is a chimera, a political theory which could be realised in Utopia or in the Golden Age the poets write of, where it would not be needed. The result is that of all the sciences which are intended for use, the theory of politics differs more from its practice than any other, and no men are thought less fit for governing a state than the theorists or political philosophers!" Spinoza's politics are to be scientific. He is going to study human nature with the same freedom of mind as men study mathematics. He has tried " not to laugh at human actions or to weep over them or alter them but to understand them."

The first result of this attitude of impartial scientific inquiry is a position curiously like that of Hobbes. In some ways no two men are more unlike than Hobbes and Spinoza, but they are agreed in this that the business of the political theorist is to take men as he finds them, to describe political society as it arises out of men's actual needs and desires. Mr Laski has pointed out that Hobbes was the first political theorist to try to found the State not on what men ought to do, but on what they wanted. The old basis of the State had been one of moral authority and, because it had been that, it required a common recognition of moral authority. " Toleration of divers religions " had been a political impossibility. In the seventeenth century it had become a political necessity, and political theory, if it was to have any reality, had to recognise the new situation. Hobbes no doubt had met the new situation by a theory which really denied morality. But for much of what he says he had more immediate justification than is ordinarily admitted. He might well have replied to his critics that he was trying (as they were not) to meet the facts of the situation : that it was no use appealing to moral authority when men would not acknowledge a common authority, and that in his account of the Laws of Nature he had admitted to the full the importance of moral behaviour for the State. " The Laws of Nature are immutable and eternal: for injustice, ingratitude, arrogance, pride, iniquity, acceptance of persons, can never be made lawful. For it can never be that war shall preserve life and peace destroy it." But at the same time he would have said moral laws only make for peace when they are commonly observed, and in all the confusion of moral standards and moral behaviour we can find a sure basis for the State not in a moral authority about which men squabble, but in the common need for security of which all men are conscious.

Spinoza had a far profounder view of human nature than had Hobbes. Because he had that, he displays a far more consistent realism. He sees through Hobbes' curious legal pedantry at a glance. But for all that he begins where Hobbes begins, by taking human nature as he finds it for the fact with which he has to deal : by insisting that the business of the political theorist is not to judge, but to understand and to see how the situation as he understands it can be dealt with.

The fundamental fact for the political theorist according to Spinoza is man's desire for self-preservation. " The endeavour after self-preservation," he says in the *Ethic*, " is the primary and only foundation of virtue." No doubt he

means by self-preservation far more than Hobbes had meant
by it. When he says, " Since reason demands nothing which
is opposed to nature, it demands therefore that every person
should love himself, should seek his own profit," so much
Hobbes might have said ; but Spinoza goes on, " what is truly
profitable to him, should desire everything that leads man to
greater perfection." But if that difference in the meaning of
self-preservation is forgotten, Spinoza's statements seem little
else than a repetition of Hobbes'. Man always desires to
increase his power. That is a necessary fact which is
neither right nor wrong, good nor bad. Men have therefore
as much right as they have might. The sole object of men's
actions, and in particular the sole object of their social relations, is increase in human power or might. That is a position
not unlike Hobbes' when he describes men as actuated by
" a restless desire of power after power."

Spinoza agrees also with Hobbes that you cannot turn men
from following the bent of their nature by a contract or promise,
if that would make them act against their own interests. Men
cannot in the nature of things act against their interests as they
conceive them. Further, Spinoza holds that, so far as men act
under the domination of their passions, they seek not what
will really give them happiness, but conflicting interests. If
men understood the real nature of things, they would see that
nothing increases a man's power or might so much as other
men, and that men acquire power in so far as they seek a common good and are weak and impotent when they seek rival
goods. That is what reason teaches, and if men were all
guided by reason, they would be in harmony and form an ideal
society. But few men are so guided by reason. Most men
seek not their real interests, but the objects which their passions
incite them to desire. Because they do that, their interests
clash, and therefore Spinoza like Hobbes can say that men
are naturally enemies. Thus we get a picture of the origin
of society not unlike that of Hobbes. Men are naturally
enemies, because led by their passions to conflicting ends, and
reduced by that mutual conflict to impotence. The purpose of
the State is to increase men's power. It does that in two ways:
positively by enabling men to unite together for common purposes and thus giving them an immensely greater power over

nature; negatively by restraining men from the conflicts into which their passions drive them, applying to passionate men the sort of sanctions which alone passionate men can understand. To effect this end government is necessary, and government is impossible without power. From the institution of government alone actions become just and unjust: for justice is what aids the ends of government and injustice what hinders them. A state or a Government, like an individual, has right in so far as it has might. There is no sense in saying that a state can act in such and such a way, but it has no right so to do. If it has might, it has right. A state, like an individual, must act according to its own interests as it conceives them, and can therefore no more than an individual be bound by a promise when its interests and the keeping of the promise conflict.

So far Spinoza and Hobbes use the same language. Because Spinoza did so he seemed to his contemporaries to take his stand along with Hobbes and Machiavelli as a cynical realist, to join with them in seeking to overthrow all the noble structure of moral authority and the Law of Nature which have been for so long regarded as the basis of the State. But in truth the agreement is only on the surface. Spinoza thought that might was right, but he had a far other view than Hobbes of the real sources of might, and that difference transforms his political theory.

Passion is impotence, and reason is might. Men are weak when their passions incite them to conflict, strong when reason unites them in pursuit of a common good. If we are to be realists and proclaim that " things are what they are and their consequences will be what they will be," we must recognise this most fundamental law which governs all human nature and human relations. Unity alone is strength, and unity is impossible without unity of mind, and unity of mind is found in the knowledge of God alone.

Man has right in so far as he has might, but he only has might in so far as he understands human nature in himself or in others. The State has a right to do all that it has power to do; but there are many things which States attempt which in the nature of things they cannot do and which they have therefore no right to do.

Spinoza, I have said, is a greater realist than Hobbes. This is seen at once in his treatment of Hobbes' doctrine of the unlimited right of the sovereign power. Hobbes had seen the necessity of a Government with power enough to enforce peace. He had realised that men's natural powers are so equal that no man can of himself " keep other men in awe." He had seen therefore that the power wielded by the sovereign could not be his own power but must somehow be given him by his subjects. But he had treated that giving of power to the sovereign as a mysterious legal process, a giving over of power which must be absolute and unconditioned and cannot be retracted. Spinoza dismisses with ease all the legal sophistry on which the doctrine of absolute sovereignty is based. The sovereign has right in so far as he has might ; but his might is grounded on the support men give him, on his success in making men seek common aims, in strengthening concord and furthering their real purposes. If he so governs that men would rather risk the evil consequences of civil war than go on tolerating the oppression of an evil sovereign, he has reached the limits of his might and therefore of his right. The power of a sovereign may be legally unlimited, but that means little or nothing. His power has real and actual limitations rooted in the facts of human nature. " For we must notice in the first place that as in the State of Nature that man is most powerful and has most right over himself who is led by reason, so too that State will be most powerful and have most right which is founded on and directed by reason. For the right of the State is the power of the common people when they are led and determined as by a single mind. And union of minds is only possible where the State aims always at that which sound reason teaches to be useful for all men."

From this standpoint Spinoza develops a doctrine of the limits of State action which is of universal application and of which men still need to be reminded. The limitations of State action are determined by the nature of that action. "Subjects are in the power of the State in so far as they fear its power or threats or love the civil State. From which it follows that all those things to which men cannot be induced by rewards or threats are not in the power of the State." The State ought not to control opinion, because it cannot control opinion: it ought not to enforce religion, because religion cannot be enforced. We cannot object to this argument that if the State cannot control opinion, it does not matter whether it tries to do so or not. For the real force of Spinoza's argument is that, though a State cannot make men moral or religious, it can only be strong if men are moral and religious, and they can be that only or more easily if the State will do its proper work. " Liberty of mind or fortitude is a private virtue. The virtue of government is security." Spinoza's teaching separates ethics and politics, but it also insists that politics depends upon ethics : and just because it depends upon ethics it cannot do the work of ethics; it cannot and therefore has no right to make men moral.

The union of mind which gives the State its strength comes not from men being forced together in external bonds, but from each man being true to his own inner nature. It is men's external relations—their passions—which disunite them. The external action of the State may control these passions in the interests of reason. The action of the State is the action of men united by reason against men disunited by passion : it is therefore man's rational nature controlling his irrational nature. But however true it may be to say that the State represents man's rational nature, it is rational nature using irrational because external instruments, and it can never have power over the real nature of the individual. His springs of happiness and sources of power are in himself.

Thus Spinoza's political theory, which seems on the surface but to reproduce the barren individualism of Hobbes, proves on closer examination to contain the core of that idealist theory of the State which is ordinarily thought to have been first proclaimed by Rousseau and was developed by Hegel and the Hegelians, and yet it never countenances that exaltation of the State over the individual which is the defect of much idealist theory of the State. " The right of the State is the power of the common people when they are led and determined as by a single mind." That contains the essence of Rousseau's theory of the general will and of the organic conception of the State. But Spinoza combines with that idealism Hobbes' respect for mere facts and actual difficulties, which makes him more anxious

than most idealists to do justice to the legal and external side of
the State.   To that combination he adds the message—which
is perhaps peculiarly his own—that the purpose of all institutions is to control external relations by reason, but especially to
promote in their members the greatest of all goods—liberty
of mind.

A. D. LINDSAY

BIBLIOGRAPHY

A. PRIMARY SOURCES

SPINOZA, BENEDICT DE :

    Opera quæ supersunt omnia (especially vols. ii and iii).   Leipzig, 1846.
    Chief Works, translated from the Latin with an Introduction by R. H. M.
        Elwes.   1883.
    Ethic of Benedict de Spinoza, translated from the Latin by W. Hale
        White and Amelia H. Stirling (3rd edition).   1899.

B. SECONDARY SOURCES

CAIRD, JOHN : *Spinoza* (" Blackwood's Philosophical Classics ").   1891.
DUFF, R. A. : *Spinoza's Political and Ethical Philosophy.*   1903.
GUNN, J. A. : *Benedict Spinoza.*   1925.
JOACHIM, H. H. : *Study of the Ethics of Spinoza.*   1901.
MARTINEAU, JAMES : *A Study of Spinoza.*   1882.
POLLOCK, F. : *Spinoza : his Life and Philosophy.*   1880.